Herefordshire
Place-Names

Herefordshire
Place-Names

by

Bruce Coplestone-Crow, F.S.A., F.R.Hist.S.

Logaston Press

LOGASTON PRESS
Little Logaston Woonton Almeley
Herefordshire HR3 6QH
logastonpress.co.uk

First published by Logaston Press 2009
Copyright © Bruce Coplestone-Crow 2009

ISBN 978 1906663 21 6

Typeset by Logaston Press
and printed in Great Britain by
Bell & Bain Ltd., Glasgow

To the memory of
Dr Margaret Gelling OBE
1924-2009

Contents

Foreword

Lack of easily available information about Herefordshire place-names has for many years been a serious problem for historians, archaeologists, geographers and toponymists. There are detailed surveys for two other counties which border on Wales: A.H. Smith's *Place-Names of Gloucestershire* (English Place-Names Society 38-41) and J. McN. Dodgson's *Place-Names of Cheshire* (EPNS 44-48,54). For Shropshire an extensive archive has been assembled during the last thirty years, and the first volume of the EPNS survey is now ready for publication. Work on this scale for Herefordshire has only recently been embarked upon. It has been undertaken by John Freeman, who will probably eventually be responsible for the EPNS survey of the county. That will be many years hence, however, and in the meantime Bruce Coplestone-Crow's material does something to fill the gap. Place-name spellings are to some extent a by-product of his studies on other aspects of Herefordshire history, so the coverage is not systematic, as it would be in a collection by an EPNS editor, but many names are documented here which are not found in Eilert Ekwall's *Dictionary of English Place-Names* or in A.T. Bannister's pioneering work, *The Place-Names of Herefordshire*, published in 1916. The early spellings for these additional names, and the brief etymological comments which I have supplied, will enable more use to be made of the place-name evidence for this county than has hitherto been possible. In the fullness of time Mr Freeman will extract a great deal more material from a wider range of sources, and by a longer and more concentrated study he will doubtless modify some of my 'one-liner' etymologies. But Mr Coplestone-Crow's studies of regional names, such as Archenfield, Leen, Maund and Straddle, are, I think, unlikely to be bettered, and his knowledge of estate history, which has led to sounder identifications for many early spellings, will remain unsurpassed. We have been most fortunate in having Richard Morgan's help with some of the Welsh names.

I believe this to be a useful production, and I am happy to have played a part in making it available.

Margaret Gelling

Preface to the First Edition

This book is a result of many years study of manorial and tenurial history in Herefordshire. It is thus a product of an incidental collection of place-name spellings rather than of a deliberate toponymic survey of the county. This fact may account for some of its shortcomings, many of which I am only too well aware of. Most obvious among them must be the choice of sources. These are heavily weighted towards the period before 1350 because that is the era I have studied most closely. While the result is still, I hope, an adequate statement of the origins of the major place-names of Herefordshire, my unfamiliarity with later medieval and early modern sources has meant that for one or two place-names (Evesbatch for instance) how precisely their modern forms arose is not explored. However, the advantages I see in being able to identify lost places or difficult spellings through a detailed knowledge of the medieval land-units of the shire and their tenurial histories will, I hope, go some way towards making up for this and other shortcomings.

The purpose of the book is to offer an up-to-date survey of the major place-names of Herefordshire, pending a full survey by the EPNS. Two previous attempts at collecting place-name forms for the county have been made and these should be mentioned here. Though they collected forms separately, Canon A.T. Bannister and Mr W. StC. Baddeley both published their results in 1916 (see PNHe). While both studies are commendable in the context of their time (especially Bannister's), the advances in the study of place-names made in the intervening 70 or so years considerably diminishes their present usefulness.

Like the two earlier authorities I can in no way count myself an expert in the field of place-name studies, and here it has been my privilege to rely on Dr Margaret Gelling, one of our leading experts in the field. It should be pointed out straight away, however, that any controversial identification of a particularly early spelling with a later or modern form is entirely my doing and not Dr Gelling's. Similarly, any criticisms of the sometimes highly personal interpretation of the evidence for the location of 'lost' places or land-units, and of the boundaries of the various districts, should also be directed at me.

The place-names are listed alphabetically by modern (pre-1974) civil parish. Where possible each place-name is given a National Grid reference number, which in every case will be preceded by the letters SO. Where we have not been able to improve on the forms and derivations given by Eilert Ekwall in his *Oxford Dictionary of English Place-Names* we have said so.

It is my very great pleasure now to record my thanks to the various people who have helped me in this project. To Dr Margaret Gelling, without whom the whole thing would have been impossible, I owe a very great debt of gratitude. Her constant kindness and forbearance over many years I shall not easily forget. The Revd David Walker, formerly of University College of Wales, Swansea, very kindly made available to me his transcription of Balliol College Oxford MS 271 (the St Guthlac Cartulary) and Dr Julia Barrow allowed me to see in advance of publication her edition of the *acta* of the bishops of Hereford. To both I am extremely grateful. To Mrs Elizabeth Taylor I am grateful for transcripts of some of the deeds in Hereford Record Office and in the Mynde Collection and to Mrs Phyllis Williams for access to original documents concerning Whitbourne and neighbouring parishes. Mr Richard Morgan, formerly of Llandrindod, now of Cardiff, has been of great assistance with the many place-names of Welsh origin. His deep knowledge of the subject is appreciated by both Dr Gelling and myself. Finally, it is a pleasure to put in writing my thanks to Mr Peter Russell for drawing the maps. His superlative cartography has graced other peoples' work before mine and I count myself extremely fortunate in having secured his services for the present book.

Preface to the Second Edition

In this second edition I have taken the opportunity to revise many of the entries so as to focus them more clearly on the etymological matter. I have also added-in those new forms I have come across where they expand on, or support, suggested etymologies. Very few of these latter have been changed. I have also included English translations of the boundary clauses from the *Book of Llan Dâv*, and it is my pleasure to record the assistance Mr Richard Morgan (whose book *Dictionary of the Place-Names of Wales* (co-authored with Hywel Wyn Owen) came out in 2007) has given me with these. They are based on those given in Evans and Rhys's version of *Book of Llan Dâv* and by William Rees in *Liber Landavensis* (1840), but with considerable modification. I have revised the dating of all the material from this source to bring them into line with the dates suggested by Professor Wendy Davies in *The Llandaff Charters*. Finally, I would like to thank Andy Johnson of Logaston Press for the opportunity to revise and reissue this book.

Notes

The same order of place-names has been maintained in this edition as in the last. However, where prefixes such as Little, Much, Upper, Welsh etc. were ignored (so as to maintain strict alphabetical order), for ease of reference such place-names are now listed alphabetically as per their prefix, giving the page number where the entry is in fact to be found. Also there are now two comprehensive indexes, one for place-names and one for persons, peoples and organizations.

Use of an asterisk before a word (e.g. **ecles*) or a personal name indicates that the item is not recorded, but is inferred from place-names or other philological evidence.

Use of an apostrophe at the end of a place-name or personal name indicates that it appears in an abbreviated Latin form in the original document, meaning it is not always possible to deduce exactly what the ending of the extended version should be.

Hypocoristic refers to the Welsh custom of affixing *ti-* (meaning 'you') to a personal name when a familiar or 'pet' form is appropriate.

A simplex place-name is an uncompounded one, e.g. Moor, Hide, etc.

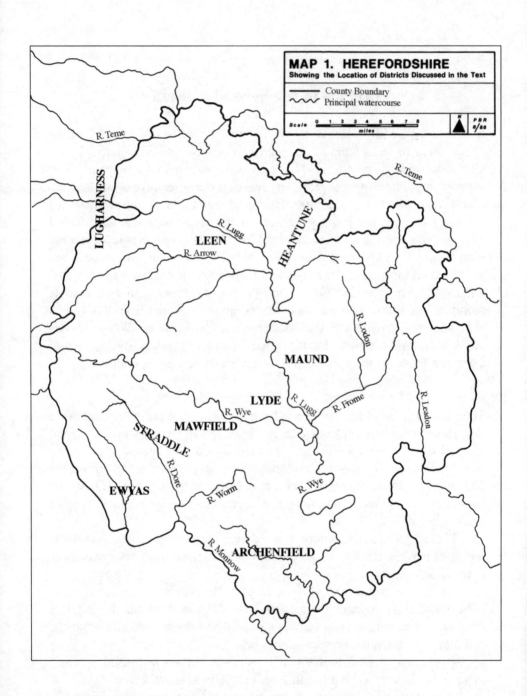

MAP 1. HEREFORDSHIRE

Showing the Location of Districts Discussed in the Text

——— County Boundary
〜〜〜 Principal watercourse

Scale 0 1 2 3 4 5 6 7 8
              miles

PBR
8/88

Abbreviations

Abbr = *Placitorum Abbreviatio*, Record Commission, 1811.

AC = J.H. Round (ed.), *Ancient Charters, Royal and Private, Prior to 1200,* Pipe Roll Society, 1888.

AcornC = 'Acornbury Priory Cartulary', *8th Report of the Deputy Keeper of the Public Records*, Appendix II, 1847

AD = *Catalogue of Ancient Deeds*, 6 vols., P.R.O., 1899-1915; also 'Lists of Ancient Deeds', as published in the volumes of the *List and Index Society.*

Adigard de Gautries = J. Adigard de Gautries, 'Les nomes de lieux de la Manche attestés entre 911 et 1066', *Annales Normand*, **1** (1951).

AncCorr = J.G. Edwards (ed.), *Calendar of Ancient Correspondence Concerning Wales*, 1935.

AncPet = W. Rees (ed.), *Calendar of Ancient Petitions Relating to Wales*, 1975.

AncWood = S. Robinson, 'The Forests and Woodland Area of Herefordshire', TWNFC (1923).

Anderson = O.S. Anderson, *The English Hundred Names*, Lund, 1913.

AnnCamb = J. Williams ab Ithel (ed.), *Annales Cambriae*, Rolls Series, 1860.

ASC = M. Swanton (ed. & trans.), *The Anglo-Saxon Chronicles*, 2000.

ASCh = A.J. Robinson (ed.), *Anglo-Saxon Charters*, 1939.

AW = R. Bromwich, A.O.H. Jarman & B.F. Roberts (eds.), *The Arthur of the Welsh*, 1991.

Banco = *Index of Placita de Banco*, P.R.O. Lists and Indexes, 1909.

Banks = R.W. Banks, 'Notes on the Early History of the Manor of Huntington', *Archaeolgia Cambrensis* (1869); and 'Notes to the Account of Cwmhir Abbey, Radnorshire, *ante* (1888).

Barrow = J. Barrow, *English Episcopal Acta VII: Hereford 1079-1234*, 1993.

BCS = W. de Grey Birch, *Cartularium Saxonicum*, 3 vols., 1885-93.

BeauchampC = E. Mason (ed.), *The Beauchamp Cartulary: charters 1100-1268*, Pipe Roll Society, 1980.

Berks Eyre = M.T. Clanchy (ed.), *The Roll and Writ of the Berkshire Eyre of 1248*, Selden Society, 1973.

BM = H.J. Ellis & F.B. Bickley (eds.), *Index to Charters and Rolls in the Department of Manuscripts, British Museum*, 2 vols., 1900-12.

BMFacs = G.F. Warner & H.J. Ellis, *Facsimiles of Royal and Other Charters in the British Museum*, 1903.

Book of Seals = L.C. Loyd & D.M. Stenton, *Sir Christopher Hatton's Book of Seals*, Northants Record Society, 1950.

Bothe = A.T. Bannister (ed.), *Registrum Caroli Bothe, Episcopi Herefordensis*, Canterbury and York Society, 1921.

Bracton = Henricus de Bracton: *Note Book* (ed. F.W. Maitland), 1887.

BreconC = R.W. Banks (ed.), 'Cartularium Prioratus S. Johannis Evang. de Brecon', *Archaeologia Cambrensis* (1882) & (1883).

Brockworth = S.E. Bartlett, 'History of the Manor and Advowson of Brockworth', *TBGAS*, **7** (1882).

Bromyard = J.G. Hillaby & E. Pearson, *Bromyard*, 1970.

c = circa

Cant = R.G. Griffiths and W.W. Capes (eds.), *Registrum Thome de Cantilupo, Episcopi Herefordensis*, Canterbury and York Society, 1907.

Capes = W.W. Capes, *Charters and Records of Hereford Cathedral*, 1908.

CartAntiq = L. Landon (ed.), *The Cartae Antiquae Rolls 1-10*, Pipe Roll Society, 1939 and J. Conway Davies (ed.), *The Cartae Antiquae Rolls 11-20*, Pipe Roll Society, 1946.

CathDign = Z.N. and C.N.L. Brooke, 'Hereford Cathedral Dignitaries in the Twelfth Century – Supplement', *Cambridge Historical Journal*, **8** (1946).

CBSS = W. Rees, *The Lives of the Cambro-British Saints*, 1853.

CGH = D. Whitehead, *The Castle Green at Hereford: a landscape of ritual, royalty and recreation* (2007).

Ch = *Calendar of Charter Rolls*, 6 vols, P.R.O, 1903-27.

Chadwick = H.M. Chadwick, 'The Foundation of the Early British Kingdoms' in N.K. Chadwick (ed.), *Studies in Early British History*, 1954.

Charl = W.W. Capes (ed.), *Registrum Thome de Charlton, Episcopi Herefordensis*, Canterbury and York Society, 1913.

Charles = B.G. Charles, 'The Welsh, Their Language and Place-Names in Archenfield and Oswestry' in *Angles and Britons*, O'Donnell Lectures, 1963.

ChR = *Rotuli Chartarum*, Record Commission, 1837.

Chronicle = J.C. Dickinson & P.T. Ricketts (eds.), 'The Anglo-Norman Chronicle of Wigmore Abbey', *TWNFC* (1969).

CirenC = C.D. Ross (ed.), *The Cartulary of Cirencester Abbey*, 2 vols., 1964.

Cl = *Calendar of Close Rolls 1272-1422*, P.R.O., 1900-32.

ClR = *Rotuli Litterarum Clausarum*, 2 vols., Record Commission, 1833-44.

CMAD = J.T. Gilbert (ed.), *Chartularies of St Mary's Abbey, Dublin*, 2 vols., Rolls Series, 1884-5.

Court = *Court Rolls*, P.R.O. Lists and Indexes, 1896.

CRCG = W.H. Stevenson (ed.), *Calendar of the Records of the Corporation of Gloucester*, 1893.

Croft = O.G.S. Croft, *The house of Croft of Croft Castle*, 1949.

Cur = Sir Francis Palgrave, *Rotuli Curiae Rolls*, 2 vols., Record Commission, 1835 and *Curia Regis Rolls*, P.R.O, 1922-in progress.

Davies = W. Davies, *The Llandaff Charters*, 1979.

Davies (Unciae) = W. Davies, 'Unciae: Land Measurement in Liber Landavensis', *Agricultural History Review*, **21** (1973).

DB = *Domesday Book*, Vol. 1, ed. Abraham Farley, Record Commission, 1783.

Delisle = L. Delisle & E. Berger (eds.), *Receuil des Actes de Henri II, Roi d'Angleterre et Duc de Normandie*, 4 vols. in 3, Paris, 1909-27.

DEPN = E. Ekwall, *The Concise Oxford Dictionary of English Place-Names*, 4th ed., 1960.

DiversAccs = F.A. Cassel (ed.), *Roll of Divers Accounts; Account of Escheats; Wardrobe Receipt Roll; Reign of Henry III*, Pipe Roll Society, 1982.

DM = A.S. Wood, 'The Domesday More', *TWNFC* (1963).

DMV = Deserted Medieval Village.

DPNW = H. Wyn Owen and R.Morgan, *Dictionary of the Place-Names of Wales*, 2007.

Dugdale = Sir William Dugdale, *Monasticon Anglicanum*, 6 vols. in 8, 1856.

Duncumb = J. Duncumb and continuators, *Collections towards the History and Antiquities of the County of Hereford*, 6 vols., 1804-1915.

Early Deeds = W. StC. Baddeley, 'Early Deeds Relating to St Peter's Abbey, Gloucester', *Trans of the Bristol and Gloucestershire Archaeological Soc.*, **37** (1914) & **38** (1915).

ECH = A. Malpas, J. Butler, A. Davis, S. Davis, T. Malpas and C. Sansom (eds.), *The Early Church in Herefordshire: Proceedings of a Conference Held in Leominster in June 2000*, 2001.

ECWM = H.P.R. Finberg (ed.), *Early Charters of the West Midlands*, 1961.

EH = A.T. Bannister, *The History of Eywas Harold, Its Castle and Priory*, 1902.

EHC = 'Cartulary of Ewyas Harold Priory' as calendared in EH and WalkerReg.

EpActs = J. Conway Davies, *Episcopal Acts and Cognate Documents Relating to Welsh Dioceses*, 2 vols., 1946-8.

ERN = E. Eckwall, *English River Names*, 1928.

ET = original charter transcribed by Mrs E. Taylor.

EWGT = P.C. Bartrum, *Early Welsh Genealogical Tracts*, 1966.

Ex = *Excerpta è Rotuli Finium*, 2 vols., Record Commission, 1835-6.

Eyton = R.W. Eyton, *The Antiquities of Shropshire*, 12 vols., 1854-60.

FA = *Feudal Aids*, 6 vols., P.R.O., 1899-1920.

Faraday = M.A. Faraday, Feet of Fines for Pembridge and Other Places in Herefordshire, 1509-1714 (MS in Birmingham Central Library), 1969.

Fees = *The Book of Fees*, 3 vols., P.R.O., 1920-31.

FF = *Feet of Fines of the Reigns of Henry II and Richard I*, Pipe Roll Society, 1894 and *Feet of Fines 1196-7*, Pipe Roll Society, 1896.

FFW = A.H. Lamont, 'Fords and Ferries of the Wye', *TWNFC* (1921).

von Feilitzen = O. von Feilitzen, 'Old Welsh *Enniaun* and the Old English Personal Name Element *Wen*', *Modern Language Notes*, **62** (1947).

First Century = F.M. Stenton, *The First Century of English Feudalism*, 2nd ed., 1961.

Foliot = A. Morey & C.N.L. Brooke (eds.), *The Letters and Charters of Gilbert Foliot*, 1967.

Fr = J.H. Round (ed.), *Calendar of Documents Preserved in France*, P.R.O., 1899.

Free Fisheries = F.R. James, 'The Wye Free Fisheries Case', *TWNFC* (1916).

FW = B. Thorpe (ed.), *Florenti Wigorniensis monachi Chronicon ex Chronicis*, 2 vols., 1848-9.

Galbraith = V.H. Galbraith, 'An Episcopal Land-Grant of 1085', *English Historical Review*, **44** (1929).

Gallia Christiana = P. Piolin (ed.), *Gallia Christiana*, Vol. XI, Paris, 1874.

GEC = G.E. Cockayne, *The Complete Peerage*, Vol. 10, 1945.

Geoffrey = Geoffrey of Monmouth: *The Historia Regum Brittaniae* (Trinity College, Cambridge, MS 1125), ed. A. Griscom, New York, 1929 and *The Historia Regum Britanniae of Geoffrey of Monmouth* (Bern, Burgerbibliothek MS 568), ed. N. Wright, 1985.

Gerald of Wales = Gerald of Wales: *The Journey Through Wales*, ed. L. Thorpe, 1978.

GloucC = W.H. Hart (ed.), *Historia et Cartularium Monasterii Sancti Petri Gloucestriae*, 3 vols., Rolls Series, 1863-7.

Grundy = G.B. Grundy, 'The Ancient Woodland of Gloucestershire', *TBGAS*, **58** (1936).

Harris = S.M. Harris, 'The Kalendar of the 'Vitae Sanctorum Wallensium' (Vespasian A xiv)', *Journal of the Historical Society of the Church in Wales*, **3** (1953).

Hart = C.E. Hart, 'The Metes and Bounds of the Forest of Dean', *TBGAS*, **66** (1945).

HB = Nennius: *Historia Brittonum*, ed. J. Morris, 1980.

HDB = V.H. Galbraith & J. Tait (eds.), *The Herefordshire Domesday Book 1160-70*, Pipe Roll Society, 1950.

Hillaby = J.G. Hillaby, 'The Origins of the Diocese of Hereford', *TWNFC* (1976).

Holtzmann = W. Holtzmann, *Papsturkunden in England*, 3 vols., Berlin, 1930-52.

Howse = W.H. Howse, 'A farm Indenture of 1481', *TWNFC* (1957)

HRO = Hereford Record Office.

HT = M.A. Faraday (ed.), *Herefordshire Taxes in the Reign of Henry VIII* (2005).

InqMisc = *Calendar of Inquisitions Miscellaneous*, P.R.O., 1916-in progress.

Inspeximus = R.W. Banks, 'Inspeximus and Confirmation of the Charters of Wigmore Abbey', *Archaeologia Cambrensis* (1882).

Ipm = *Calendar of Inquisitions Post Mortem*, P.R.O., 1898-in progress.

IrishC = E. StJ. Brooks (ed.), *The Irish Cartularies of Llanthony Prima and Secunda*, Dublin, 1953.

Jack = G.H. Jack & A.G.K. Hayter, 'Excavations on the Site of Caplar Camp', *TWNFC* (1925).

Johansson = C. Johansson, 'The Place-Names of a Herefordshire Charter', *Studia Neophilologica*, **4** (1977).

Jones = T. Jones, *A History of the County of Brecknock*, 2 vols., 1805-9 (one vol. version by E. Davies, 1898).

JW = John of Worcester: *Chronicle*, ed. J.R.H. Weaver, 1908.

Kemp = B.R. Kemp, 'Hereditary Beneficies in the Medieval English Church: a Herefordshire example', *Bulletin of the Institute of Historical Research*, **43** (1970).

KinRR = Rentals and Surveys of Kinnersley 1359-69 and 1400-01: P.R.O., SC 11 Rolls 556 and 557.

Kirby = I.M. Kirby, *A catalogue of the Records of the Dean and Chapter [of Gloucester], Including the Former St Peter's Abbey*, 1967.

Kirby'sQuest = Sir Henry Barkly, 'Kirby's Quest for Gloucestershire 1283-6, *TBGAS* **11** (1886-7).

KPC = J. Amphlett (ed.), *The Kyre Park Charters*, Worcestershire Historical Society, 1905.

KR = information from Dr Keith Ray, County Archaeologist.

Lacy = J.H. Parry (ed.), *Registrum Edmundi Lacy, Episcopi Herefordensis*, Canterbury and York Society, 1918.

Lancaster = W. Rees (ed.), *A Survey of the Duchy of Lancaster Lordships in Wales, 1609-13*, 1953.

Land of Lene = Lord Rennell of Rodd, 'The Land of Lene' in I.Ll. Foster & L. Alcock (eds.), *Culture and Environment*, 1963.

Larking = C.B. Larking (ed.), *The Knights Hospitaller in England: Being the Report of Prior Philip de Thame to the Grand Master Elyan de Villanova for AD1338*, Camden Society, 1857.

Layamon = Layamon: *Brut or Hystoria Britonum*, ed. & trans. W.R.J. Barron & S.C. Weinberg, 1995.

LBS = S. Baring-Gould & J. Fisher, *The Lives of the British Saints*, 4 vols., 1907-13.

Lees = B.A. Lees (ed.), *Records of the Templars in England in the Twelfth Century*, British Academy, 1935.

Leland = L. Toulmin Smith (ed.), *The Itinerary of John Leland*, 5 vols., 1907-10.

LeomC = K.M. Morgan (ed.), An Edition of the Cartulary of Leominster Priory Up to the Mid-Thirteenth Century, University of Wales MA Thesis, 1972.

Liebermann = F. Liebermann (ed.), *Gesetze der Angelsachsen*, 3 vols., Halle, 1903-16.

LL = J.G. Evans & J. Rhŷs (eds.), *The Book of Llan Dâv*, 1893 (facsimile ed. 1993).

Löfvenberg = M.T. Löfvenberg, *Studies in Middle English Local Surnames*, Lund, 1942.

LostC = A.T. Bannister, 'A Lost Cartulary of Hereford Cathedral', *TWNFC* (1917).

Loyd = L.C. Loyd, *The Origins of Some Anglo-Norman Families*, Harleian Society, 1951.

LWE = N. Fryde, *List of Welsh Entries in the Memoranda Rolls 1282-1343*, 1974.

LWSS = G.H. Doble: *Lives of the Welsh Saints*, ed. D.Simon Evans, 1971.

MA = M.A. Faraday, *Herefordshire Militia Assessments 1663*, Camden Society, 1972.

MB = F.C. Morgan, 'The Manor of Buttas, King's Pyon, 1638', *TWNFC* (1946).

MAW = O. Jones, E. Williams & W.O. Pughe, *The Myvyrian Archaiology of Wales*, 3 vols., 1801-7 (one vol. version 1870).

ME = Middle English.

MemR = *The Memoranda Roll of the King's Remembrancer for 1230-1*, Pipe Roll Society, 1933.

MonC = P. Marchegay (ed.), *Chartes Anciennes du Prieuré de Monmouth en Angleterre*, Les Roches-Baritaud, 1879.

Murray'sMap = *Map of Herefordshire by T.L. Murray*, 1831.

Myllyng = A.T. Bannister (ed.), *Registrum Thome Myllyng, Episcopi Herefordensis*, Canterbury and York Society, 1920.

n.d. = undated.

NonInq = *Nonarum Inquisitiones*, Record Commission, 1807.

OblR = *Rotuli de Oblatis et Finibus*, Record Commission, 1835.

ODR = F. Noble, *Offa's Dyke Reviewed*, ed. M. Gelling, BAR, 1983.

OE = Old English.

Old Rectories = J. Lloyd, 'Old Herefordshire Rectories and Tithes 1558', *TWNFC* (1901).

ON = Old Norse.

OrdVit = Orderic Vitalis: *The Ecclesiastical History*, ed. & trans. M. Chibnall, 6 vols., 1969-80.

Orig = *Rotulorum Originalium Abbreviatio*, 2 vols., Record Commission, 1805-10.

Orl = A.T. Bannister (ed.), *Registrum Ade de Orleton, Episcopi Herefordensis*, Canterbury and York Society, 1908.

OS = Ordnance Survey, First Edition 1" maps.

OseneyC = H.E. Salter (ed.), *Cartulary of Oseney Abbey*, 5 vols., Oxford Historical Society, 1935.

Owen = E. Owen, *Catalogue of Manuscripts Relating to Wales in the British Museum*, 4 vols. in 2, Cymmrodorion Record Series, 1900-08.

Owen's Pembrokeshire = H. Owen (ed.), *The Description of Pembrokeshire by George Owen of Henllys 1602*, 4 vols. in 3, Cymmrodorion Record Series, 1897-1936.

OxfordFacs = H.E. Salter (ed.), *Facsimiles of Early Oxford Charters in Oxford Muniment Rooms*, 1929.

P = Pipe Roll, as published by the Pipe Roll Society by regnal year.

(p) = place-name used as a personal name or surname.

Painswick = W. StC. Baddeley, *A Cotteswold Manor; Being a History of Painswick*, 1907.

Palgrave = Sir Francis Palgrave, *Parliamentary Writs*, 2 vols. in 4, Record Commission, 1827-34.

Pat = *Calendar of Patent Rolls*, P.R.O., 1906-in progress.

Patterson = R.B. Patterson (ed.), *Original Acta of St Peter's Abbey, Gloucester, c1122-1263*, Bristol and Gloucestershire Archaeological Society, 1998.

Pleas = D.M. Stenton (ed.), *Pleas Before the King or His Justices 1198-1212*, 4 vols., Selden Society, 1953-67.

PNGl = A.H. Smith, *The Place-Names of Gloucestershire*, 4 vols., English Place-Names Society, 1964-5.

PNGw = R. Morgan, *Place-Names of Gwent*, 2005.

PNHe = A.T. Bannister, *The Place-Names of Herefordshire*, 1916 and W. StC.Baddeley, 'Herefordshire Place-Names', *Trans. of the Bristol and Gloucestershire Archaeological Soc.*, **39** (1916).

PNRa = R. Morgan, *A Study of Radnorshire Place-Names*, 1998.

PNRB = A.L.F. Rivet & C. Smith, *The Place-Names of Roman Britain*, 1979.

PNWo = A. Mawer & F.M. Stenton, *The Place-Names of Worcestershire*, English Place -Names Society, 1927.

Price = J. Price, *An Historical and Topographical Account of Leominster*, 1795.

P.R.O. = Public Record Office publications (now The National Archives).

P-RW = G.R.J. Jones, 'Post-Roman Wales' in H.P.R. Finberg (ed.), *The Agrarian History of England and Wales*, Vol. 1, Pt. 2, 1972.

PT = C.C. Fenwick (ed.), *The Poll Taxes of 1377, 1379 & 1381, Part 1; Bedfordshire -Leicestershire*, British Academy, 1998.

QD = *List of Inquisitions ad quod damnum*, 2 vols., P.R.O. Lists and Indexes, 1906-8.

QW = *Placita de Quo Warranto*, Record Commission, 1818.

RATD = J.T. Gilbert (ed.), *The Register of the Abbey of St Thomas, Dublin*, Rolls Series, 1889.

Rawlinson = R. Rawlinson, *The History and Antiquities of the City and Cathedral of Hereford*, Appendix (original documents), 1717.

RBE = H. Hall (ed.), *The Red Book of the Exchequer*, 3 vols., Rolls Series, 1896.

RBH = J. Rhŷs & J.G. Evans (eds.), *The Text of the Bruts from the Red Book of Hergest*, 1890.

ReadingC = B.R. Kemp (ed.), *Reading Abbey Cartularies*, 2 vols., Camden Society, 1986-7.

Red Book = A.T. Bannister, 'A Transcript of the Red Book of Hereford' in *Camden Miscellany*, 1929.

Red Book MS = copy of ff.88-96 of Red Book lent by Mrs Phyllis Williams.

Rees = W. Rees, *A History of the Order of St John of Jerusalem in Wales and On the Welsh Border*, 1947.

ReesMap = W. Rees, *Map of South Wales and the Border in the Fourteenth Century*, Ordnance Survey, 1932.

Reeves = N.C. Reeves, *The Town in the Marches: a history of Leominster and its environs*, 1972.

Regesta = H.W.C. Davis, C. Johnson, H.A. Cronne & R.H.C. Davis (eds.), *Regesta Regum Anglo-Normannorum*, 3 vols., 1913-68.

RH = *Rotuli Hundredorum*, 2 vols., Record Commission, 1812-18.

RMSS = *Report on Manuscripts in the Welsh Language*, Historical Manuscripts Commission, Vol. 1 (3 parts) 1898-1905 and Vol. 2 (4 parts) 1902-10.

Robinson = C.J. Robinson, *A History of the Mansions and Manors of Herefordshire*, 1872 and *A History of the Castles of Herefordshire and Their Lords*, 1869.

Rodd = Lord Rennell of Rodd, *Valley on the March*, 1958.

Roderick = A.J. Roderick, 'Villa Wallensica', *Bulletin of the Board of Celtic Studies*, **13** (1948-50).

Rollason = L. Rollason, The Boundaries of the Herefordshire Charters of the Book of Llandaff, University of Birmingham, B.A. Dissertation, 1975.

Rolls = D.M. Stenton (ed.), *Rolls of the Justices in Eyre for Gloucestershire, Warwickshire and Staffordshire, 1221-2*, Selden Society, 1940.

RotLib = *Rotuli de Liberate ac de Misis et Praestitis*, Record Commission, 1844.

RotNorm = *Rotuli Normanniae*, Record Commission, 1835.

SalopEyre = A. Harding (ed.), *The Roll of the Shropshire Eyre of 1256*, Selden Society, 1981.

SalopFF = W.G.D. Fletcher (ed.), 'Shropshire Feet of Fines, 1196-1248', *Transactions of the Shropshire Archaeological and Natural History Society* 2nd series **10** (1898), 3rd series **6** (1906) & **7** (1907).

Sanders = I.J. Sanders, *English Baronies*, 1960.

Select Cases = G.O. Sayles (ed.), *Select Cases in the Court of King's Bench Under Edward I*, 2 vols., Selden Society, 1936-8.

Sheppard = J. Sheppard, *The Origins and Evolution of Field Settlement Patterns in the Herefordshire Manor of Marden*, Department of Geography, Queen Mary College, University of London, Occasional Papers, No.15, December 1979.

Skidmore = W. Skidmore, *The Scudamores of Upton Scudamore*, Akron, Ohio, 1982.

Slocombe = I. Slocombe, Pencombe: Medieval Settlement Pattern (MS in Bromyard Public Library).

SMR = Sites and Monuments Record.

Spofford = A.T. Bannister, *Registrum Thome Spofford, Episcopi Herefordensis*, Canterbury and York Society, 1919.

SR = R.E. Glasscock (ed.), *The Lay Subsidy of 1334*, British Academy, 1975.

Staffs Pleas = G. Wrottesley, 'The Plea Rolls of the Reign of Edward I', *Staffordshire Record Society*, **5** (1885).

Stanbury = J.H. Parry & A.T. Bannister (eds.), *Registrum Johannis Stanbury, Episcopi Herefordensis*, Canterbury and York Society, 1919.

Stanford = S.C. Stanford, 'The Function and Population of Hill-Forts in the Central Marches' in F. Lynch & C. Burgess (eds.), *Prehistoric Man in Wales and the West*, 1972.

StGC = Balliol College, Oxford, MS 271 ('Cartulary of St Guthlac's Priory, Hereford').

St Katherine = A.T. Bannister, 'A Descriptive Catalogue of Manuscripts Dealing with St Katherine's, Ledbury', *TWNFC* (1923).

Subs = F. Jones, 'The Subsidy of 1292', *Bulletin of the Board of Celtic Studies*, **13** (1950).

Supplement = 'Original Documents' supplement to *Archaeologia Cambrensis* (1877).

Swin = W.W. Capes (ed.), *Registrum Ricardi de Swinfield, Episopi Herefordensis*, Canterbury and York Society, 1909.

Tax = *Taxation Ecclesiastica*, Record Commission, 1802.

TGW = J. Rhys, 'The Goidels in Wales', *Archaeologia Cambrensis* (1895).

Thorn = F. & C. Thorn, *Domesday Book: Herefordshire*, Phillimore, 1983.

Treago = T. Wright, 'Treago and the Large Tumulus at St Weonard's', *Archaeologia Cambrensis* (1855).

Trill = J.H. Parry (ed.), *Registrum Johannis de Trilleck, Episcopi Herefordensis*, Canterbury and York Society, 1912.

TWNFC = Transactions of the Woolhope Naturalists' Field Club, Herefordshire.

Two Lives = M.R. James, 'Two Lives of St Ethelbert, King and Martyr', *English Historical Review* **32** (1917).

VCH = *Victoria County History of Herefordshire*, Vol.1, 1908.

VE = *Valor Ecclesiasticus*, 6 vols., Record Commission, 1810-34.

VR = A.T. Bannister (ed.), 'Visitation Returns of the Diocese of Hereford in 1397', *English Historical Review*, **44** (1929) & **45** (1930).

VSBG = A.W. Wade-Evans (ed.), *Vitae Sanctorum Britanniae et Genealogiae*, 1944.

VSD = 'Vita Sancti Dauid' in VSGB.

VSM = 'Vita Sancti Mildburgae' in BL Lansdowne MS 436, printed in J. Capgrave, *Nova Legenda Angliae* (ed. C. Horstmann, 2 vols., 1901), supplemented by Leland's extracts from the earlier BL Additional MS 34,633, printed in his *De Rebus Britannicis Collectanea* (ed. T. Hearne, 3 vols., 1770-7).

VSMev = 'Vita Sancti Mevenni' in G.H. Doble, *The Saints of Cornwall*, Part 5 (ed. D. Attwater), 1970.

Wace = Wace: *Roman de Brut: A History of the British*, ed. & trans. J. Weiss, 1999.

WalkerCh = D. Walker, 'Charters of the Earldom of Hereford, 1095-1201', *Camden Miscellany*, 1964.

WalkerReg = D. Walker, 'A Register of the Churches of the Monastery of St Peter's, Gloucester' in *An Ecclesiastical Miscellany*, Bristol and Gloucestershire Archaeological Society, 1976.

WalkerSC = D. Walker, 'Some Charters Relating to St Peter's Abbey, Gloucester' in P.M. Barnes and C.F. Slade (eds.), *A Medieval Miscellany for Doris Mary Stenton*, Pipe Roll Society, 1962.

Whitbourne = P. Williams, *Whitbourne: a bishop's manor*, 1979.

Whitehead = D. Whitehead, 'Pipe and Lyde, Herefordshire: an unrecorded castle', *TWNFC* (1979).

Williams = D.H. Williams, *White Monks in Gwent and the Border*, 1976.

Winforton = Mrs Dawson, 'Notes on Border Parishes: Winforton', *Archaeologia Cambrensis* (1898).

Wms = personal communication from Mrs P. Williams of Whitbourne.

WorcC = R.R. Darlington (ed.), *The Cartulary of Worcester Cathedral Priory*, Pipe Roll Society, 1968.

WorcsSR = *Lay Subsidy Rolls for the County of Worcester, c1280-1603*, Worcester Records Society, 1893-1902.

YearBook = A.J. Horwood (ed.), *Year Books of the Reign of Edward I: Years 20 and 21*, Rolls Series, 1866.

Y Cymmorodor = *Transactions of the Honourable Society of Cymmrodorion*.

District-names

Archenfield/Erging

Ercic(g), Ercig, Ercycg (regionis), Ergic mid 6th to late 9th (c1130), 1128,
  1129 LL; *Ercychi (regionis),* mid 6th (c1130) LL; *Ercin(c)g* early 9th HB,
  1129 LL; *E(i)rgin(g)* late 11th VSD, c1130, 15th LL; *Ergyn(g)* 958/9
  (c1130), c1130 or later LL, 1377 PT (p), 15th LL; *Erchin* 1129 LL;
  Her(e)ging late 11th or 1135-54 (post 1275: *ex* 'Liber Abbatis de
  Feversham') RBE, c1130-6 Geoffrey; *Hergin* c1155 Wace; *Erchyng* 15th LL.
Orcheus (pagus in Guenta provincia) early 12th VSMev; *Orcanie*(?) c1155
  Wace.

Brankamffeld, Briencandafelda, Erenkandefeld 823-62 BCS, GloucC, ECWM;
  Arcenefelde 1086 DB; *Urceneuelda* 1130 LL; *Erchenesfeld* 1131 EpActs;
  (H)erchen(e)feld(am) 1137 AC, 1139-48 Foliot, 1143-55 BreconC, c1170
  MonC, 1174 P; 1197 CAR; *Urchene(s)feld* 1147 EpActs, 1188 Gerald,
  1212 Fees; *Irc(c)hen(e)feld(e)* 1160-70 HDB, 1221 P, 1249/50 Fees, 1323
  Orig; *Irchyn(e)f(f)eld(e)* 1160-70 or later HDB; 1334 AncPet; *Erchinefeld*
  1174 P; *Urchinefeldia* 1220 Bracton; *Hirchenefeld(e)* 1253 InqMisc;
  Irchunfeld 1292 QW; *Irchingeld* 1302-3 LWE; *Erchynfeld* 15th LL;
  Irdynfelde 1506 BM.
Yrcingafelda 915 ASC

See also Bryngwyn in Much Dewchurch, Map 2.

The Welsh name *Ergyn(g)* is a development from Roman-British Ariconium, the
name of the settlement at Weston under Penyard. The etymology of Ariconium
is obscure, see PNRB.

The English name Archenfield has as its first element an early form
of *Ergyn(g)*. Smith's suggestion (PNGl) that the form *Yrcingafelda* in ASC
contains an OE folk-name in which *–ingas* was added to the Welsh name is not
convincing, as none of the other spellings supports it. The other forms suggest
a straight forward compound of the Welsh name with OE *feld*. There may have
been occasional scribal association with *–inga-* names.

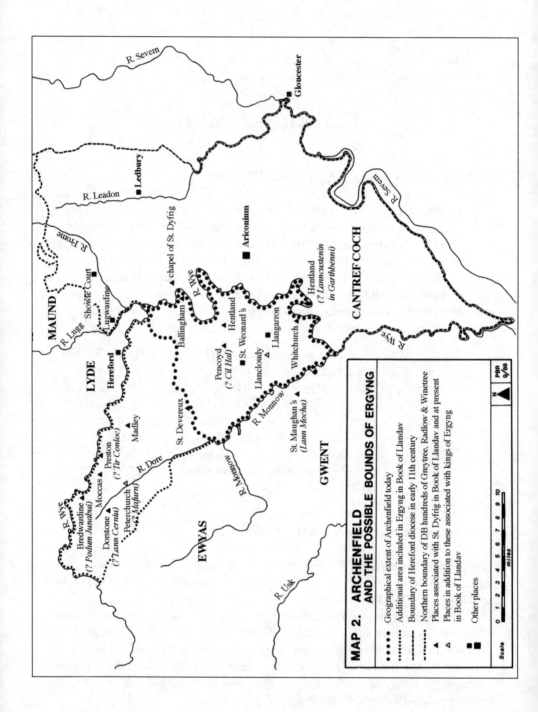

MAP 2. ARCHENFIELD
AND THE POSSIBLE BOUNDS OF ERGYNG

Scale

0 1 2 3 4 5 6 7 8 9 10
miles

•••••• Geographical extent of Archenfield today
•••••• Additional area included in Ergyng in Book of Llandav
- - - - Boundary of Hereford diocese in early 11th century
- - - - Northern boundary of DB hundreds of Greytree, Radlow & Winetree
▲   Places associated with St. Dyfrig in Book of Llandav and at present
△   Places in addition to these associated with kings of Ergyng
        in Book of Llandav
■ ■   Other places

N

PBR
9/88

Archenfield is the English name for the area bounded by the rivers Wye, Monnow and Worm. The post-Roman kingdom of Ergyng, from which the first part of the English name is derived, covered Archenfield and also wide lands east of the Wye. Ergyng's precise extent is problematic, but certain documentary evidence makes an approximation of its bounds possible.

The *Book of Llan Dâv* contains charter evidence dating from the last century of the kingdom or Ergyng's existence (Davies). These show that in the 6th and early 7th centuries the kingdom covered all Archenfield plus the area north of it as far as the Wye, and also the upper Dore Valley (see Map 2). Its chief saint was Dubricius or Dyfrig, and the greatest concentration of places associated with him and of churches dedicated to him occurs in this area on available evidence.

There are, however, other indications that Ergyng also included lands on the east bank of the Wye that because of its tendentious origins the Book of *Llan Dâv* does not mention. First among these is the obvious fact that because it is named from the Romano-British settlement at Ariconium in Weston under Penyard, east of the Wye, that place must once have been within its territory. Second, there was until the 16th century a chapel of St Dyfrig at Lower Buckenhill in Woolhope, which is also east of the Wye. Third, there is a possibility that the place-name Yartleton in Aston Ingham (and in Longhope, just across the border in Gloucestershire) has a version of Ergyng as its first element. Fourth, Welsh traditions speak of a *Cantref Coch* or 'Red Cantref' stretching from the Wye as far east as 'the bridge of Gloucester', by which is meant the bridge over the Severn outside the west gate of the city (RMSS; Y Cymmrodor, **9** (1888); MAW). This way also went the bounds of Hereford diocese as defined in an early 11th century document (ECWM). This boundary went down the Wye from Monmouth to the Severn and along the Severn to Gloucester, from where it went up the river Leadon to Dymock and then struck off north-east and north to follow the line of the Malvern Hills. Since this boundary is recognized as being very old (Hillaby) it may represent the limits of Ergyng in this direction. A boundary for Ergyng this far to the east embraces Ariconium, the chapel of St Dyfrig in Woolhope and the 'Red Cantref'.

It also draws within its ambit the settlement site at Ledbury, which may once have held an episcopal seat. In the 1170s bishop Gilbert Foliot of London, a former bishop of Hereford, wrote to the bishop-elect of Hereford asking him to preserve the church at Ledbury having regard to the episcopal see it long since held and to the bishops whose bodies lie buried there (Foliot; CGH). Ledbury has not held an episcopal seat since the coming of the English, as far as we know, although the settlement-site it represents may have when it was part of Ergyng.

If the eastern boundary of Ergyng lay on the Severn and the Malvern Hills, then the boundary between the Malverns and the Wye near Hereford will also need defining. Here again there are clues. Canon Doble, for instance, has noted (LWSS) that in 1330 Lugwardine Church, east of the Wye, had had the chapels of Hentland, Llangarron and St Weonard's, west of it, attached to it 'since time out of mind'. As he also points out, 'these medieval ecclesiastical arrangements are of great antiquity, often going back to Celtic times, and the subjugation of a group of churches of St Dyfrig and other Celtic saints to what has been for ages an unimportant country parish may prove to be a valuable clue to the early history of this part of Herefordshire'. The arrangement certainly goes back to DB, when the king had Lugwardine and the three Archenfield churches (whose priests bore his dispatches into Wales) in his hands, and may date back to the time when all four places were part of Ergyng (see also Orl; ChR; Foliot). Similarly, it is difficult to see how in 1334 Showle Court in Yarkhill could have been an outlier of Archenfield (and even given its name to a liberty of the same: SR) unless it too had been joined to it at one time. In 1086 Lugwardine lay in Greytree Hundred, Showle Court in Radlow Hundred and Ledbury in Winstree Hundred. The northern boundary of these three hundreds draws a rough line between the Malverns and the river Lugg by Lugwardine that may represent the ancient limits of Ergyng in this direction.

These approximate boundaries for Ergyng seem to form a natural land-unit surrounding Ariconium on all sides. Within it lay a major iron-producing area of late-Roman times, and it may have been control of this valuable industry that ensured the survival of a post-Roman state centred on Ariconium. What, if any, post-Roman authority lay on its northern borders is unknown. Possibly Powys spread as far south as the Wye by Hereford, although it is equally likely that Ergyng once included lands much further north. Wilmott has argued (TWNFC (1980) & (1985)) that the natural hinterland of the Romano-British town of Magnis (Kenchester) was across the Wye to the south rather than into the broken, hilly country to the north. If this was the case, then the possibility that this area was controlled by Ergyng in the 6th and early 7th centuries may indicate that any post-Roman authority there had collapsed. The siting right on the Wye of some of the lands given to the local bishop by the kings of Ergyng in those centuries (e.g. Bredwardine, Moccas and Preston on Wye) suggests that either the people on the other side of the Wye were friendly or, indeed, that the opposite bank was also in Ergyng. An objection to this may be that the *Book of Llan Dâv* contains no grants of land from that area, but this may be because the bishop who commissioned it had no interest in it, not because such grants were not made.

Echoes of the ancient unity of lands either side of the Wye below Hereford under the rule of Ergyng seem to be preserved in the legal tract known as The Ordinance Concerning the Dunsaete, which dates from after the English arrived in the area. This Ordinance seems to show that a semi-independent Anglo-Welsh people inhabited both banks of the Wye between Hereford and Monmouth between the late 8th and early 10th centuries (Liebermann; English version now available in ODR). The tract was drawn up by king Athelstan, in consultation with the Welsh, while at Hereford in 926, probably, although certain aspects suggest that it is a reworking of a much older law-code perhaps dating from the time when Mercia was the dominant power on the Welsh border. In fact, it was probably the presence of the Dunsaete as a sort of buffer-state between Mercia and the Welsh that made it unnecessary for king Offa to construct his boundary dyke through their territory (see ODR). In 1066 the Welsh of Archenfield paid their royal dues at the king of England's manor of Linton rather than the much nearer royal estate of Wilton/Cleeve, most of whose lands lay within Archenfield (DB). As, however, Linton included the site of Ariconium it might be possible to suggest that they were merely continuing an arrangement that dated back to the time when the kingdom based on that town embraced lands on both banks of the Wye. In which case, it can be seen that the Dunsaete were the unifying force that saw this arrangement through the testing times when relations between Welsh and English were at their most violent.

Ewyas

Ewyas mid-10th (c1130) LL, 1148-55 WalkerCh (p); *Ewias* late-11th or early 12th RBE; c1143-68 Skidmore, c1160 BreconC (p), 1166 RBE (p); *Euias* 1115-20 BreconC ; *Eugias*, Evias n.d. (c1130) LL; *Euwyas* 1300 EHC; *Evyas* 1375-8 RBH; *Euas* c1400 RBH.

Ewyas is explained in DEPN as a Welsh name meaning 'sheep district'. As a commote it was included in the earliest list of cantrefs and commotes (Welsh administrative divisions) dating from c1100 (RBE). It stretched in area from Cusop Hill on the north to the river Mynwy in the south, and from the valley of the Grwyne Fawr (now in Monmouthshire) in the west to the river Dore in the east. The Dore was only its eastern boundary in its lower reaches, however, above Bacton its natural boundary being the high ground west of the Dore, approximately along the western boundary of the modern parishes of Turnastone, Peterchurch and Dorstone. The heartland of Ewyas seems to have been the vicinity of Clodock and Longtown in the Olchon valley.

The Normans divided the commote into two lordships, Ewyas Lacy (*Ewyas Lascy* 1219 InqMisc) and Ewyas Harold (*Ewyas Haraldi* 1219 InqMisc), these suffixes coming from the surname of the family who held the lordship of Ewyas Lacy and from the Christian name of the man who held Ewyas Harold soon after 1086.

Ewyas Harold was always the much smaller of the two lordships. Its administrative centre was the castle at Ewyas Harold. In 1086 is castlery covered

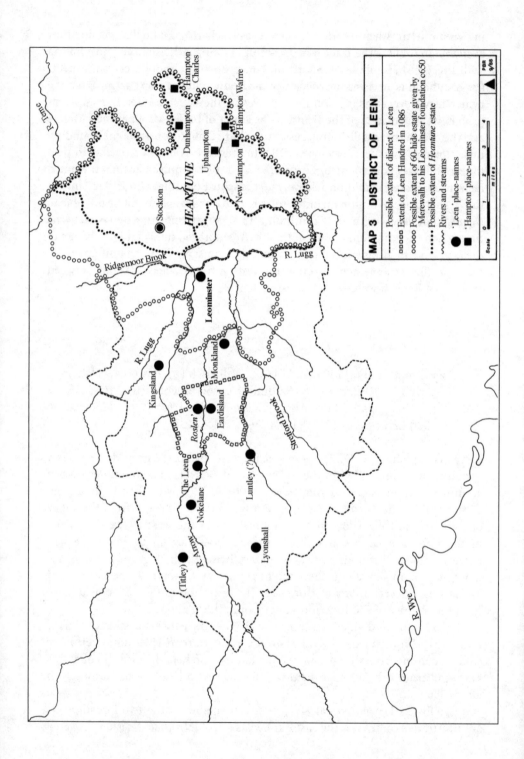

MAP 3 DISTRICT OF LEEN

- - - - Possible extent of district of Leen
ᗪᗪᗪᗪ Extent of Leen Hundred in 1086
ooooo Possible extent of 60-hide estate given by
       Merewalh to his Leominster foundation c650
∙∙∙∙∙ Possible extent of *Heantune* estate
~~~~~ Rivers and streams
● 'Leen' place-names
■ 'Hampton' place-names

Scale

miles
0   1   2   3   4

PBR
9/88

R. Teme

Hampton
Charles

Dunhampton

Uphampton

New Hampton   Hampton Waffre

HEANTUNE

Stockton

Ridgemoor Brook

R. Lugg

Leominster

R. Lugg

Kingsland

Monkland

Eardisland

Roslen

Shetford Brook

The Leen

Luntley (?)

Nokelane

Lyonshall

(Titley)

R. Arrow

R. Wye

the modern parishes of Ewyas Harold, Rowlestone, Llancillo, Walterstone, Kenderchurch, Dulas and the part of Abbey Dore lying west of the Dore. Earl in the 12th century Rowlestone, Llancillo, Walterstone and Dulas were acquired by the Lacys and added to Ewyas Lacy, while Kenderchurch reverted to episcopal ownership.

Ewyas Lacy covered about 90% of the commote of Ewyas. Its administrative centre in 1086 was the motte-and-bailey castle at Walterstone, then within Ewyas Harold's castlery. By about 1100, probably, this had been moved closer to the old Welsh centre of the commote, to a motte-and-bailey castle at Pont Hendre in Clodock, and by 1200 to the castle at Longtown. Longtown and its small borough were known in medieval times by the name of the lordship: *Eweias Lacy* (1275 RH).

Leen

Lion(hina gemæres) 958 BCS; *Leonis (monasterium)* 1080-90 VSM; *Lene* 1086 DB.

See also Luntley in Dilwyn, Eardisland, *Roslen'* in Eardisland, Kingsland, Leominster, Lyonshall, Monkland, Nokelane Head in Pembridge and Titley, Map 3.

This name survives in modern English form at The Leen, a farm in Pembridge (GR 383591), which was simply *Leen* in 1832 (OS Map). The modern Welsh form is perhaps reserved in the second element of Llanllieni, which is the Welsh name for Leominster.

Leen is considered to be a Welsh name meaning something like 'district of the streams'. The distribution of lost and surviving place-names containing this element (see Map 3) suggests that these 'streams' were the rivers Lugg and Arrow and the Pinsley Brook, around and to the west of Leominster. Its natural limits were probably the high ground all around that could be seen from Cursneh Hill in Leominster. It would thus have embraced the modern parishes of Shobdon, Lucton, Kingsland, Eyton, Leominster, Newton, Hope under Dinmore, Birley, King's Pyon, Weobley, Sarnesfield, Dilwyn, Stretford, Monkland, Eardisland, Pembridge, Staunton on Arrow, Titley and Lyonshall. By 1086 the district-name had become the name of a hundred covering just one manor, Eardisland, and of the manors of Kingsland and Monkland, which were then in Hazletree Hundred.

The late-11th century author of the 'Life of St Mildburg' (VSM; ECH) says that the district of *Leonis* (a name which he mistakenly assumes is a version of Latin *leo* 'lion') was ruled by king Merewalh, father of Mildburg. After his conversion to Christianity in 660 by the Northumbrian missionary Eadfrith (a process that includes a morally edifying story of the pagan king, the 'lion', being 'tamed' by Christianity) Merewalh founded a monastery for his daughter at a place known afterwards as *Leonis monasterium*. His initial endowment consisted of 'thirty ploughlands' and these are possibly the estate within Leen called *Heantune* or Hampton (OE *heantune*, 'at the high settlement') which occupied the high ground to the east of Leominster. In this area there are five place-names containing the element 'hampton' – Hampton Charles, Dunhampton (in Hatfield), Uphampton (in Docklow), Ne Hampton and Hampton Wafre. DB suggests that there were approximately thirty hides of land in this area, which would tie-in well with the 'thirty ploughlands'. Its conjectural area would cover the modern parishes of Hampton Charles, Hampton Wafre, New Hampton, Docklow, Humber, Hatfield, Kimbolton, Middleton on the Hill, Leysters, Pudlestone and the parts of Little Hereford south of the Teme. The monastic church was initially founded at Stockton (in Kimbolton), apparently, before Merewalh gave up the remainder of Leen to his daughter, whereupon it was moved to Leominster. A nunnery at Leominster was dissolved by Edward the Confessor in 1046 and forty years later the royal manor of Leominster, with its many 'members' and outliers that represented its landed endowment, was said to contain eighty hides. Possibly, therefore, the Leen estate given up secondarily contained an additional fifty hides, to go with the thirty given before.

Lugharness

Luggeharneys 1357, *Loggarnes* 1368, *Lughharness* 1399 Ipm; *(dominium de) Lugharney* 1546 BM.

'Lordship on the river Lugg', -harness is OE *(ge)herness* 'obedience, jurisdiction', Lugharness was another name for the marcher lordship of Stapleton, which covered the modern parishes of Stapleton, Willey, Kinsham, Combe, Rodd-Nash-and-Little Brampton, Titley and the western parts of Staunton on Arrow, all in Herefordshire, plus Stanage in Radnorshire (now Powys).

The lordship belonged to the lord of Richard's Castle in the later middle ages. As early as 1204-19 that lord was claiming his 'liberty' in his lands astride the Lugg. A survey of the boundaries of Herefordshire undertaken in 1219 contained the following statement: 'Stretford Hundred. The lands of the lord of Richard's Castle in the valley of the Lugg used to come to Rowe Ditch beneath Pembridge to hear pleas of the crown, etc., … and they have been withdrawn by Robert de Mortimer since the beginning of the war' (InqMisc). Robert de Mortimer was de facto lord of Richard's Castle from 1204 until his death in 1219. The 'war' referred to is therefore the one between king John and his barons 1215-16.

In another instance of the use of OE *(ge)herness* in Herefordshire, Leland adds it to Ewyas Harold to give *Ewisharneis*. See Ewyas Harold, page 94.

Lyde

(in regione que appellatur) Lydas c675 (copy) ECWM.

See also Arundel Farm, Lower Lyde Court and Farm, and Upper Lyde, all in Pipe and Lyde, Map 4.

There seems to have been a district taking its name from the Lyde Brook (see page 183 under Arundel Farm in Pipe and Lyde). In about 675 king Merewalh (who seems to have been fond of his thirty-hide units) gave Wenlock Abbey *terram triginta manencium in regione que appellatur Lydas*. Finberg (EWCM) thought that *Lydas* might to refer to the place-name Lyde north of Hereford, and in fact the DB organization of estates in this area does tend to confirm this. In medieval times Lyde lay in the deanery of Hereford, and deanery boundaries often preserve ancient lines of demarcation. The western boundary of this deanery north of the Wye ran from the Lugg by Moreton on Lugg to the Wye by Breinton Common, thus cutting off an angle of the Lugg and Wye (see Map 4) that contained 46½ hides, or approximately a half-hundred, in 1086. In origin this half-hundred may have been a Welsh multiple-estate or commote that the English named *Lydas* after its principle aquatic feature. Within it lay four DB estates called Lyde, one of which, 'Lyde Arundel', belonged to the bishop and formed part of a larger episcopal estate embracing Hampton Bishop, Tupsley, Shelwick, Holmer, Pipe and Lyde, Huntington, Warham and Breinton, within which lay approximately thirty hides. This would seem, therefore, to represent Merewalh's gift to Wenlock. No bishopric of Hereford existed in Merewalh's day, but when one was established Wenlock may have given the estate to the bishop.

Maund

(loco qui nominatur) Magana c675 (copy) ECWM.

See also 'Maund Aubin' (Rowberry), Maund Bryan, Dudales Hope and Whitechurch Maund in Bodenham; Rosemaund in Felton; Marden; Freen's Court in Sutton; and Nunnington in Withington, Map 4.

The difficult problems raised by the name Maund are discussed in Gelling, *Signposts to the Past*, 102-5. In amplification of what is said there it seems possible from place-name evidence to define the extent of the district of Maund fairly

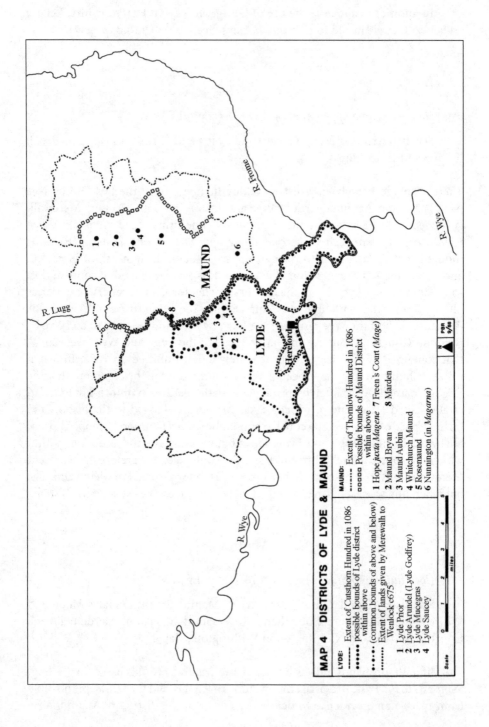

MAP 4 DISTRICTS OF LYDE & MAUND

LYDE:
- ●●●●● Extent of Cutsthorn Hundred in 1086
- •••••• possible bounds of Lyde district within above
- •••••• (common bounds of above and below) Extent of lands given by Merewalh to Wenlock c675

1 Lyde Prior
2 Lyde Arundel (Lyde Godfrey)
3 Lyde Mucegras
4 Lyde Saucey

MAUND:
- ······ Extent of Thornlow Hundred in 1086
- □□□□□ Possible bounds of Maund District within above

1 Hope *juxta Magene* 7 Freen's Court (*Mage*)
2 Maund Bryan 8 Marden
3 Maund Aubin
4 Whitchurch Maund
5 Rosemaund
6 Nunnington (in *Magarna*)

Scale

0 1 2 3 4 5
miles

N PBR 9/88

R. Lugg

R. Frome

R. Wye

MAUND

LYDE

Hereford

R. Wye

20

closely. Sheppard suggested that Maund was the name of a district surrounding Sutton Walls hillfort, an area whose approximate bounds are recognizable in the boundary of the DB hundred of Thornlaw. On strictly place-name evidence, however, this area seems too large. 'Maund' names survive, or are known to have existed, only in the area covered by the modern parishes of Bodenham, Marden, Sutton, Felton, Preston Wynne and Withington, all of which lay in Thornlaw Hundred, as did Ocle Pychard, Pencombe, Ullingswick and the Dinmore outlier west of the Lugg, but in none of these parishes do 'Maund' names occur, either now or in the past. In the six central parishes of Thornlaw listed above there were in 1086 about forty-two hides, plus a number of hides in Marden not accounted for in DB. Later evidence points to there being about five of these hides, which brings the total 'central' hides to nearly fifty. Perhaps, therefore, the district of Maund was in origin a half-hundred based on a Welsh fifty-*trefi* multiple-estate or commote, based on Sutton Walls hillfort, similar to the one assumed to lie behind the district of *Lydas*.

Mawfield

Mais Mail Lochou 6th (c1130), *campo Malochu* 7th (c1130) LL.
Mal(e)feld 1232 Dugdale, 1371 Ipm; *Makfeld* c1250 AD; *Malghfeld* 1306 AD; *Maufelt* 1327 Dugdale.

See also Mawfield in Allensmore, Map 5.

Mais Mail Lochou or its English equivalent Mawfield (the first element of which is a reduction of the Welsh *Mail Lochou* or *Malochu*) covered a small area within the hypothetical bounds of the larger district of Straddle (see below). This area bore the alternative name of *Insulam Ebrdil* ('Ynys Efrddyl') in early Welsh sources. Its approximate limits can be deduced. LL, for instance, says that Madley was in both *Mais Mail Lochou* and *Insulam Ebrdil*, while a church called *Lannguoruoe* (?Eaton Bishop) was in *Campo Malochou*. Likewise, Moccas was situated *in angulo insule Ebrdil* and *Tir Conloc* (?Preston on Wye) *infra insulam Ebrdil*. Regarding Mawfield, the English name for the same district, lands in Godway in Peterchurch were said c1250 to extend as far as *divisae quae sunt versus Makfeld* (AD), while the only place that today bears the English or Welsh versions of the name Mawfield lies in Allensmore. The boundary of the district would therefore seem to lie on the Wye to the north and the high ground separating the Wye plain from the Golden Valley on the west, while on the south and east its boundary must have been defined by the forested area of Treville and Haywood (see Map 5). In modern terms its approximate extent would seem to have been the parishes of Moccas, Blakemere, Tyberton,

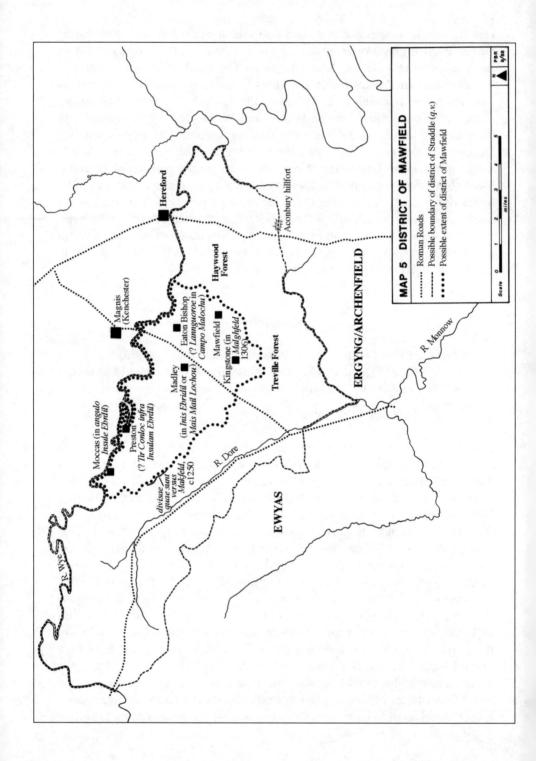

MAP 5   DISTRICT OF MAWFIELD

········· Roman Roads
--------- Possible boundary of district of Straddle (q.v.)
••••••••• Possible extent of district of Mawfield

Scale
0   1   2   3   4   5
        miles

N

PBR
9/88

R. Wye

Moccas (in angulo Insule Ebrdil)

Preston (? Tir Conloc infra Insulam Ebrdil)

divisae quae sunt versus Makfeld, c1250

R. Dore

Madley (in Inis Ebridil or Mais Mail Lochou)

Kingstone (in Malghfield

Mawfield (in Malghfield 1306)

Eaton Bishop (? Lannguoroe in Campo Malochu)

Magnis (Kenchester)

Hereford

Haywood Forest

Treville Forest

Aconbury hillfort

ERGYNG/ARCHENFIELD

R. Monnow

EWYAS

Preston on Wye, Madley, Kingstone and Eaton Bishop, plus the western parts of Allensmore and Clehonger.

'Ynys Efrddyl' or 'Efrddyl's Island' (*ynys* here being used in the sense 'raised land in water meadows') is thought by some to be named after the mother of St Dyfrig, who gave birth to him at Madley. If such a person did exist they are more likely to have been a male saint into whose traditions Dyfrig was 'born' and whose successor he was (LWSS). In LL Dyfrig is made heir to *total insule Ebdril* by a king of Ergyng. Monasteries were founded at Moccas and at *Lannguoruoe* (?Eaton Bishop) in *Campo Malochu*, abbots of whom are named in LL.

Professor Sir John Rhŷs suggested more than a century ago (TGW) that the *Lochou* element in *Mais Mail Lochou* and *Campo Malochou* is to be identified with Llacheu, a mythical son of Arthur (see 'Llygad Amr' in Garway for another mythical son of Arthur's). His few appearances in Arthurian legend strongly suggest that he is a euhemerised version of a pre-Christian god of fire and water. These two elements figure prominently in the story of Efrddyl and Dyfrig told in LL, and since *Insulam Ebrdil* and *Mais Mail Lochou* are one and the same, they can probably be seen as Christian versions of a Celtic deity whose cult was assimilated to their own legendary origins. This Celtic god's twin attributes of fire and water make him an appropriate cult figure in the kingdom of Ergyng, whose wealth, as we have supposed, was founded on the iron industry. Evidence of both crafts has been found at Ariconium and at Magnis (Kenchester) (TWNFC (1965) & (1985)) and at these places furnaces for smelting iron-ore are found within a few feet of troughs for quenching and tempering the hot metal. Another centre of the iron industry at Madley may have given rise to a popular cult of Efrddyl and Dyfrig in Mawfield.

Straddle

'Straddle Valley'
(*valle de*) *Stradelei, Stratelie* 1086 DB; (*vallis de*) *Stra(t)d(e)ley(e)* 1279 Ch, 1337 Ipm, 1359 Ipm.
Strad(d)el(l)e c1100 FW, 1219 InqMisc, 1291 Tax, 1302 Pat, 1341 NonInq, 1390 Ipm, 1409 Cl, 1517 Bothe; *Estradel* 1127 EpActs; *Straddil, -ul* 1316 Ipm, 1349 Trill.
(*valle de*) *Strada* 1169 P.
Stradyvale 1338-61 Court.
Stradhull(e) 1370 AD (p), 1388 Ipm, 1435 Spofford.

'Straddle Hundred'
Stradel H'd' 1086 DB; *Stradeh'dr'* 1175 P; (*fugitorum de*) *Strada* 1175 P.

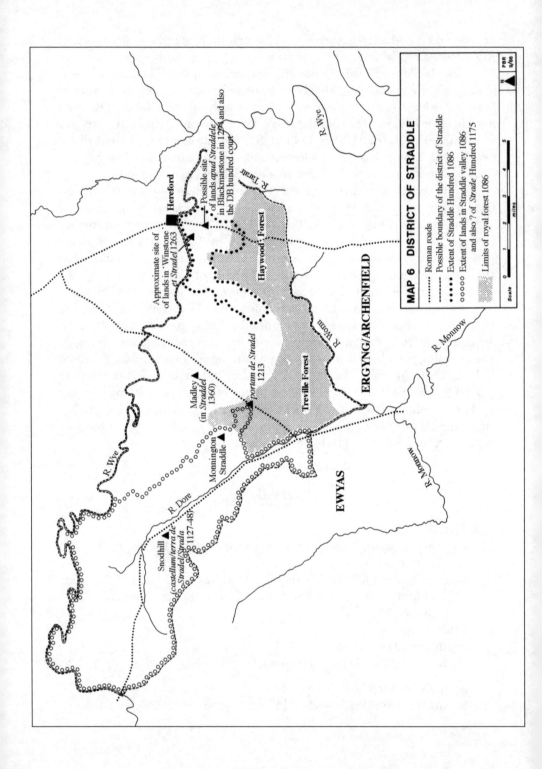

Hereford

Approximate site of of lands in 'Winstone et Stradel 1263

Possible site of lands *apud Straddele* in Blackmarstone in 1294 and also the DB hundred court

R. Wye

R. Wye

R. Taratt

Haywood Forest

R. Worm

portam de Stradel 1213

Madley ▲ (in *Stradel* 1360)

Monnington Straddle ▲

Treville Forest

ERGYNG/ARCHENFIELD

R. Monnow

EWYAS

R. Monnow

R. Dore

Snodhill ▲ (*castellum/terra de Stradel/Strada* 1127-48)

PBR 9/88

N

MAP 6 DISTRICT OF STRADLE

.... Roman roads

‒‒‒‒‒ Possible boundary of the district of Straddle

••••• Extent of Straddle Hundred 1086

ooooo Extent of lands in Straddle valley 1086 and also ? of *Strade* Hundred 1175

▨ Limits of royal forest 1086

Scale

0   1   2   3   4   5
miles

Snodhill Castle and Manor
(terra de) Strada 1127 Regesta; *Strate (cum pertinenciis cum castello)*
    1196 P; *(honor de) Stradie* 1243 Fees.
(castellum de) Stradel 1136-48 Brockworth.

See also 'Straddle' in Hereford, *Portam de Stradell'* in Abbey Dore, Madley
and Monnington Straddle in Vowchurch, Map 6.

A possible way of explaining the geographical spread of this name is to consider
the final element to be OE *leah* used in its early sense of 'forest'. Development
to Straddle instead of Stratley/Streatley/Streetly can be explained partly by
association of the valley-name with late OE *dæl*; but this treatment of –*leah* is
evidenced elsewhere in Herefordshire, in the name Marcle. The first element
is probably *stræt* 'Roman road', perhaps in the plural since three such roads
traverse the area.

Straddle was the name of a district that seems to have covered all the land
south and west of the Wye between Clifford in the west and Dinedor in the east
and extending as far south and west as the rivers Worm and Dore. A large part
of the area was wooded in 1086 and this formed the royal forests of Treville
and Haywood. It was crossed by three Roman roads. Iter XII of the Antonine
Itinerary between Magnis (Kenchester) and Gobannium (Abergavenny) crossed
the plain of the Wye by Madley. Branching off it at Bacton in the Golden Valley,
a road (locally called Fine Street) went up that valley, through Peterchurch, to
the banks of the Wye opposite the Roman fort at Clyro. A third road forded the
Wye at Hereford and went south through Archenfield to Blestium (Monmouth).
The name Straddle shows a fairly even distribution across this area.

In 1086 Straddle Hundred covered a much smaller area south of Hereford.
It contained just seven hides of land and was entirely in the hands of the bishop.
Its hundred-court may have met at the point where the Roman road running
south of Hereford crosses the Bailey Brook (505382), which lies close to a
locality called 'Straddle' in the late 13th century and which was the site of one
of eight general inquisitions annually held by the bailiff of the city of Hereford
(Duncumb; Bailey Brook is not now visible at this location, having been
culverted to pass under housing estates). The city did not extend its boundary
to include this area until the 13th century and when it did the bailiff may simply
have adopted the former hundred-moot as the site of one of his inquisitions.
Straddle Hundred did not survive the reorganization of the hundreds of the
shire in the time of Henry I, its place being taken by Webtree Hundred.

Madley, further west than Straddle Hundred, was said to be in *Straddel*
in 1360 (Ipm) and in 1213 the place where the Roman road (Iter XII) entered
the Wye plain from the south-west was called *portam de Stradell* (Cl; *Strathel*
in Ch). Close by this locality is Monnington Straddle, the only modern place to
retain the ancient district name in its title.

Monnington Straddle lies in Vowchurch parish which, with the parishes of Bacton, Turnastone, Peterchurch, Dorstone, Bredwardine, Cusop and most of Clifford, was in what is called *Valle de Stradelei* in DB. This former English name for the Golden Valley began in the 12th century to be confused with Welsh *ystrad* 'valley', Ystrad Dour being its Welsh name. Thus, in 1127 the land of Snodhill is called *terra de Strada*, although in 1136-48 the castle there is called *castellum de Stradel*. In 1136-48 probably (and certainly in 1175), there was a hundred called *Strade* or *Strada*, which almost certainly had the same extent as the lands said in 1086 to be in *Valle de Stradelei*. This hundred was probably a creation of the time in Henry I's reign that the hundreds of the shire were reorganised. By 1243 it had been amalgamated with Webtree Hundred, which covered most of the rest of the old district of Straddle (Fees). The *Strade* theme was continued at Snodhill, however, its castle and honour being called *Strate* in 1196 and *Stradie* in 1243, although the Golden Valley was still being called *vallis de Stradeleye* as late as 1359 (Ipm).

The survival of Straddle as a district name has not been traced beyond 1360. In its earliest form the district may have been a Welsh land-unit or commote comparable with neighbouring Ewyas and Ergyng/Archenfield. Within its bounds was a smaller district called *Mais Mail Lochou* or Mawfield: see the District Name Mawfield. In the 6th and 7th centuries the whole lay within the post-Roman kingdom of Ergyng.

Abbey Dore (387303)

> *Abbey Dore* 1831 OS.

This is a new name that came into use between 1727 and 1831. Abbeycwmhir in Radnorshire (now Powys) is a similar case (PNRa). Its elements are from the abbey that was founded here in 1147 and the name of the river Dore, for which see ERN.

Earlier names associated with this land-unit are:-

1. 'Llangernyw'.
   Lann Cerniu c580, c625 (c1130) LL.
   Cenubia Cornubium id est Lann Cerniu super ripam Dour c745 (c1130), LL.

   'Church of Cernyw'.

Bounds of *Lann Cerniu* c580 (c1130) LL: '... *or nant dylicat nant yreguic, onant ireguic cehit inant dirheith tir rud ini perued ircoit behit pan a nir halmelen ynhiaun behet pan cuid in lost irinis, o lost irinis hit bronn iralt.*'

'... from the steam to the source of the brook *Ewic*. From the brook *Ewic* the length of the stream to the red barley-ground to the centre of the wood; the wood till it reaches yellow moor, straight on to where it rises to the tail of the island. From the tail of the island to the breast of the wooded slope.'

Egerton Phillimore (in Owen's Pembrokeshire) followed by ECWM and Davies equates *Lann Cerniu* 'on the banks of the Dore' with *Cum Barruc* in Dorstone. However, the grant of king Ithel of Gwent which he uses as authority for this, though very obscure in places, nowhere makes *Cum Barruc* and *Lann Cerniu* one and the same. Evans (LL) suggested that it might be the site of Dore Abbey and this is quite possible, although the bounds do little to confirm or deny it, unless the unnamed 'stream' in line one is the Dore and *Ewic* is the name of the brook that meets the Dore at 386310, north of Abbey Dore. 'The breast of the wooded slope' may then be the ridge of high ground separating Abbey Dore from Dulas on the west.

2. *Blancheberbshale* c1120-5 WalkerReg; *Blancbrahel* 1195 P (p).
   Blancharbesal 1232 Dugdale; *Blakelarbestall* n.d. Williams.
   Blak Berats Haulle c1540 Leland.
   Blakeconersham n.d. Williams.

This obscure name might have OE *halh* (dative *hale*) as its final element. One sense of *halh* is 'tongue of land between rivers'. Abbey Dore and Ewyas Harold occupy such a tongue between the river Dore and Dulas Brook.

Robert of Ewyas, founder of Dore Abbey, gave *Blancharbesal* as the site of the new church. The name may refer to the parts of Abbey Dore parish lying west of the Dore. The abbey later extended its lands to include large tracts of Treville Forest east of the Dore and these now form the parts of Abbey Dore parish lying east of that river.

Batchy Farm (396368)

> *Baggeshagh'* 1214 ClR.
> *Baddeshage* c1217, *Baddissawe* c1220 Capes (p); *Baddesawe* 1275 RH; *Badeshagh'* 1281 Select Cases (p); *Baddesshaue* 1322 Ipm (p); *Bad(d)es(c)hawe* 1327 Banco, 1400 Duncumb; *Buddeshawe* 1327 Dugdale.
> *Baldesane* c1270 Skidmore (p).
> *Bacho* 1831 OS.

'Bæddi's projecting wood', second element OE *sceaga*.

(lost, but probably at c429341)

> *Fernilegh in Hoppilegh, La Sallonere in Hoppilegh* 1227 Ch.

In 1227 king Henry III confirmed to Dore Abbey lands on the eastern side of Treville Wood. The bounds of this land indicate that these places lay south-west of Grithill (430341) near the grid reference given.

The two –*lēah* names probably have plant-names in –*ig* as first elements; thus 'ferny wood/clearing' and 'wood/clearing where wild hops grow'. *La Sallonere* is obscure; if it were amended to *Sallouere*, a derivative with –*er* of *salh* 'willow' might be considered, perhaps 'willow clump'.

(Brampton Hill 402355)

> *Portam de Stradell'* 1213 Cl; *gate of Strathel* 1227 Ch.

For the name, see District Name Straddle. The bounds of the land confirmed to the abbey in 1227 by king Henry III show that the 'gate of Straddle' lay at Brampton Hill.

(lost, but probably at c412339)

> *Bathlegh* 1227 Ch; *Baddeslegh* 1316 FA.

Again, the bounds of king Henry's grant show that this place lay at the approximate grid reference given.

If the later form is more reliable, then 'Bæddi's wood/clearing', with the same personal name as Batchy, two miles to the north-west. The earlier form suggests a derivation from OE *bæth* 'artificial pool'.

❧ ACONBURY ☙

Aconbury (516336)

'Fort inhabited by squirrels', see DEPN, the reference being to Aconbury hillfort.

(Aconbury Hill 330504)

> *Cair Rein* 1128, *Cayr Rein* c1130 LL; *Arauaio monte* c1135 Geoffrey; *munt d'Arave* c1155 Wace; *munte of Ravinite* c1190 Layamon.

The boundaries of the diocese claimed by bishop Urban of Llandaff (1107-33) in LL include *Caer Rein* on the northern border of Archenfield. Its position on those boundaries indicates that this is a reference to Aconbury hillfort. It bears the name of Rhain Dremrudd, eponymous ruler of the kingdom of Rhieinwg in the 6th century, for which see BBCS, **24** (1970). Jones (P-RW) notes that this hillfort dominates the *maenor wrthir*, or upland *maenor*, of a Welsh commote in Ergyng: see Much and Little Birch. Geoffrey of Monmouth refers to *Cair Rein* c1135 as *Aruaio monte*, the place where Arthur slew the giant *Retho* (Rhain), and in Master Wace's version of this fabulous history (c1155) the giant is *Riton* and the location of his death *munte d'Arave*. Layamon, a local man from Arley Kings on the Severn writing c1190, greatly expanded Wace's version, and in his tale it is king *Riun* whom Arthur slays on 'the mount of *Ravin*' (Wace; Layamon).

Caldicott (526378)

> *Caldecote* mid-13th *StGC*

'Cold cottages', a common name.

Merryvale Farm (517324)

> *Muraule* 1294 Swin; *Mury Wale* 1388 Duncumb; *Merivalefeld* 1415 Duncumb; *Merryfold* 1831 OS.

This and Merryvale Farm in Eye, Moreton and Ashton (which see) are well-known as doublets of Merevale, Warwickshire. The spellings for the Herefordshire names supports a hybrid late OE/French origin from *myrig* 'pleasant' and French *val* 'valley'. Merryvale in Aconbury is at the head of a stream-valley. In the Warwickshire name, the spellings show that *myrig* was associated with a Latin *mira* 'wonderful' and the possibility of a Latin name *mira vallis*, coined for Merevale Abbey, has been noted. The Herefordshire doublets make an English/French origin, not necessarily connected with the abbey, seem more probable. All three names are likely to be post-Conquest.

🙣 ACTON BEAUCHAMP 🙥

Acton Beauchamp (679503)

'*tūn* by the oak(s)', with the well-known family name affixed: see DEPN.

🙣 ADFORTON 🙥

Adforton (402710)

> *Alfertintune* 1086 DB; *Alfarton* 1292 BM.
> *Aufreton'* 1243 Fees.
> *Eatforton, Etferton* 1272-1307 BM.
> *Atforton* 1292 Subs; *Atfreton* 1304 Ipm; *At(t)ferton(e)* 1397 VR, 1648 KPC.
> *Atfordton* 1535 VE.

Perhaps OE *Ealdfrithingtūn*, 'estate associated with Ealdfrith'.

(site of Wigmore Abbey 411712)

> *Beodun* 1148-63 (14th) Chronicle.

'Bee hill'. OE *dūn* is appropriate for the low, whale-backed hill which runs south-west from the abbey site. According to Chronicle, *Beodun* was the final site chosen for this much-moved abbey.

Paytoe (412715)

> *Peyton'* 1249 Inspeximus.
> *Paytowe* 1529-30 Court; *Petytone* 1547 HT.
> *Peyto* 1649 KPC.

Peyton' is possibly a mistranscription for *Peytou'*. A name ending in *hōh*, 'hill spur', would suit the site, as the hill mentioned under *Beodun* has a sharp point at this end. But the first part of the name *Pegethōh* would be obscure. It is simpler to accept *Peyton* as evidence for an etymology 'Pæga's settlement' (with *-tūn*), and to assume influence from *hoh*.

Stanway (399710)

> *Stanewei* 1086 DB; *Stanwey(e)* 1180/1-1214 (14th) Chronicle, 1249
> Inspeximus, 1412 Capes; *Stanway* 1397 VR.

'Stone way'. This name is more likely to refer to the road to Letton than the Roman road, which runs a mile to the east.

℀ ALLENSMORE ℀

Allensmore (467359)

> *More* 1086 DB.
> *Aleinesmore* 1220 Cur; *Aleynesmore* 1368 Capes, 1428 FA.
> *Moralayn* 1265 Cl; *Mora Alani* c1285 Red Book, 1320 Capes, 1346 Ipm;
> *More Alani* 1341 NonInq.

OE *mōr* in the sense 'wet, low-lying ground'. The presence of another settlement of the same name on the north-west side of Hereford probably encouraged the use of the affixes *Aleyn-*, *Alani-*.

The bishop of Hereford's DB manor of *More* in Straddle Hundred is almost certainly Allensmore, rather than The Moor in Clifford (cf. PNHe; Thorn). He did have another manor of Moor near Hereford, but this was at Canon Moor, north-west of the city and outside Straddle. Straddle Hundred belonged entirely to the bishop in 1086 and as we have established above this hundred lay south of the city (see District Name Straddle, page 23) and as Allensmore was always in episcopal hands in the medieval period, Allensmore almost certainly represents it. To distinguish it from the other episcopal manor of Moor it acquired an affix from Alan fitzMayn (fl. 1141 WalkerCh) who was the bishop's subtenant there.

Hungerstone (444352)

> *Hungareston* 1137-9 HDB; *Hun(i)egarestun'* 1243, 1249 Fees; *Honga(r)ston*
> 1316 FA, 1345 Ipm.
> *Hungaredeston* 1251-2 Fees (p).

Probably '*Hūngar's settlement'. DEPN suggests *gærstūn* 'paddock' compounded with personal name *Huna*.

31

Mawfield (Upper and Lower Mawfield Farms 452367)

> *Malfelle* 1086 DB; *Mal(e)feld* 1160-70 HDB, 1281 Select Cases, 1316 FA,
>   1327 Banco, 1334 SR, 1346 AD; *Maldfeyld* 1514 HT (p).
> *Malcfeld(e)* 1243 & 1249 Fees.
> *Machefeld* 1303 Swin (p).

> See District Name Mawfield.

Winnall (453343)

> *Wilehal(l)e* 1086 DB, 1160-70 HDB.
> *Wylenhall'* 1265 Cl; *Wyllenhale* 1361 Ipm; *Willenhall* 1371 Ipm; *Wilnehale*
>   1485 Ipm.

Probably 'willow nook', from OE **wiligen* 'growing with willows' and *hale*,
dative of *halh*.

﹏ **ALMELEY** ﹏

Almeley (332515)

> *Elmelie* 1086 DB, 1137-9 HDB; *Helmeley* 1222 Cur.
> *Almeleia* 1165-73 Delisle; *Almali(e)* 1278 Cant, 1303 FA; *Almaly* 1291 Tax,
>   1400-1 *KinRR*; *Allmeley* 1308 AD, 1610 BM.
> *Aumeley* 1243 Fees; *Aumaleye* 1266 AD.
> *Almalaley* 1543 HT.

'Elm wood', identical with Elmley in Kent and Worcestershire. There are pre-
Conquest spellings for the two Worcestershire Elmleys, so *elm* is certainly the
first element, but both Worcestershire names have ME *Alm-*, *Aume-* forms like
this one.

Almeley Wooton (333525)

> *Wutton'* 1206 P; *Wouton* 1308 AD; *Wotton* 1429 Ipm.

'Settlement near a wood', OE *wudu-tūn*.

Eccles Alley (344520)

> *Eckl(e)y(s)* 1359-60 *KinRR*; *Ek(k)eley* 1400-1 *KinRR* (p), 1407 AD (p);
>   *Eccleys, Nekyllys* 1492 Ipm.

On the face of it, another 'Ecca's wood or clearing' as at Eccles Green in Norton Canon. However, it should be noted that the township is on the western side of a Roman fort (recorded by the Herefordshire SMR) in Camp Field (349522), so there is at least an outside chance that it involves OE *ecles* 'church'. Alley has been added to the genitive of this place-name, presumably because of a special characteristic of the road on which the hamlet stands which causes it to be referred to in this way.

Hopley's Green (341526)

> *(H)oppeleye* 1359-60 *KinRR*; *Hopeley* 1379 PT (p).
> *Hopleyse Grene* 1543 HT.

Probably 'wood or clearing in a secluded valley, from OE *hop* and *lēah*.

Logaston (348514)

> *Lugastone* 1328 PNHe; *Leugarston'* (p), *Lengaston'*, *Lenharston(e)* 1359-60
>   *KinRR*; *Lengaston* 1400-1 *KinRR*.

Possibly 'paddock with a shelter', from OE *hlēo* and *gæstun*. But the personal name *Lēofgar* + *tūn* might appear as *Levgarstone* in the 14th century. Hungerstone in Allensmore presents an analogous problem.

Oldcastle (327520)

> *Veteri Castro* 1303 GEC (p).
> *Old(e)castel(l)* 1359-60 *KinRR* (p), 1392 QD (p), 1429 Ipm.

There is an 'old castle' with slightly earlier spellings in Malpas, Cheshire.

Upcott (326508)

> *Up(p)cote* 1160-70 HDB, 1339 Ipm; *Uppekote* 1243 Fees.

'Higher cottage(s)'. DB says of Almeley that 'the men of another village work in this village' and HDB names that village as Upcott.

Woonton (352522)

> *Wen(n)etun(e)* 1086 DB, 1130-5 LeomC; *Wentona* 1160-70 HDB.
> *Winnet(una)* 1123, 1148-63 LeomC.
> *Woneton(e)* 1359-60 *KinRR*, 1389 AD.

'Pasture settlement', from OE *wynne* + *tūn*, or 'Wynna's settlement'. **wynne* is a rare element in place-names; when it does occur it is most frequently a first element, not a generic.

❧ ASHPERTON ☙

Ashperton (642415)

> *Sp(er)tune* 1086 DB
> *Aspreton(i)a* 1144 MonC, 1186 Fr; *Ashp(er)ton'* 1224 Cur, 1291 Tax;
>   *Asperton(e)* 1336 Ipm, 1347 KPC, 1397 VR.
> *Espertona* 1160-70 HDB; *Espreton'* 1174-86 Fr.

The spellings suggest OE **peretūn* 'pear orchard' with *æsc* 'ash tree' prefixed. DEPN suggests *tūn* added to OE *æscbeorh* 'ash hill', *æscburna* 'ash stream' or *Æscbeorht* personal name; but none of these suits the spellings so well, and *burna* is a very rare element in Shropshire and Herefordshire.

Walsopthorne (651424)

> *Walesapeldor(na)* 1086 DB, 1160-70 HDB.
> *Walsop(e)thorn(e)* 1243 Fees, 1317 Ipm, 1334 SR; *Walshopesthorne* 1346 FA.
> *Walshipton* 1291 Ch.
> *Walesthorn, Walnesthorp* 1407 Ipm.

The DB form suggests 'Welshman's apple-tree', from OE *Walh* (genetive *Wales*) and *apuldor, apuldre*, and this may have been the original name. If so, it was refashioned in the belief that it contained *hop* 'secluded valley' and *thorn* 'thorn- tree'.

❧ PIPE ASTON ☙

Aston (461718)

> *Hesintune* 1086 DB, - *id est Asciston* 1160-70 HDB.
> *Assiston* 1291 Tax, 1527 Court.
> *Aston* 1305 Ipm, - *in Wigmoresland* 1349 Trill, 1434 KPC, 1535 VE.

This name is explained in Thorn as 'estate called after the ash-tree(s)', with OE **Escingtūn* alternating with **Æscestūn*. The development to Aston instead of ***Ashton may have been assisted by the position of the settlement east of Burrington. The material available throws no light on the origin of the affix 'Pipe'.

❧ ASTON INGHAM ☙

Aston Ingham (6833236)

> *Estune* 1086 DB; *Estona* 1175 P; *Estone* 1256 Capes; *Astone* 1300 Swin.
> *Estun' Ingan* 1243 Fees.

'East settlement', perhaps named in distinction to Weston under Penyard: they lie east and west of the site of the Roman town of Ariconium (646238). Richard Ingan had this manor in 1212 (Fees), although the affix probably comes from his ancestor, Hingan, who was living in 1127 (AC). See also Ashe Ingen in Bridstow.

Yartleton Farm (688219)

> *Yarkeltone* 1345 Trill (p).

This place-name also occurs in the neighbouring parish of Longhope in Gloucestershire. PNGl considers its first element to be **Arc-*, **Ærc-*, a stem-formation from an OE folk-name derived from the district name Ergyng (Archenfield), and the second element *dūn* 'hill'.

❧ AVENBURY ☙

Avenbury (661531)

> *Agnanbyrig* 873-915 ECWM.
> *Aweneburi* 1086 DB.
> *Agenebir(ia)* 1137-9 HDB, 1211-12 RBE; *Agn(e)bur(i)(a)* 1141-3 StGC,
>   1148-63 Foliot, c1240 StGC; *Haghenebir'* 1196 P (p); *Aygnebur'* 1199
>   StGC; *Agnebury* c1250-c75 St Katherine (p).
> *Aveberi* 1166 RBE.
> *Aunebir'* 1210 RotLib (p); *Auuebur'* early 13th StGC.
> *Avenebir'* 1210 RotLib (p); *Aveneby(ry)* c1220 DiversAccs, c1250 Capes (p);
>   *Avenebur(y)* 1241, 1273 Capes, 1334 SR.

The connection between *Agnanbyrig* and Avenbury is made in ECWM and this is amply supported by later forms. Its second element is *byrig*, dative of *burh*, probably in the sense 'manor house'. The first element is likely to be an OE personal name. There is an OE name-theme *Ægen-*; and a weak simplex **Ægena* would be a reasonable conjecture. The Avenbury forms require **Agena*, however, and it can only be hazarded that this might have been a side-form of **Ægena*.

Whether or not the first element is a personal name, the OE form of Avenbury is likely to have been *Agenanbyrig*. The –*g*- was vocalised to –*u*-, and the name was later refashioned as if the –*u*- were a spelling for the consonant –*v*.

'Debitots Barn' (now Upper Munderfield 615546)

Said to be named after the d'Abbetot family, who also provided the 'Abbey' affix for Rowden Abbey in Winslow (TWNFC (1893-4)). They were from St-Jean-d'Abbetot, between Le Havre and Lillebonne, dépt. Seine-Maritime (Loyd).

Little Froome Farm (652535)

See 'Frome' in Wolferlow.

The Greeve (654518)

Grefes Momfeld 1268-75 *Red Book MS*.

OE *græfe* 'copse', and Munderfield (below).

Hackley Farm (653533)

Hakel(e) 1231 Cur, 1268-75 *Red Book MS* (p); *Hakeley(e)* 1357 (p) 1452
   Slocombe.
Nether Hakeleye 1379 *Slocombe*; *Netherhecluid* 1413 *Slocombe*.

Also to be associated with this name, perhaps, is the following surname, which is normally preceded by 'of' or 'de':-

Hakelitil 1263 Pat; *Hakelittel* 1276 Swin; *Hakelut(t)el* 1285 Ch, 1304 Swin.
Hakelite, Hakeluyte c1285 Red Book; *Hakelut* 1327 Banco.

Possibly a compound of *lēah* 'wood or clearing' with *haca* 'hook', to which was added OE *lȳt* 'little', alternating with *lȳtel*. It is possible that *Hakele* 1231 and *Netherhecluid* 1413 refer to two separate settlements. If so, the family came from the one that was distinguished as 'little'. The ridge on the end of which Hackley Farm stands might have been called *Haca* 'Hook'.

Munderfield Farm ('Munderfield Hagurnel' 645570)

Mandefeld 1194 P (p); *Monderfeld* 1224 Cur, 1268-75 *Red Book MS* (p);
   Mundrefeld 1224 Cur.
Mundrefeld Hagghernel 1285 Cl.

'Munda's open land', OE *Mundanfeld*. Mundham, Sussex ('Munda's village'), is *Mundreham* 1086 *et seq.*, *Mondreham* 1187. The *re-* has been explained as an Anglo-French development of *–ne-* from earlier *–an-*, *-en-*, and this explanation suits Munderfield also. The affix comes from the family of Hagurner or Hagurnel, which had lands at nearby Lower Hopton ('Hopton Hagurnel') in Stoke Lacy.

Munderfield Harold (622549)

Munderfeldeherald 1424 AD.

The affix may be from the family of John Harold who was a cleric of Bromyard in 1383 (Capes).

The Venn (Lower Venn Farm 665506)

Fac' 1160-70 (c1219?) HDB (p).
Fenna 1211-12 RBE (p), 1243 Fees; *La Fenne* c1220 DiversAccs, 1265 Ch
    (p), 1277 Cant, 1295 Ipm; *- juxta Frome Episcopi* 1346 FA.
La Venne Inferior 1372 Ipm.

'Fen'. The two affixes were to distinguish it from The Venn (Vennwood) in Bodenham.

༇   AYLTON   ✄

Aylton (658377)

Merchelai DB.

Ailmeton(e) 1137-9 HDB, 1267 Ipm; *A(y)lmeton(e)* 1251-2 Fees, 1291 Tax,
    1334 SR.
Eilinetona 1160-70 HDB; *Ayleuentun'* 1250 Fees; *Aylyinton* 1284 AD;
    Aylineton 1294 Ipm; *Alynetone* 1309 Swin (p); *Aylyneton* 1352 Trill.
Eleuetun' 1243 Fees; *Aylvichetone* 1283 Swin.
Alyston 1341 NonInq.
Aeltone 1397 VR.

'Æthelgifu's estate'. The personal name is feminine. In 1086 the estate was in the king's manor of Much Marcle: HDB distinguishes it as Aylton.

Aymestrey (426652)

> *Elmodestreu* 1086 DB.
> *Eilmundestro vel Bedmodestreu* 1160-70 HDB; *Aylmondestres* c1140 (14th)
>   Chronicle; *Ailmondestre* 1291 Tax, 1353 Trill.
> *Aymondestre* 1303 FA.
> *Aelmenstre* 1397 VR; *Ailmestre* 1419 BM, 1428 FA.

'Æthelmund's tree'. A note in Thorn says of the 1160-70 reference that the indication is that the place then had another name, 'Beadumund's tree'.

Gatley Park (450684)

> *Gat(e)ley(e)* 1275 Cant, 1566 BM; *Gatelegh* 1301 Pat; *Gathele* 1424 Ipm.
> *Gattelyth* 1292 QW; *Gatelith* 1304 Ipm.

'Goat's slope', second element OE *hlith*, which is used in place-names for a concave hill-slope. There is, or was, another Gatley in Eastnor.

Lye, Upper and **Lower** (395658 and 405667)

> *Liya* 704-9 ECWM.
> *Lecwe* 1086 DB.
> *Lega, -e* 1086 DB, 1243 Fees; *Legham, Leghe* 1219 InqMisc.
> *Leye* 1243 Fees, 1316 FA, 1527 Court; *(L)Eye* 1148-9 (14th) Chronicle.

> (?)*Feverlege* c1540 Leland.

> *Leye Inferior* 1292 Subs (p).
> *Netherleye* 1303 FA, 1305 Ipm; *Nether Lighe* 1560 Court.

> *Overley(e)* 1263 Pat, 1303 FA, 1305 Ipm; *Ov'lee* 1535 VE.

'Clearing', OE *lēah*.

King Coenred of Mercia gave lands in Lingen and *Liya* to a certain Feleburga, who seems to have founded a religious house (ECWM). This house may be the one that Leland calls *Feverlege* and which he says was 'suppressed *olim*' and its lands given to Wigmore Abbey and Limebrook Priory. Wigmore was a Mortimer foundation and received lands in Lower Lye from them. The nunnery at Limebrook was founded in Lingen by Mortimer subtenants; the site chosen for it perhaps being influenced by foreknowledge of Feleburga's house and its location. It is possible that *Feverlege* preserves a local form in which the lady's name, *Feleburh*, was used as an affix to the simplex place-name.

Shirley Farm (384653)

> *Sirelei* 1086 DB; *Shorley* 1275 Cant; *Shurley* 1546 HT.
> *Schurlet* 1305 Ipm; *Sherlythe* 1399 PNHe.

'Bright concave hill-slope', from OE *scīr* and *hlith*. It is interesting to have two names in this parish containing the comparatively rare generic *hlith*.

Sned Wood (405661)

> *Sutsned* 1256 Salop Eyre (p).

Sned is OE *snǣd*, probably 'detached piece of woodland'. *Sut-* in the early form is probably 'south'.

Woodhampton Farm (408672)

> *Wodehampton* 1256 Salop Eyre (p); *Woodarton* 1275 Cant.

'Woodland settlement', from OE *wudu* and *hāmtūn*.

Yatton (430668)

> *Yetton(a)* 1179 Inspeximus, 1292 Subs, 1336 Ipm; *Yeaton* 1631 KPC.
> *Yetton' inferior* 1249 Inspeximus.

'Settlement at a pass through hills', first element OE *geat*. The A4110 between Hereford and Kington, a Roman road in origin, passes through a ridge of hills just to the south, by Aymestrey. 'Inferior' perhaps to distinguish it from Yatton near Much Marcle.

❧ BACTON ☙

Bacton (371323)

> *Bachetone* 1086 DB; *Baketon(e)* 1188 P (p), 1224 Cur, 1291 Tax, 1316 FA,
>   1341 NonInq, 1428 FA; *Bactone* 1397 VR.
> *Bakinter* c1115-c25 GloucC (p); *Backingtona* c1132 EpActs; *Ba(s)kinton(a)*
>   1160-70 HDB, 1166 RBE, 1206, 1210 Cur (p), 1213 ClR (p), 1235 Cl,
>   1230-58 CirenC (p); *Bachintune* c1220 BreconC; *Bakynton* 1317 Ipm.

'Bacca's estate'; an unusually clear instance of the genitival construction (OE *Baccantūn) alternating with the use of connective –ing- (*Baccingtūn).

Tremorithic (359315)

(land in) *Moreduc* 1216-72 AD.
Mordicston 1287 AD; *Mordekeston* 1291 Tax; *Tremoreiddig* 1831 OS.

'Mordoc's estate'; Welsh *tref* probably alternating with OE *tūn*.

℀ BALLINGHAM ℀

Ballingham (576316)

Baldinga' 1160-70 HDB; *Baldingesham* 1162 Holtzmann; *Badelingeham*
1215 ClR; *Balding(e)ham* 1244-6 StGC, 1251 Ch, 1412 BM; *Baldyngham*
1297 Duncumb.
Ballingham 1237 StGC; *Balinge(s)ham* 1291 Tax, 1457, 1519 Owen;
Ballyngham 1334 SR.
Balincham 1535 VE.
Belynyan 1558 BM.

This name probably does not contain the Welsh name *Budgualan*, for which
see Carey, below. It is more likely to be an OE name *Badelingaham* 'land in a
river-bend belonging to the followers of Badela'. The 1535 spelling shows palatalisation (development of –ing- to –inch-) that is common in Shropshire and
Herefordshire names.

Carey (564310)

(capella de) Cari 1162 Holtzmann; *Kary* 1237 StGC; *Cary* 1272-1307, 1523
Owen; *Care* 1519 Owen; *Kery* 1534 Owen.

The 'chapel of Carey' may originally have been called: *Podum Sancti
Budgualan* c620 (c1130); *Lann Budgualan in hostio Crican super Guy* c860 (c1130);
Lann Budgual 1045-1104 (c1130) LL. The bounds (incomplete) of *Podum Sancti
Budgualan* c620 (c1130) are given in LL: 'A uado selinam super ... transuersum
usque influmine magno iuxta riuulum circhan incircuitu fluminis guy, totus angulus
datus est ...', 'From the willow ford ... upwards as far as the great river near the
Circhan brook; the whole angle within the circuit of the Wye is given'.
Regarding the bounds, Davies (Unciae) and *Rollason* suggest that the 'ford
by the willow' (*vado selinam*) stood on the Careybrook at Lower Witherstone
in Little Dewchurch (557317) and that the boundary then crossed over the Wye

('great river'; *fluminis magno*) at 565327 near 'Abertar' in Bolstone. They then took in the circuit of the Wye round to the mouth of the Careybrook (*rivulum Circhan*) before going up that brook back to *vado selinam*. *Rollason* further suggests that the site of *Podum Sancti Budgualan* or *Lann Budgualan* within these bounds was at Carey rather than Ballingham, and that the ecclesiastical centre of the estate only later moved to its present site. A site at Carey would certainly fit the description *...in hostio Crican super Guy* better than Ballingham. If *Lann Budgualan* did change its site this could have taken place in the 11th century, when bishop Herewald dedicated or rededicated a number of Archenfield churches, apparently after they had become deserted.

However, the problem with equating *rivulum Circhan* with Careybrook is that the names are different, and Carey looks like the original, British name of the brook, identical with Carey, Devon, Cary, Somerset and some other examples in DEPN (Ekwall did not realise that the Herefordshire Carey was an ancient one).

Somewhere in Ballingham there was an *Oldeton*' (1268 *StGC*) which gave its name to *Oldetunesmedewe* and *Oldestonefeld* (mid 13th *StGC*). There was also an *Olde Wrthin* (mid 13th *StGC*).

BARTESTREE

Bartestree (568406)

> 'Beorhtweald's tree'; see DEPN.

WELSH BICKNOR

Welsh Bicknor (592177)

> *Garthbenni Lanncusthennin ... Lann Idoudecsent in eodem cimiterio*
>   1066-87 (c1130) LL.
> *Ecclesiam Sancti Custenin de Biconovria* 1144 MonC.

Bicknor is probably 'ridge with a beak'. The affix is to distinguish it from English Bicknor on the other side of the Wye in Gloucestershire.

Both Welsh and English sources of the 12th century refer to the church of Welsh Bicknor as St Constantine's. It is likely, however, that before the 11th century, when bishop Herewald was busy dedicating and rededicating churches in Archenfield, St Constantine's church in *Garthbenni* stood at Hentland in Goodrich (which see) and that before St Constantine's was transferred to Welsh Bicknor and combined with it 'in one cemetery' the church of Welsh Bicknor was known as *Lann i Doudec Sent* 'the church of the Twelve Saints'.

(**Hill** at 578182)

> *Holston* 1537, *Howlston* 1571, *Houlston* 1608 Duncumb.

Perhaps a compound of **hugol* 'hillock' with *stān* 'stone'.

⁂ MUCH AND LITTLE BIRCH ⁂

Much and **Little Birch** (504305 and 512312)

> *Mainaure* 1086 DB

> *Birche(s)* 1160-70 HDB, 1251-2 Fees, 1535 VE; *La Birich* 1162 Holtzmann;
> *Burchis* 1257 StGC (p).

> *Briches Beate Marie* 1291 Tax; *Seyntmariebirches* 1302-3 LWE.
> *Little Byrche* 1523 AD.

> *Byrches Sancti Thomas* 1334 SR
> *Magna Byrche* 1543 HT.

> 'Birch trees'.

The DB estate called *Mainaure* is annotated *Birches* in HDB. Later information makes it almost certain that the DB estate is a remnant of a much larger land-unit represented in the 14th century by the 'liberty of Showle' within Archenfield (SR). This 'liberty' included Aconbury, Ballingham, Bolstone, Little Dewchurch, eastern Much Dewchurch, Dewsall, Callow and Hoarwithy, as well as Much and Little Birch. Jones (P-RW) suggests that this large composite estate was the *maenor* (*Mainaure* in DB) *wrthir*, or 'upland *maenor*' of Ergyng and that it was centred on the hillfort at Aconbury. A corresponding *maenor fro*, or 'lowland *maenor*', was probably centred on Hentland (below).

Athelstan's Wood (520310)

> *bosco de Alston'* 1237 Cl; *Elstaneswod* 1251 Ch; *Adhelstaneswude* 1265
> InqMisc; *Elystanewode* 1348 Duncumb; *Aylstones Wood* 1573 AncWood.

The wood was in episcopal hands until the 12th century, when it became crown property. It seems likely, therefore, that it is named from Athelstan, the bishop of Hereford who died in 1056.

Bigglestone (517302)

> *Vigliston* 1388 Duncumb (p).
> *Buggleston* 1442 Ipm; *Bygylston* 1525 HT (p); *Begelston* 1545 HT; *Biggleston* 1663 MA.
> *Biddlestone* 1831 OS.

Possibly 'Biccel's tun', with the change of *–c–* to *–g–* seen in Biggleswade, Bedfordshire, though this does not manifest itself until 1486 in the Bedfordshire name. Earlier spellings are required for a safe etymology.

Bromley (532299)

> *Brompley* 1334 SR

Perhaps 'bramble wood/clearing'.

Rowlston's Barn (526305)

> *Rolveston(e)* 1275 AcornC, 1276 InqMisc, 1277 AD, 1304 Ipm; *Rolston* 1429-32 Court.
> *Rouleston* 1290 ET; *Rovelestone* 1294 Swin; *Roulueston* 1400 Duncumb.

'Hrōlf's estate', identical with Rolleston in Leicestershire, Staffordshire and Wiltshire. There is also a parish called Rowlestone in Herefordshire (below).

❧ BIRLEY ❧

Birley (568406)

> 'wood/clearing by a fort', see DEPN.

Lye Court (458527)

> *Leghe* 1372 Ipm.

'clearing', OE *lēah*.

❧ BISHOP'S FROME ❧

See page 100.

Bishopstone (415439)

> *Malveshill* 1086 DB
>
> *Bissopeston(a)* 1135-54 OxfordFacs, 1169-70 HDB, 1286 Ipm, 1328 Banco
> (p); *Biscopestone* 1166 RBE (p), 1210-12 RBE.
> *Bissopesden'* 1196 Cur (p).

'Bishop's estate', once part of a larger land-unit called Mansell, for which see Mansell Gamage and Mansell Lacy. The bishop's part of it is identified as Bishopstone in HDB.

Bunshill (431424)

> *Bunesulle* 1086 DB; *Bunneshulle* c1270 AD (p); *Bunshull'* 1334 SR.
> *Boneshulla(m)* 1142 Holtzmann, 1160-70 HDB; *Boneshill* 1198 CartAntiq;
> *Boneshull(e)* 1258 AD, 1280 Cant (p), 1294 Swin.
> *Bunehilla* 1185 P (p); *Bunhulle* 1283 Capes (p).
> *Bounshyll* 1505 AD.
>
> *Overbunshill* 1398 AD.

Probably 'Bun's hill'. The hill is a projection of the Garnon's Hill massif, which is shown clearly by the hachuring on the 19th century 1" map.

In spite of the 1505 spelling the vowel of the first element was probably short. It is either a personal name *Bun* (a strong form of the recorded *Buna*) or a hill-name. OE *buna* 'cup' is not out of the question; an *–s–* genitive would be ungrammatical for the word, but possible if the word had become a hill-name.

ᴥ **BLAKEMERE** ᴥ

Blakemere (362411)

> 'Black mere', see DEPN.

ᴥ **BODENHAM** ᴥ

Bodenham ('Bodenham Devereux' 530509)

> 'Boda's land in a river bend'. DEPN prefers 'Boda's village', but the situation is a classic *hamm* and *hamm* is always likelier than *hām* in this county.

The part of Bodenham at this location was also known as:

Chyrcharde 1389 AD; *Chircheyord* 1428 AD.
Bodenham Devereux 1588 BM.

This manor, which contained the parish church, came into the hands of William, progenitor of the Devereux family in Herefordshire. He was from Évreux, dépt. Eure, Normandy.

Bodenham Moor ('Bodenham Furches' and 'Bodenham Roger' 544505)

Le (La) More 1254 InqMisc, 1360 AD; *Mora* 1318 AD.
Le (la) Nethermore 1409, 1508 AD.
Bodeham Rogeri 1243 Fees.
Bodenham F(o)urches 1249 Fees, 1363 Ipm.

Bodenham 'Roger' was held by Roger of Bodenham in 1243. The family of Furches was widespread in Herefordshire after the Conquest. Herbert de Furches had part of Bodenham in 1086 and in 1249 William de Furches had Bodenham Furches.

Bowley Town (583532)

Bolelei 1086 DB.
Bolege, Bolis c1220-30 BreconC (p).
Balleleg 1225 Cur.
Bol(l)ey(e) 1305 Orig, 1322 Orl (p), 1324 Capes (p), 1334 SR.

Perhaps 'tree-stump clearing', OE **bola-lēah*, but the personal name *Bol(l)a* is obviously possible as first element.

Broadfield (Broadfield Court 546531, Lower Broadfield 545525 and Riffin's Mill 544519)

Bradefeld(e), -(a) 1086 DB, 1148-55 Foliot, 1204 Cur, 1307 Ipm, 1334 SR.

Hure Bradefeld 1265-72 Duncumb.
Bradefeld Superior 1378 BM.

Bradfield Inferior 1547-53 Court.

Bradefeld Ryffeyn 1377 BM.

'Broad open land'. Broadfield 'Superior' is now Broadfield Court. Robert de Ruffin was living in 1220 (Cur) and his family's manor became Riffin's Mill. The family probably came from Ruffin, near Nogent-le-Roi, dépt. Eure-et-Loire.

Brockington (543511)

> *Brokhamton* 1334 SR.

'Brook settlement'. There are two other 'Brockhamptons' in Herefordshire.

Butford (543537)

> *Bedeford* c1170-94 BreconC.
> *Bodeford, Boteford* c1230 BreconC.

The ford was presumably where a bridge crosses a small tributary of the Humber Brook, north of the farm. More spellings are needed for the elucidation of the first element.

Dudales Hope Farm (560517)

> *Dudidale* 1254 InqMisc, late 13th AD (p); *Dodidale* 1268-75 *Red Book MS* (p); *Dodydale* 1334 SR.

> *La Hope* c1158-c81 *StGC*, 13th AD.
> *Hope iuxta Magane* c1179-86 Barrow.

> *(villa de) Dudidale et Hope* 1264 Capes; *Hope Dodydale* 1409 AD; *Dodydaleshope* 1427 KPC; *Duddedals Hope* 1654 BM.

There were apparently two settlements, one of which was called *Hope* 'remote enclosed valley'. The other may have been OE **Dudingdæl* 'hollow associated with Duda'. ME *dale* 'valley' would suit the long, narrow stream-valley in which the place lies; but it is very doubtful whether OE *dæl* was used in this sense before it was influenced by ON *dalr*, and a formation with a personal name, *-ing* and *–dæl* in the sense 'valley' seems improbable. If the name is of late OE or early ME origin (which would remove the objection to the second element meaning 'valley'), an adjective in *–ig* might be considered for *Dudi-*; but there is no recorded word from which such an adjective could derive.

Hope *iuxta Magane* is perhaps to distinguish this Hope from Lower Hope in Ullingswick because it lay slightly nearer to Maund Bryan (*Magene Brian* in 1243, see below) than Lower Hope.

Heath Corner (553538)

> *Hetham* 1219-34 Capes, *(La) Hethe* 1334 SR, 1219-34 Capes, 1256 Salop Eyre (p).

'Heathland'.

46

Houghton (559510)

Hutune late 13th AD (p); *Huton* 1303 FA; *Houton(e)* 1307 Swin (p), 1334
SR, 1357 Ipm, 1366 AD (p), 1409 AD (p), 1431 FA; *Hueton* c1360-93 AD
(p); *Howton* 1366 AD (p).

'Settlement on a hill-spur', OE **hōh-tūn*, a common place-name.

Maund Bryan (562499)

Magne Nicholai 1195 P; *Maw(e)n(e) Nichol(l)* 1303 FA, 1327 Ipm, 1346 FA,
1431 FA.
Magene Brian' 1243 Fees.
Marssh Mawene 1388 IPM; *Marshe Mawne* 1523 HT.

See District Name Maund. This place-name took its first affix from Nicholas
'of Maund' who was living 1143-55 (WalkerCh) and its second from his son Brian
(BreconC).

Rowberry Court ('Maund Maurice', 'Maund Aubin' (559492)

Ruberh' 1148-55 Foliot; *Rughebur'* c1230 StGC; *Rubir'* 1249 Fees; *Roberwe*
1283 StGC; *Roubury* 1361 AD; *Rowberye* 1579 KPC.
Magena Maur' 1160-70 HDB; *Magene Mauricii* 1243 Fees.
Magene Albini 1243 Fees.

Rowberry is 'rough hill', second element OE *beorg*. For Maund, see District
Name Maund.

Maurice 'of Maund' was living in 1148-62 (BreconC) and Robert *de Sancto
Albino* had lands at Rowberry at the same date (Foliot). His family were perhaps
from Saint-Aubin-de-Vieil-Évreux, the place of origin of William fitzOsbern, earl
of Hereford and the man who carried out the Norman conquest and settlement
of the shire.

Swainshill (568514)

Swonild 1318 AD (p).

Probably 'herdsman slope', second element *helde*.

The Venn (Vennwood 548490)

(La) Fenne 1086 DB, 1148-54 Foliot, 1265 Cl (p), 1470-4 Court, 1295 Ipm;
La Venne 1381 QD; *Vend* 1470-4 Court.

'Fen'. There is another Venn in Avenbury.

The Vern (519508)

> *(La) Ferne* 1086 DB, 1205 P 1291 Tax; *Ferna* 1143-55 BreconC (p); *Ferne alias Verne* 1470-4 Court.

'Ferny place'.

Whitechurch Maund (564492)

> *Manneswyteschirche* 1317 Ipm; *Manewhiteschirche* 1336 Ipm; *Whitechurche Magne* 1428 Ipm.
> *Wytechirch'* 1334 SR.
> *Great Whytechurche* 1422 Ipm.

'White church', cf. the parish of this name. See District Name Maund. If the *Man(n)e-* parts of the 1317 and 1336 forms are versions of *Magene*, etc. (i.e. Maund), as the present place-name suggests, then the 1422 and 1428 examples may have arisen because of a mistaken belief that Latin *magna* 'great' was involved.

BOLSTONE

Bolstone (552327)

'Bola's stone'. DEPN prefers the personal-name Bula. Ekwall cites an alternative form *Boulstone*, but the name is *Bolstone* on the 19th century OS map.

'Abertar' (565327)

> *Abethtarada* 1191 P; *Abbertaret* 1230 P; *Abetarader* c1260 *StGC.*
> *Abboteratis Myll* 1544 Free Fisheries; *Abbot Tarretts Mill* 1639 Ballingham.

'Mouth of the river Tar'. Welsh *aber* was misunderstood as 'abbot' when the mill was named. The mill stood at the above grid reference and 'Taradr', now Tar, is the name of the brook that joins the Wye nearby.

BOSBURY

Bosbury (695434)

'Bosa's manor-house', see DEPN.

Catley (681444)

> *Catesley* 1243 Fees; *Cattelegh* 1251 FA; *Cattele(e)* 1279 Ipm, 1279 Cant (p); *Catteley* 1279 Ipm, 1334 SR, 1371-3 BM.
> *Kantel* 1234 Fees.

'Cat's wood'; the same name occurs in Lincolnshire.

Upleadon Court (665421, and **Temple Court** 692433)

> *Ledene* 1086 DB.

> *Upleden(e)* 1017-41 (c1090) Dugdale, 1137-9 HDB, 1291 Tax, 1329 St Katherine, 1334 SR; *Huppleidun'*, *Upleidene* 1200 Pleas (p); *Hupleden(e)* 1219 InqMisc, 1256 BM; *Uppledone* 1304 Swin.

The DB manor of *Ledene* may have been centred near the river Leadon (from which it is named), perhaps at Temple Court, with the centre of gravity only later moving to its present site at Upleadon. Upleadon is slightly 'up' from Temple Court topographically speaking. Temple Court was the site of a Preceptory of the Knights of the Temple (the Templars) established after the great earl William Marshal, who died in 1219, gave it to that Order.

❧ BRAMPTON ABBOTTS ☙

Brampton Abbotts (601265)

'Broom settlement', see DEPN. 'Abbotts' from the abbot of Gloucester, who owned the manor.

Gatsford (616264)

> *Gedesford'* 1137-9 HDB.
> *Gadelesford, Gedelesford* 1160-70 HDB.
> *Gatesford* 1364 AD, 1438 AD; *Gaitforde* 1524 HT.

Perhaps 'Gæddel's ford'. The personal name is not on record, but would be a diminutive of the recorded *Gadd*.

Netherton (599258)

> *Nethert(h)on* 1300 EH (p), 1443 Ipm.

'Nether settlement', i.e. lower than Brampton Abbotts.

❧ BRAMPTON BRYAN ❧

Bramton Bryan (370725)

'Broom settlement', see DEPN. The affix is possibly from Brian fitzUnspac who had the manor c1157-8.

Pedwardine (Upper 365708 and Lower 368703)

> *Pedewr(d)e* 1086 DB,1151-63 Foliot (p); *Pydewrthyn* 1256 Salop Eyre (p); *Pedwardyn(e)* 1291 Orig, 1462 BM; *Pederwardyn* 1292 Subs (p); *Pe(d)d(e)wardyn(e)* 1305 Ipm, 1493 BM.

> *Parva Pedewardyn* 1292 QW.

> 'Pēoda's settlement', second element *worthign*.

❧ BREDENBURY ❧

Bredenbury (at Bredenbury Court 611561)

> *Brideneberie* 1086 DB; *Bridenebiria* 1160-70 HDB; *Bri(n)deneburch* 1180 P; *Briden(e)bury* 1276 Swin, 1341 NonInq; *Brydinbury* 1428 FA; *Brydenburye* 1585 BM.

> 'Boarded manor-house'.

Noakes Farm (633552)

> *Ach* 1086 DB; *(H)akes* 1198 Fees, 1243 Fees, 1251-2 Fees.
> *Lacre* 1086 DB; *Lac* 1160-70 HDB; *Lake* 1243 Fees (p).
> *Ok(es)* 1267 Swin (p), 1268-75 *Red Book MS* (p), 1295 Ipm, 1344 InqMisc, 1345 Ipm; *La (Le) Okes* 1303 Ipm, 1387 Ipm; *Le Okes by Bromyard* 1317 Ipm.

'Oak trees'. The modern form is from the ME phrase *atten okes* 'at the oaks'. This manner of referring to the place may have been current locally, though it was not used in writing, at any rate, till after 1387. Some forms have the French definite article prefixed. '– by Bromyard' to distinguish it from Court of Noke in Pembridge.

Sawbury Hill (626553)

> *Salberga* 1086 DB; *Sal(e)biri(a)* 1137-9 HDB, 1243 Fees; *Salbur'* 1249 Fees.
> *Sargeberie* 1086 HDB.
> *Sauberi* 1204 Cur.

'Sallow-willow hill', second element OE *beorg*.

Wicton Farm (629559)

> *Wigetune* 1086 DB; *Wyggetone* 1268-75 *Red Book MS* (p); *Wigton* 1663 MA.

'Wicga's settlement'. The same name has become Wigton in Cumberland. DB *Wigetune* is here and not Wickton in Stoke Prior as PNHe suggests.

⁂ BREDWARDINE ⁂

Bredwardine (335445)

> *Brocheurdine* 1086 DB.
> *Brodewordin* 1160-70 HDB.
> *Brerdewordin* c1175-89 BM.
> *Bredewrhin* 1185-9 BMFacs; *Bredewerthin* late 12th BreconC; *Bredewerdin*
>   c1200 BreconC; *Bredewardin* 1291 Tax, *Bred(e)wardyn* 1292 QW, 1328 QW,
>   1328 Banco, 1355 Ipm.
> *Brudewrthin* c1200 BreconC.
> *Brad(e)w(o)rthin* 1200 Cur, 1265 Cl (p); *Bradew(a)rdin* 1219 InqMisc,
>   1216-72 BM; *Bradwardyn* 1397 VR.

Probably 'plank settlement', from OE *bred* 'board' (perhaps in the genitive plural) and *worthign*. The DB form is perhaps best classified as a chance genitive bad spelling, though John Freeman (Thorn, notes) makes a case for the settlement having alternative names. DEPN, citing the form *Brerdewordin*, gives an etymology involving OE *brerd* 'brim, bank', but this is the only spelling so far found with *Brerde-*, and unless others come to light it seems reasonable to regard it as aberrant.

Bredwardine is probably the site of *Lann Iunabui* c585, c625, c745 (c1130) LL. The bounds of *Lann Iunabui* c585 (c1130) are given in LL: '*Or rit diuch ilan dirguoiret huch irguduit dir bronn ir alt recte trus ircecg usque dum descendit guar irhennrit issid arifrut inircoit maur, per siluam recte disguartham campull. Orcampull recte usque Guy.*' 'From the ford above the church downwards above the honeysuckle to the breast of the wooded slope, straight over the ridge till it [the boundary] descends above the old ford on the stream in the great wood, through the uppermost part of the Cambwll; from the Cambwll straight to the Wye.'

Egerton Phillimore (LL) suggests that the church of Bredwardine could represent *Lann Iunabui*. Davies follows Bannister PNHe in placing it at Llandinabo in Archenfield, but this appears elsewhere as *Lann Hunapui* and is not on the Wye.

The bounds fit a location at Bredwardine for *Lann Iunabui* quite well. They start at 'the ford above the church' (*rit diuch i lan*) and this could be the ford across the Wye by Bredwardine castle referred to in a charter of c1200 (BreconC: *veteri villa super ridd*). The castle stands very close to the church. From this ford the boundary will have gone via Finestreet Dingle (323440) to Bredwardine Hill (318446) ('breast of the wooded slope'; *bronn ir alt*) and then to Merbach Hill (303447) ('the ridge'; *ir cecg*), whose English name involves OE *mearc* 'boundary'. West of Merbach Hill the Bach Brook ran through a large wooded area now represented only by the place-name Middlewood (289447). On this brook in the 'great wood' (*coit maur*) may have stood the 'old ford', (*ir henn rit*), close to which the boundary ran. Descending through the wood past the ford the boundary comes to the 'uppermost part of the Cambwll' (*guartham Cambwll*). In the 6th-8th centuries, the estate called Middlewood in DB included lands that now lie north of the Wye. In those days the river divided itself at 293463 to run both north and south (with the northern arm carrying its the main flow) of an island on which there was formerly a hermitage of St Cynidr. Where the Bach Brook disgorges into the Wye at Clock Mills (290455) there was a ford that gave access to this island. The northern arm of the Wye that cut off the island was quite irregular in its course and may once have been known as Cambwll ('curved pool'). It is now drained and marked only by a series of small lakes going past Court Barn (302463) and The Wydenhams (306464) to a point on the Wye at 322468. From there the boundary will have gone along the Wye back to the ford by the church.

Benfield Farm (322445)

> *Benethfeld* c1175-89 BM.
> *Ben(e)feld(um)* 1218 Robinson, 1224-9 AD, 1232 Dugdale, 1273 AD;
>   *Benefield* 1227 Ch, 1285 QD; *Benfylde* 1537 Dugdale.

> *Benfeld montayn* 1498 AD.

Perhaps 'open land where bent grass grows', from OE *beonet* and *feld*; but more spellings with *Benet-* would be required for certainty. The first element could be 'bean', but crop-names are rare with *feld* when used in settlement-names (as opposed to field-names). *Montayn* probably refers to Bredwardine Hill.

'**West Bredwardine**' (now **Weston Farm** 323457)

> *Westbradewardin* 1286 Ipm; *Westbredward'* 1288 AD.
> *Weston Bradwardyne* 1340 Ipm; *Weston on Weye* 1374 Ipm; *Weston* 1440 Ipm.

❧ BREINTON ☙

Breinton (473395)

> *Br(e)untune* 1200-19 Capes.
> *Brehintone* c1215 Capes (p); *Brahintone* 1252 Capes.
> *Breinton'* 1218 P; *Breynton(e)* 1272, 1332 Capes, 1291 Tax, 1316 FA, 1328
>   Banco (p), 1341 NonInq, 1347 AD.
> *Broyntun'* 1243 Fees (p).
> *Brenton, Brounton* 1291 Tax.
> *Braynton* 1375 QD; *Brainton* 1663 MA.
> *Breyngton'* 1377 PT.

Possibly 'settlement by the hill called *Bræge*'. There is reason to suppose that Primitive Welsh *brez* could become OE *bræg*, and such a name might be treated as a weak noun, giving a genitive **Brægan*. This is a very tentative suggestion. DEPN's **Bryning(a)tun* ('settlement of Bryni's people') does not suit the spellings.

Warham (482392)

> *Werham* 1086 DB, 1322 Ipm, 1327 Banco (p); *War(e)ham* 1160-70 HDB,
>   1379 QD, 1535 VE; *Warrham* 1179-86 Capes; *Weham* 1334 SR.

'River-meadow by a weir', OE *wer* and *hamm*. The second element could be *ham* 'village', but *hamm* is generally to be preferred in this county.

❧ BRIDGE SOLLERS ☙

Bridge Sollers (414426)

The forms in PNHe are adequate. The Sollers family were from Soliers, a short distance south-east of Caen, dépt. Calvados.

❧ BRIDSTOW ☙

Bridstow (585248)

> *Lann sanfreit* 1056-104 (c1130); *Lannsanbregit* 1066-87 (c1130) LL;
> *(parrochia) Sancte Brigide (in Erchenfelde)* c1150 Fr.

> *Bridestowe* 1291 Tax, 1346 Trill, 1428 FA.

> 'Church of St Bride' and 'Holy place of St Bride'.

Ashe Ingen Court (580260)

> *Ascis* 1086 DB; *Esse(s)* 1160-70 HDB, 1219-27 Barrow (p), 1242 GloucC;
> *Aisse* 1283 Swin (p); *Assch(e)* 1300 Swin, 1364 AD.
> *Esse Hingani* 1137-9 HDB.

'Ash trees'. As in the case of Aston Ingham (above), the affix is probably taken from Hingan, who was living in 1127.

Moraston House (570257)

> *Meredicheston'* 1334 SR.

> 'Maredudd's estate'.

Wilton (590243)

> 'Estate among the willows', see DEPN.

❧ BRILLEY ☙

Brilley (261492)

> *Brunlege(e)* 1219 InqMisc, 1267 Ipm; *Brunley* 1252 Duncumb, 1397 VR.
> *Bromlegh(e)*1233 Cl, 1333 Capes, 1337 Ipm.
> *Brumleg(h)* 1248 Berks Eyre, 1255 Cl; *Brumleye* 1299 Ipm; *Brumleie* 1337 Ipm.
> *Brynlegh* 1259-60 Banks.
> *Brilleis* 1532 Supplement; *Brilley* 1535 VE.

'Broom clearing'. This compound of OE *brōm* and *lēah* usually becomes Bromley or Bramley. Early *Brun-* forms can, however, be paralleled in Bromley, Essex, and Bromley, Surrey; and the Essex name is Brynley in 1506.

54

(lost)

Crydesleah 1016-35 ASCh; Curdesleg(e) 1086 DB, 1137-9 HDB.

There is a rare place-name element *cryd(e)*, the meaning of which has not been firmly established, which may be the first element in this name. The best available discussion of *cryde* is in Helge Kökeritz, *The Place-Names of the Isle of Wight* (1940), 135.

(lost)

Mateurdin 1086 DB, Mathewordin 1137-9 HDB; Mathewurdam, Mawerdin 1160-70 HDB.

Second element *worthign* 'enclosed settlement'. The forms are insufficient for the identification of the first element.

In 1086 Brilley was represented, for the most part, by settlements with these two lost place-names. This can be deduced from the fact that they were then held, wholly or partly, by Gruffudd ap Maredudd, pretender to the throne of the kingdom of Deheubarth (south Wales), and from the tenurial descent of all the lands Gruffudd had in Herefordshire. Johansson says that DB *Curdeslege* is the same place as *Crydesleah* in ASCh rather than Cradley, as suggested in PNHe and ASCh, and she is certainly right in this. In the charter of 1017-35 a certain Edwin son of *Enneawne* sued his mother for lands in Wellington and *Crydesleah* that the mother had in dower from Edwin's father. *Enneawne* is the Old Welsh name *Enniaun*, now Einion (von Feilitzen). This Edwin son of Einion is almost certainly the one who appears in the genealogy of the ruling house of Deheubarth, that is, Edwin son of Einion ab Owain (died in 984), grandson of Hywel Dda. Edwin ab Einion had three sons, only the youngest of who, Owain, had living issue. His grandson was the above Gruffudd ap Maredudd, so it seems that the estate had passed down this branch of the royal family of Deheubarth. After Gruffudd's death in 1091 (in a failed attempt on Deheubarth's throne) all his lands in Herefordshire were given to William de Braose of Radnor (HDB), and *Curdeslege* and *Mateudin* (Brilley) eventually became part of the Welshry of the marcher lordship he and his family had at Kington (later Huntington). The motte-and-bailey castle at Cwmma (277513) may mark the site of one of these lost places.

Welshwood Farm (277492)

Walelege 1086 DB.

'Wood of the Welshmen'. The DB place-name is not represented by modern Ailey in Kinnersley as previously thought (e.g. VCH, PNHe), as this has a different etymology. As with *Curdeslege* and *Mateurdin*, this manor passed to the Braose family of Radnor and became part of the Welshry of the lordship of Kington or Huntington.

𝒩𝓈 BRIMFIELD ❧

Brimfield (526676)

> *Brum(e)felde, Brom(e)felde* 1086 DB, 1174-86 Kemp, 1212 Fees, c1212-17
>   RBE, 1219-34 *LeomC*, 1302 Ipm, 1327 Banco, 1347 BM 1397 VR;
>   *Brumuelde* 1317 BM; *Bromfeud* 1200-50 *LeomC.*
> *Brumesfelda* 1123 ReadingC.
> *Bromesfeld'* 1141 Regesta.
> *Bremesfelda* 1158-61 Foliot.
> *Brimfield* 1174-86 Barrow; *Brimfeud* 1249 Ipm; *Brymfeld'* 1334 SR.
> *Bremfeld* 1401 OseneyC.
> *Bremell alias Bremfeld* 1576 AD.

Most of the spellings indicate 'broom' as the first element, as in Bromfield, Shropshire, six miles to the north-west (which was *Brimfield* in 1826). In *Bremell alias Bremfeld* 1576, *-ell* is probably a reduced form of *–feld*. (DEPN has *Bremelfelda* in the place of the 1123 version from *LeomC*, but this is incorrect.)

Drayton (Upper 539669 and Lower 537674)

> *Dreiton* 1123 *LeomC.*
> *Draiton* 1200-50 *LeomC*; *Drayton* 1317 BM.

DEPN divides examples of Drayton into two groups: those which refer to a portage between two rivers, and those which refer to a position on a steep hill. This Drayton seems to be a good example of the second meaning.

Nun Upton (542666)

> *Upton* 1291 Tax.
> *Nunneupton* 1542 Dugdale.

'Higher settlement'. Its affix refers to the nuns of Limebrook, who received this manor from the Mortimers of Wigmore.

Wyson (520678)

> *Wystetone* 1347 BM.

More spellings are required. It is probably a personal name + *-tūn*.

❧ BRINSOP ☙

Brinsop (442448)

> *Hope* 1086 DB.
> *Brun(e)shop(e)* early 12th OrdVit, 1103-7 BreconC, 1283 *StGC* (p), 1305 Orig.
> *Brun(e)hop(e)* 1143-55 WalkerCh (p), 1178 P, 1185-90 BreconC, late 12th
>   CirenC (p), c1215 Capes (p), 1243 Fees, 1308 Capes.
> *Brinhope* late 13th BM.
> *Brimeshope, Broneshope* late 13th BM.
> *Bromhop* 1291 Tax.
> *Bron(e)s(s)op* 1328 Banco; 1341 NonInq.
> *Bryn(e)shope* 1446 BM, 1465 AD, 1535 VE.
>
> *Ouerebrymeshope* late 13th BM.

Probably 'Bryni's sheltered valley', with some influence from OE *brōm* 'broom'. Brinsop Court, north of the village, occupies a classic *hop* site.

❧ BROBURY ☙

Brobury (345444)

> *Brocheberie* 1086 DB.
> *Brogebir'* 1158-64 *LeomC* (p); *Brogeberia* 1158-65 ReadingC.
> *Brokebiria* 1160-70 HDB; *Brokeburi* 1183-5 StGC, *Brokeb(u)r(y)* 1208 Cur
>   (p), 1317 Ipm.
> *Brocberi* 1201 Pleas; *Brocbire* 1243 Fees; *Brocbury* 1291 Tax, 1317 Ipm.
> *Brekebir'* 1209 P (p).

Apparently 'manor by a brook'; but this does not suit the present position. Brobury overlooks the Wye, which would by referred to as *ēa* 'river', not *brōc*. Letton Lake, 1½ miles north, is the sort of stream which might have been called *brōc*.

BROCKHAMPTON-BY-BROMYARD

Brockhampton (683549)

> *Brochant(one)* 1166 RBE (p), 1219-27 Barrow (p); *Broc(h)amton(e)* 1268-75 *Red Book MS* (p), late 13th AD; *Brockhampton* 1283 Swin (p); *Brok(e)hampton(e)* 1304 Swin (p), 1431 FA.

'Brook settlement'. The moated site north of the village is by a fairly substantial stream. There is another Brockhampton, by Ross, and 'Brockhampton' in Bodenham has become Brockington.

The Grove (formerly **Studmarsh** 695557)

> *Stobmarshe, Stobmershe, Stubmarsh* 1268-75 *Red Book MS*.

'Tree-stump marsh'.

Lower Norton Farm (685570)

> *Nor(t)hin(e)ton(e)* 1200-15 Barrow (p), 1268-75 *Red Book MS* (p); *Norhmpton* 1268-75 *Red Book MS* (p).

'Place in the northern part of the manor', OE *north-in-tūne*. Its southern counterpart was at Southington Farm in Linton-by-Bromyard. They lie north and south of Brockhampton, which is thus, probably, the 'manor' in question. There was another 'Northington' (now Netherton) in Ledbury.

BROCKHAMPTON-BY-ROSS

Brockhampton (site of old church 598317)

> *Brocham(p)ton(a)* 1160-70 HDB, 1274 StaffsPleas (p).

Another 'brook settlement', to go with those in Bodenham (now Brockington) and by Bromyard. Brockhampton was in the estate called *Caplefore* in DB; see Capler Camp in Woolhope.

Fawley Chapel (591295)

> *Falileam* 1142 Holtzmann; *Faliley* 1292 QW.
> *Filileam* 1158 Holtzmann.
> *Feneleia* 1159 Holtzmann.
> *Felileie* 1166 RBE; *Felileyam* 1198 CartAntiq.

Feleleg' c1170-c80 *StGC.*
Falley(e) 1284 AD, 1334 SR; *Fallaye* 1316 FA; *Ffalley* 1534 Owen;
    Faley 1663 MA.
Folley 1641 BM.

'Hay clearing', OE (Mercian) *fælethe-lēah. Little Ffawley* (1586 Owen) was at Fawley Court (578301).

৯৫০   **BROMYARD**   ৫৪

Bromyard (655548)

'Broom enclosure'; see DEPN.

৯৫০   **BUCKTON AND COXALL**   ৫৪

Buckton (384733)

Bucton(e) 1086 DB, 1383 BM; *Bocton* 1199 Cur (p), 1305 Ipm, 1272-1307
    BM; *Buketon* 1292 QW.

'Bucca's estate'.

Coxall (371743)

Cok(k)eshalle 1249 Inspeximus, 1397 VR; *Cocheshale,* 1292 QW; *Cockesale*
    1529-30 Court.
Colkehale 1291 Tax.
Coteshall 1292 QW.

Perhaps 'nook of the woodcock', second element *halh. Cocc* may be used as a personal name, however.

Adley Moor (380746)

Adelactune 1086 DB; *Ad(e)lacton(e)* 1292 QW, 1249, 1535 Inspeximus.
Adelestune 1086 DB.
Edelactune 1086 DB.
Adelahton 1305 Ipm, 1527 Court; *Ad(e)laghton* 1359 Ipm, 1524 BM, 1535 VE.
Adlaton 1527 Court.

'Eadlāc's estate'. The same name has become Allastone in Staffordshire.

🙦 LOWER BULLINGHAM 🙤

Lower Bullingham (519383)

> *Neathere Bullynghope* 1265 InqMisc; *Netherebolinghope* 1298 AD, 1322 Ipm;
>   *Netherbolynghop* 1315 Orig.
> *Bullyng(es)hop(e) Inferior(i)* 1316 FA, 1341 NonInq.

Probably 'marsh enclosure connected with Bulla'. This name, and others of the same type, is discussed in M. Gelling, *Place-Names in the Landscape* (1984), 117ff. Bullinghope in Grafton, formerly Upper Bullinghope (*Bollynghope Superior* 1316 FA), remains spelt that way. Early forms of both place-names are in PNHe.

🙦 BURGHILL 🙤

Burghill (479445)

> *Burgelle* 1086 DB.
> *Burch(e)hull(e)* 1103-7 BreconC, 1142 Holtzmann, 1148-63 HDB (p), 1198
>   P (p), 1219-34 Barrow, 1243 Fees; *Burchella* early 12th OrdVit;
>   *Burchhulla* 1194 -1224 RATD (p).
> *Burechulle* 1166 RBE (p).
> *Burchil* 1169 P.
> *Bukilla* 1160-70 HDB.
> *Burghull(e)* 1211-12 RBE (p), 1278 Orig, 1303 FA, 1328 Banco (p), 1459 BM;
>   *Borghulle* 1377 KPC (p); *Burghyll* 1535 VE.
> *Burhull(e)* 1247-72 AD, 1331 QD; *Burhyll* 1547-53 Court.
> *Burghill alias Burfield* 1663 MA.

'Fort hill', OE *burh-hyll*. The reference must be to the large hillfort in nearby Credenhill Wood.

Burlton Court (485440)

> *Burg(h)elton(e)* 1215 Cl, 1334 SR.
> *Burweltun'* 1243 Fees; *Burwelton* 1303 FA.
> *Borleton* 1316 Ipm, 1373 Ipm; *Burleton* 1328 Banco, 1346 FA.

'Settlement by the fort hill'.

Tillington Court (471457)

>*Tul(l)inton(e)* c1170-85 Treago (p), 1271, 1309 Ipm; *Tulintun'* 1243 Fees.
>*Tillinton'* 1188 P (p).
>*Tullington* 1229 Cur, 1271 Ex; *Tullyn(g)ton* 1304 Ipm, 1328 Banco, 1535 VE.

>'Settlement associated with Tulla', OE **Tullingtūn*.

❧ BURRINGTON ☙

Burrington (443721)

>*Boritune* 1086 DB; *Boriton* 1333 Ipm, 14th Chronicle; *Boryton* 1527 Court.
>*Buriton* c1250-72 BM.
>*Borenden* 1211 Cur.
>*Buryntone* 1397 VR.
>*Beryngton* 1535 VE.

OE *byrigtūn* 'settlement at a fort'. This is one of a cluster of names by the river Teme which derive from *byrigtūn*; the others have the modern form Berrington. Nineteenth-century historians speak of a 'camp' or fort here, but nothing is visible today.

Bringwood (460733)

>*Buringwode* 1301 Pat, *Boryngwode* 1333 Ipm.

This may be a shortened and slightly corrupt version of an OE **byrigtūn-wudu* 'Burrington Wood'.

❧ BYFORD ☙

Byford (397429)

>*Buiford* 1086 DB, 1141-3 (p), c1170 *StGC* (p).
>*Buford(')* 1217-19 Barrow, 1291 Tax, 1317 Ipm.
>*Biford* 1286 Swin; *Byford* 1291 Tax, 1328 Banco, - *et Bystede* 1399 Ipm, 1425
>   Cl.

'Ford at a river bend', OE **byge-ford*. The outline of the parish boundary follows an old, very sharply curving, course of the Wye. *Bystede* 'site of the bend' may be an alternative name, coined after the river-course change.

Byton (371641)

> *Boitune* 1086 DB.
> *But(t)on* 1287 Ipm, 1291 Tax, 1349 Ipm.
> *Bitton* 1307 Ipm.
> *Buyton(e)* 1386 BM, 1393, 1410 Capes (p).
> *Beyton(e)* 1397 VR, 1547-53 Court.
> *Byton* 1479-80 Rodd; *Bytu'* 1535 VE.

'Bend settlement', referring to the course of the river Lugg. Cf. Byford.

ॐ   **CALLOW**   ☙

Callow (494344)

> *Calue (in trenchato Hereford)* 1175 WorcC; *Calwa (in haio Hereford)* 1185-6
> WorcC; *Kalewe* 1193 WorcC; *(La) Caluwe* 1285 Ipm (p), 1338 Larking;
> *Calowe* 1292 QW, 1341 NonInq; *(La) Calewe* 1300 Swin, 1322 Ipm (p),
> 1328 Banco (p), 1346 Duncumb.

'Bare hill', from *calewe*, a derivative of OE *calu* 'bare'.

Also to be associated with Callow, probably, is:

> *Ferdeldel* 1191 P; *Ferthendel'* 1199 P, 1200 RBE; *Ferdend'* 1231 MemR.

'Quarter', OE *feorthan-dæl*. This term is better evidenced as a field-name, but it occurs as a settlement-name in Fardel in Devon (which is a DB manor).

This place appears on the Pipe Rolls from 1191 onwards in association with Bolstone and with *'Abethtar'* in Bolstone as lands in Herefordshire acquired by Worcester Cathedral Priory from *terra regis*. King Henry II (in 1175) and king Richard I (1189-99) were the grantors, in Henry's case it was out of his 'hay [forest] of Hereford' and in Richard's out of the royal manor or hundred of Archenfield. It is possible that it is an alternative name for Callow.

Huntless Farm (513352)

> *Honteleye* 1299 AD; *Hunteley* 13th AcornC.

'Huntsman's wood'.

Twyford (506345)

> *Twiford* 1281 Ipm; *Tyford, Thwyford* 13th AcornC; *Twyford* 1316 FA.

'Double –ford', used of a road that crosses two streams. The road that passes Twyford Farm crosses the Red Brook at two places before reaching Twyford Common.

❧ CANON FROME ☙

See page 102.

❧ CANON PYON ☙

See page 189.

❧ CASTLE FROME ☙

See page 102.

❧ HOW CAPLE ☙

How Caple (612305)

> *Capel* 1086 DB; *Caple(s)* 1166 RBE (p), 1226-30 Capes (p), 1291 Tax, *Capele* mid 13th *StGC*, 1300 Ipm.
> *Huwe Caples* 1316 Swin, 1328 Banco; *Hugh Caple* 1334 SR; *Huwecappyl* 1397 VR; *Howcaple* 1535 VE.

As pointed out in ODR, the Old Norman-French *capele* 'chapel' seems a less likely origin for 'Caple' names than DEPN's suggestion that there was probably an OE word *cape* meaning a 'look-out place'. See also Capler Camp in Woolhope. The affix is from the Christian name of Hugh of Caple, living in c1120 (GloucC), or from another of the same name living a century later (Swin).

(lost)

> *Kenardesl'* c1230 CRCG.

See Kinnersley, page 130.

King's Caple (559289)

> *Cape* 1086 DB; *Caple* 1285, 1325 Ipm.
> *Chingestaples* 1155 Dugdale; *Chingescaple* 1160-70 HDB; *Kingescapolle*
>   1205 Cur; *Kyngescaple* mid 13th *StGC* (p), 1303 Pat.
> *Capyll Regis* 1397 VR.

See How Caple and also Capler Camp in Woolhope. This manor was in the king's hands before 1066, but not after that date.

Pennoxstone (555285)

No old forms, but the name could be derived from the surname of a family active in King's Caple in the 12th and 13th centuries. In 1205 Jacob *Pennoc* or 'of *Penhoc*' claimed that Henry de Longchamps, lord of Wilton, had disseised him of certain lands (Cur; P). The manor of Wilton had a small outlier in King's Caple (DB; HDB) and this may be the land in dispute. If so, there is a possibility that it lay at Pennoxstone, which may have taken its name from Jacob's family. The surname itself could derive from Pinnock in Gloucestershire.

Ruxton (552293)

> *Roderacston*, *Rotheracston* 1304 (p); *Ruxon* 1778; *Ruckstone* 1806 Duncumb.

Probably the Welsh personal name Rhydderch and OE *tūn* 'estate'.

Clehonger (465379)

> *Cleungre* 1086 DB; *Cleyhongre* 1163-7 Capes; *Claihangre* 1200 Cur;
>   *Cle(h)angre* 1243 Fees, 1309 Orig; *Clehingre* 1291 Tax; *Clehungr(e)* 1320
>   Capes, 1327 Banco, 1341 NonInq, 1535 VE.

'Sloping wood on clay soil', a recurrent compound which has become Clayhanger, Clinger, Clingre in other counties.

Hunderton (495389)

> *Hundreton(e)* 1150-4 Capes, 1294 Swin, 1535 VE; *Hundriton* 1291 Tax;
>   *Hundertone* 1300 Swin, 1376 Capes.
> *Hunditone* 1252 Capes.

The first element is probably 'hundred', i.e. the administrative term. Though it lies not far from the lost 'Stradde' in Hereford, which was probably the site of the hundred-court of DB Straddle Hundred (see District Name Straddle), it is not apparent what special function this settlement could have in relation to the hundredal administration. After the 12th century reorganisation of the Herefordshire hundreds, the local hundred-court moved even further away, to Webtree in Allensmore.

❧ CLIFFORD ☙

Clifford (245456)

'Ford by a cliff', see DEPN.

'Broadmeadow' (now Archenfield 263422)

> *Brademedewe* 1219 InqMisc; *La Brademedue* 1250 Year Book; *Brodemedewe* 1299 Ipm, 1424 Ipm; *Broadmeadow* 1831 OS.

'Broad meadow'.

Lower Castleton Farm (282455)

> *Castelton* 1382 Ipm, 1537 Dugdale.

'Farm by a castle', or perhaps 'estate with a castle' as this is presumably a post-Conquest name.

'Gorsington' (now Upper Court 244454)

> *Gersintim* 1218-34 BreconC (p).
> *Gosinton* 1292 Subs (p), 1328 Banco; *Gosynton* 1341 QD (p), 1399 Ipm (p).
> *Gosyngton* 1321 Orl (p).

Duncumb says that Upper Court was formerly called Gorsington. It is almost certainly a manorial place-name derived from a family from Gossington, Gloucestershire, who were subtenants of the lords of Clifford.

Hardwicke (263439)

> *Herdwyc* 1272 AD (p); *Herdewyk* 1309-24 BM, 1328 Banco (p).
> *Hardwykecumbe Hey* 1537 Dugdale.

'Herd farm'. The 1537 name means 'woodland enclosure at Hardwicke coomb'.

Harewood (255429)

Harew(o)de 1086 DB, 1160-70 HDB.

Probably 'hare wood'.

Llan-y-coed (275426)

Lanercoyt 1309-24 BM.

Mr Morgan suggests Welsh *llannerch*, 'clearing, glade'.

Merbach (303454)

Mer(e)bache 1216-41 AcornC, 1292 QW.

'Stream-valley on a boundary'. The parish boundary runs along a 'batch' on the east side of Merbach Hill.

Middlewood (289447)

Midewde 1086 DB; *Midelwude* 1160-70 HDB; *Middelwode* 1299, 1382 Ipm; *Medelwood* 1537 Dugdale.

'Middle wood', a place-name that originally embraced the island in the Wye in Winforton parish that contained St Cynidr's hermitage: see also Bredwardine.

Newton (292439)

(La) Neuton 1247-72 AD, 1287 AD, 1361 Ipm.

'New farm'. The 'new' settlement here, with its motte-and-bailey castle, probably replaced an 'old' settlement at Old Castleton, which also has a castle.

Sidcombe Farm (298444)

Sybcombe 1537 Dugdale.

More spellings are needed before the first element can be identified, but the second element is *cumb* 'short, broad valley'.

Windle Park (274444)

Windhull 1247-72 AD; *Wimble Park* 1831 OS.

'Wind hill'; this compound has become Windle in Lancashire, also.

❧ CLODOCK ☙

Clodock (327275)

Cladoc 1266 EHC; *S.Cleddoc'* 1540 Dugdale.

Merthirclitauc c740 (c1130) LL.

'St Clydog', see DEPN.

The bounds of *Merthirclitauc* early 8th (c1130) LL: '*Lapis iniguoun breith, icecin inihit diriu icurum, dirmain icecin iralt arhit cecin diuinid bet imain arciueir nant trineint diguairet arihit bet in elchon arihit diguairet bet ynys alarum iniguartha dirmain tillauc dir cruc, dir cruc arall, dimynui, mynugui truio daper nant cum cinreith (i nant cum:* interlined*) nant inihit bet minid ferdun diar iralt minid ferdun, nihit dir luch ferdun iminid inihit bet blain hilin, hilin inihit bet mingui, mingui nihit diguairet bet aper finhaun bist bet iblain, oi blain ircecin iniaun iuinid dicirchu irguoun breith arcecin iminid bet imain ubi incepit.*' 'The stone in the speckled moor, along the ridge, along it to the slope *cwrw*, to the stone on the ridge of the wooded slope, along the ridge upwards as far as the stone opposite to the stream of Turnant, along it as far as into the Olchon, along it down as far as *Alarun* island at its summit, to the stone with the holes to the mound, to another mound, to Mynwy, through Mynwy to the outflow of the stream of Cwm Cynreith, along the stream throughout its length as far as Mynydd Ferddin, along the wooded slope of Mynydd Ferddin to the pool of [Mynydd?] Ferddin, along the mountain to the source of the *Hilin*, along the *Hilin* as far as Mynwy, along the Mynwy downwards to the outflow of the well (or fountain) of *Bist*, along it from its source to the ridge straight upwards making for the speckled moor on the ridge of the mountain, to the stone where [the boundary] began.'

These bounds are fairly easy to follow on a modern map. They start at a certain prominent stone at the north end of Hatterall Hill (308259: *Lapis in i guoun breith i cecin*) where there is now an old quarry. From there they go northwards along the ridge of the mountain past Rhiw Arw (310278: *riu i curum*) to a stone at 304279 (*i main*), and then onwards to another stone above Great Turnant (or Trinant; c296387). They then descend the Turnant Brook (*nant trineint*) to the river Olchon at 316293 (*digairet ar i hit bet in elchon*). Descending the Olchon the bounds come to '*Alarun* island' (*ynys alarun*), which is possibly the triangle of land below Longtown isolated by the Olchon and the Mynyw. Crossing the 'island' from perhaps the ford on the Olchon at 320288 via 'the stone with the holes' (*main tilluc*) and two 'mounds', the bounds come to the Mynwy (*myngui*) at 328287, which they cross before ascending 'stream Cwm Cynreith' (*aper nant cum cinreith*), which is probably the brook which ascends Mynydd Ferddin (Mynydd Merddin on modern maps) from 328287 to about 340287. From this brook they go to the top of Mynydd Ferddin (344286: *minid ferdun diar iralt*) and then follow

The bounds of *Merthirclitauc* early 8th (c1130) LL: '*Lapis iniguoun breith, icecin inihit diriu icurum, dirmain icecin iralt arhit cecin diuinid bet imain arciueir nant trineint diguairet arihit bet in elchon arihit diguairet bet ynys alarum iniguartha dirmain tillauc dir cruc, dir cruc arall, dimynui, mynugui truio daper nant cum cinreith (i nant cum:* interlined*) nant inihit bet minid ferdun diar iralt minid ferdun, nihit dir luch ferdun iminid inihit bet blain hilin, hilin inihit bet mingui, mingui nihit diguairet bet aper finhaun bist bet iblain, oi blain ircecin iniaun iuinid dicirchu irguoun breith arcecin iminid bet imain ubi incepit.*' 'The stone in the speckled moor, along the ridge, along it to the slope *cwrw*, to the stone on the ridge of the wooded slope, along the ridge upwards as far as the stone opposite to the stream of Turnant, along it as far as into the Olchon, along it down as far as *Alarun* island at its summit, to the stone with the holes to the mound, to another mound, to Mynwy, through Mynwy to the outflow of the stream of Cwm Cynreith, along the stream throughout its length as far as Mynydd Ferddin, along the wooded slope of Mynydd Ferddin to the pool of [Mynydd?] Ferddin, along the mountain to the source of the *Hilin*, along the *Hilin* as far as Mynwy, along the Mynwy downwards to the outflow of the well (or fountain) of *Bist*, along it from its source to the ridge straight upwards making for the speckled moor on the ridge of the mountain, to the stone where [the boundary] began.'

These bounds are fairly easy to follow on a modern map. They start at a certain prominent stone at the north end of Hatterall Hill (308259: *Lapis in i guoun breith i cecin*) where there is now an old quarry. From there they go northwards along the ridge of the mountain past Rhiw Arw (310278: *riu i curum*) to a stone at 304279 (*i main*), and then onwards to another stone above Great Turnant (or Trinant; c296387). They then descend the Turnant Brook (*nant trineint*) to the river Olchon at 316293 (*digairet ar i hit bet in elchon*). Descending the Olchon the bounds come to '*Alarun* island' (*ynys alarun*), which is possibly the triangle of land below Longtown isolated by the Olchon and the Mynyw. Crossing the 'island' from perhaps the ford on the Olchon at 320288 via 'the stone with the holes' (*main tilluc*) and two 'mounds', the bounds come to the Mynwy (*myngui*) at 328287, which they cross before ascending 'stream Cwm Cynreith' (*aper nant cum cinreith*), which is probably the brook which ascends Mynydd Ferddin (Mynydd Merddin on modern maps) from 328287 to about 340287. From this brook they go to the top of Mynydd Ferddin (344286: *minid ferdun diar iralt*) and then follow the ridge of the hill south-south-west to the 'pool of [Mynydd?] Ferddin' (*luch ferdun*) at about 339274. Descending the hill the bounds come to the source of the *Hilin* (*blain hilin*), which may be the brook that rises at a spring at 344261, which they follow as far as the Mynwy (*hilin in ihit bet mingui*: now partly the boundary between the parishes of Walterstone and Longtown) at 330254. They then ascend the Mynwy (the boundary between Herefordshire and Monmouthshire at this point) to 329259, where a small brook (possibly the *Bist*) enters the river from the west. The bounds then follow the modern county boundary, which goes up the *Bist* to its source (*bet i blain*), then onwards up the ridge (*cecin*) of Hatterell Hill (313254) and along the ridge back to a stone at 308259.

Great Bilbo (359293)

Belboga c1115-48 EHC; *Pelbog'* 1216-72 AD (p); *Bilbel* 1219-34 LostC.

Second element OE *boga* 'bow', probably in the sense 'smoothly-curving hill'. The element *bel*, which occurs in a number of place-names, has not been satisfactorily explained. There is a Black Bilbo in Rowlestone (362286), which may have gained its affix through being in the hands of the Benedictine monks of Ewyas Harold Priory, who wore black habits.

Llanwonog (324298)

No old forms.

'Holy place of (St) Gwynnog', a saint who was also celebrated at *Lann Tiuinauc* or Whitchurch (Harris).

Longtown (322290)

(Castell de Ewias et) Novi Castelli 1187 P.
Nova Villa 1232 Cur.
Longa Villa 1540 Dugdale; *Longton of Ewys* c1540 Leland.

Perhaps 'long town' because it straggled along the Hay to Abergavenny road. The earliest centre of Norman activity in Ewyas seems to have been at Walterstone, which is probably named after Walter de Lacy (died 1085). Later it moved to the motte-and-bailey castle in Clodock (326281; probably the *Castelli de Ewias* mentioned above) and finally, by 1187, to Longtown. This was at first named after the 'New Castle'. Later the town established in conjunction with the castle became known as 'New Town' and, eventually, Longtown. See District Name Ewyas.

Maes-coed (Lower 348308, Middle 337335 (in Newton) and Upper 334348 (in St Margaret's))

> *(Montis de) Maischoit* 1137-9 Painswick; *Mescott* 1201 Abbr; *Mascoit* 1227 Ch, 1377 Owen; *Mascoy(t)* 1232 Dugdale, 1327 Ch.

This Welsh name presumably contrasts the western part of the land between Escley Brook and the river Dore (which is a 'plain') with the wooded eastern part. 'Plain beside the wood' might be a fair translation. Hickling records a DMV at 327352 in Upper Maescoed (TWNFC (1972)).

❧ CODDINGTON ❧

Coddington (718427)

> *Cotingtune* 1086 DB; *Kotintone* 1276 Cant (p); *Cotinton(e)* 1291 Tax, 1296 Swin; *Cotyn(g)ton* 1334 SR, 1428 FA.

'Estate associated with Cota'. The same name occurs in Cheshire and Nottinghamshire. The personal name is usually said to be *Cotta*, but spellings for these three place-names indicate *-t-*.

❧ COLLINGTON ❧

Collington (Great 649600, Little 657598)

> *Col(l)intune* 1086 DB; *Colyntone* 1305 Swin (p).
>
> *Collinton Major'* 1291 Tax; *Colynton Magna* 1316 FA.
>
> *Parva Colintone* c1250-72 BM; *Colyntone Minoris* 1275 Cant; *Colynton Parva* 1316 FA.

'Estate connected with Cola'.

The two churches of Great and Little Collington were united at Little Collington in 1352 because 'there is scarcely maintenance for one priest so much has the plague reduced the people and impoverished the land' (Trill). Great Collington is now deserted.

Colwall (739423)

> *Colewelle* 1086 DB, 1200-19 Capes (p), 1241 Capes; *Colewella* 14th AD (p).
> *Col(l)ewall(e)* 1140-8 Capes (p), 1291 Tax, 1294 Orig, 1320 Capes, 1506 BB.
> *Colowella* late 12th BM.

> 'Cool spring'.

(county boundary at 768437)

> *Baldeyate* 1577-8 AncWood.

This name, together with a lost *Baldenhall* in Malvern, is discussed in PNWo, 210-11.

Barton Court (724409)

> *Bertone* c1174 Capes, 1286 Swin, 1397 VR; *Bart(h)one* St Katherine (p), 1577-8 AncWood.

> 'Grange', OE *beretūn*.

Brockhill Farm (755437)

> *Brochull* c1300 AD; *Brokeshull* 1381 PNHe.

'Brook hill'. This compound occurs several times as a minor name in Worcestershire.

(county boundary at 763404)

> *Brustenyate* 1577-8 AncWood.

Perhaps 'burst gap', referring to a landslip.

ᔤᔤᔤ COMBE ᔤᔤᔤ

Combe (347632)

> *La Cumbam* 1244 Inspeximus; *La Cumbe* 1263 Pat, *La Caumbe* 1287 Ipm, *(La) Coumbe* 1292 Subs (p), 1307 Ipm; *Combe* 1399 Ipm.

'Short, wide valley'. There is a suitable feature at 358630, between Combe and Combe Moor.

ᔤᔤᔤ MUCH AND LITTLE COWARNE ᔤᔤᔤ

Much Cowarne (618472), **Little Cowarne** (601511)

> *Cogre* 1017-41 Dugdale.
> *Cuure* 1086 DB; *Coura, -e* 1088(?) GloucC, 1121 AC, 1148-55 BreconC, c1158 Foliot; *Cura* c1150 Capes; *Cowra* c1250 Early Deeds.
>
> *Covene Majori* 1088(?) GloucC; *Magna Coerne* 1243 Fees; *Magna Coure* 1291 Tax; *Magna Cowern(e)* 1292 QW, 1334 SR, 1373 Ipm; *Cowarn Magna* 1397 VR.
> *Muchel Cowarne* 1429 KPC.
>
> *Parva Coura* 1145 *StGC, Parua Coura* 1148-63 Foliot; *Parva Coure* 1291 Tax.

A compound of *cū* 'cow' and *ærn*, which in place-names can be translated 'building of a special nature'. The reference is probably to an important centre of dairy produce.

Bache Farm (599460)

> *Bache* 1088(?) GloucC; *Bece* 1114 Regesta; *Bache* c1158-63 Foliot; *La Bache* 1263-84 Early Deeds (p).

The farm overlooks a little stream-valley, so probably OE *bæce*. But the name could be a refashioning of an earlier *bēce* 'beech tree'.

Leighton Court (643462)

> *Leghton* 1317 Ipm, 1324 Cl.

OE *leactūn*, which is literally 'leek enclosure', but also 'herb garden' and later 'vegetable garden'.

Cradley (736472)

> *Credelaie* 1086 DB; *Cradele(i)a* 1166 RBE (p), c1196-8 Barrow; *Credele(i)* 1189-93, 1241 Capes; *Cradeleg(h)* c1230-4 Barrow, 1317 AD; *Cradeleye* 1283 Capes, 1346 AD; *Credeleye* 1291 Tax, *Creddel'* 1292 QW.

> 'Creoda's clearing'.

Upper Barrow Farm (715498)

> *(La) Bar(e)we* 1254 Capes (p), 1338 Ipm, 1349 AD (p); *Barowe* 1575-80 Bromyard.

> Probably OE *bearu* 'grove'.

Cowleigh Gate Farm (756478)

> *Calilleg Buron* c1230-4 Barrow.
> *Coleghe* 1234 Cur (p); *Conleye* 1267 Swin (p); *C(o)uleye* 1276 AD (p), 1352 AD (p); *Couleg* c1320 AD (p); *Cowley* 1397 VR.

'Cow pasture'. Cowley, Gloucestershire has this derivation, but most instances of Cowley have other origins. *Buron* is unexplained, but may be a manorial name.

'Hanley' (at 697469)

> *Hanlie* 1086 DB; *Henlege* 1243 Fees; *Henleia* 1248 AD (p); *Haneleia* c1250 StGC; *Hanlege* 13th AD; *Han(e)ley(e)* c1250 StGC, 1349 AD (p).

'High wood', a name which sometimes becomes modern Henley or Handley, as well as Hanley.

Homehouse Farm (708463)

> *Heume* 1243 Fees (p); *La Homme* 14th AD.

OE *hamm*, used here (as in Ham Green in the adjacent parish of Mathon) for an enclosed plot in marginal land.

Ridgeway Oak (704487)

> *Oke* 1267 Swin; *(terra de) Oke* c1285 Red Book.

> 'Oak tree'.

Seed Farm (705476)

> (manor of) *La Sudde* 1349 AD.

> Löfvenberg suggests a derivation from an OE **sydde* 'mud, slough', related to the modern word 'suds'.

Storridge Farm (749488)

> *Storug(g)e* 1219 InqMisc, c1285 Red Book, c1320 AD (p).

> 'Stone ridge'.

⚜ CRASWALL ⚜

Craswall (281362)

> 'Cress stream', see DEPN. The stream rises by the remains of Craswall Priory (272377) and joins the Monnow just south of the parish church.

⚜ CREDENHILL ⚜

Credenhill (450439)

> *Cred(d)ehull(e)* 1067-71 Gallia Christiana, late 12th CirenC, 1243 Fees,
> c1250 *LeomC*, 1275 Ipm; *Cradenhille, Credenelle* 1086 DB; *Credenhull(e)*
> 1292 QW, 1306 Orig, 1385 Capes.

> 'Creoda's hill', the hill in question being the one immediately north of the village.

⚜ CROFT ⚜

Croft (450654)

> 'Enclosure', see DEPN.

Cusop (240415)

> *Cheweshope* 1086 DB; *Kiweshope* 1198 CartAntiq; *Kiveshope* 1196 Cur;
> *Kiswishop'* c1220 Divers Accounts; *Kywishope* 1292 Swin; *Kusop* 1317
> Ipm; *Cuyshope* 1543 HT.
> *Chineshope* 1142 EpActs; *Kyneshope* 1291 Tax.

Second element *hop* 'secluded valley'. For the first, DEPN suggests a Welsh stream-name *Cyw* 'chickens', identical with Chew, Somerset, but borrowed in English at a later date, which Ekwall says would account for the absence of palatalisation in *C-*.

Tylasop (248406)

> *Tyleshope* c1230-4 IrishC; *Tyllyshope* 1832 OS.

'Tilli's secluded valley'.

Little Dewchurch (529318)

> *Lytel Deuchurche (et Combe)* 1397 VR; *Dewchurch Parva* 1535 VE.

'Little' is to distinguish it from Much Dewchurch, which see. For *Combe*, see Morraston, below. See also Much and Little Birch.

Altwynt (528308)

> *Attelgunt* 1249-50 Fees; *Athelgwynt* 1334 SR; *Alztgweynte* 1409 BM;
> *Altegwynt* 1419 BM; *Halewynte* 1540 HT.

Probably 'wooded slope', from Welsh *allt* and *gwynt*.

Kilforge House (560321)

> *Kilfudus, Kylfodus, Kylfod(es)* mid 13th StGC, 1457 Owen; *Kilfodes* 1350 Trill.

A Welsh name, with first element *cil* 'hook', referring to its position on the parish boundary.

Morraston (532314)

> *Youeston* 1334 SR; *Maryheston* 1409 Owen; *Morghaston* 1534 Owen;
> *Merdisthon* 1540 HT.

Probably a compound of OE *tūn* with the personal name Morien which appears in the grant of *Cum Mouric* to the local bishop c850.

> *(ecclesia) Cum Mouric (in Ercicg)* c850 (c1130); *Cum Mouruc* 1045-1104 (c1130) LL.

The bounds (incomplete) of *Cum Mouric* c850 (c1130) LL: '... *ariuulo iguern usque as cliuium, et augmentum trans uiam dedit morgen deuilla sua ...*. '... from the *Iguern* Brook as far as the cliff. And Morien augmented it [with land] on the other side of the road in his village.'
The English seem to have known *Cum Mouric* simply as 'Combe':

> *Combe* 1334 SR; *(Lytel Deuchurche et) Combe* 1397 VR.

On the evidence of 1397 VR Little Dewchurch and 'Combe' were separate places. If 'Combe' represents *Cum Mouric* and the original ecclesiastical centre of the estate, there has been a migration of the church site here, as in other places in Archenfield.
The 9th-century donor of the estate gave land '... from the brook *Iguern*' (*a riuulo iguern*), which may be the brook running down past Altwynt, 'as far the cliff ...' (*usque ad cliuim* ...), which perhaps refers to the hill beyond the church. Along this hill runs the road from Hoarwithy to Aconbury, which is likely to be the one on the other side of which Morien had a 'vill' from which he augmented the initial gift.

Prothither (536300)

> *Portheedreth* 1409; *Porthedre* 1411; *Portheder* 1534v Owen, 1565 BM;
> *Porthether* 1548 BM; *Porthedich* 16th AD.

A Welsh name, with *porth*, presumably in the sense of 'gate'. This settlement appears on the 19th-century OS map as the focal point of the local road-system. Mr Morgan suggests a personal name *Edryd* or *Edrydd* as the second element, but points out that *edrydd* 'dwelling' is also possible.

Upper Witherstone (556319)

> *Wyther(s)ton'* mid 13th StGC; *Witherstone* 1523, *Wetherston* 1534 Owen.

If this is a pre-Conquest name, then 'Wiohthere's estate', but possibly a ME name with a surname *Wither*; or a 'stone' name from a stone resembling a wether.

Much Dewchurch (482311)

> *Lann Deui* c620, c745 (c1130), LL; *Lan deui Ros Cerion* 1045-1104 (c1130)
> LL.
> *Podii Deui* c728 (c1130) LL.

'Church of (St) David'. 'In the moor of *Ceirion*' (LL), *Ceirion* perhaps being the personal name *Câr*, as in Ceri, plus the territorial suffix *–ion*.

> *Dewischirche* 1148-55 Foliot; *Dewyeschurche* 1247 Ipm; *Deweschirch(e)* 1275
> Owen, 1334 SR, 1341 NonInq.
> *Dewchurch Magna* 1535 VE.

'(St) David's church', a straight translation of the Welsh. An abbot of *Lann Deui* is mentioned c620 and an abbot of *Podii Deui* c728 (LL).

Bryngwyn (488303)

> *Breiigwyn* 1179-1205 GloucC.

> *Villa Asmacun* 1160-70 HDB.

> *Yrcheneshome* 1291 Tax.

Bryngwyn is a Welsh name, for which more spellings are required for a safe etymology. The qualifying element might be *(g)wyn* 'white'. Mr Morgan thinks the name is *Bryn-gwyn* 'white hill', but if so the early spelling is corrupt. See also 'Wormington', below.

Bryngwyn was an estate belonging to Gloucester Abbey, Nothheard, ealdorman of the Magonsæte, having given it four *manentes* (hides) of land in Archenfield (precise location not given) in 823-5 (ECWM; GloucC). In DB the abbey's lands in Archenfield were part of the composite manor of 'Westwood', for which see below. In 1160-70, however, they were said to be at *Villa Asmacun* within 'Westwood'. Mr Freeman (in Thorn) suggests the second part of this name is a mistake for *Asmanton*, OE 'Æscman's estate', which would give modern 'Ashenton' or 'Ashminton', probably the latter in this case, as at Ashminton in Linton-by-Bromyard. Possibly, therefore 'Bryngwyn' and 'Ashminton' were the Welsh and English names for the same estate. In 1291, however, the abbey's four carucates of land in Archenfield were at *Yrcheneshome*, which seems to be 'river-meadow of Ergyng', the river concerned probably being the Worm Brook. See District Name Archenfield.

Coedmoor Farm (469346)

Coyt(t)emore 1257 Ex, 1274 Ipm; *Coitesmore* 1260 QD; *Coydemore* 1383 Ipm.

'Big wood', Welsh *coed-mawr*.

Kivernoll (568324)

Kivernon 1212/16-28 AcornC; *Kynernoc* 1230 P; *Kyuernou* 1300 Ipm;
  Kyvernow(e) 1322-3 *ET*, 1327 Banco (p); *Kyuernowe* 1400 Duncumb;
  Kevernowe 1586 *ET*; *Kevenoll* 1637 Duncumb.
Kivernewesbrugge 1300 Ipm.

In spite of the 1230 spelling, it seems likely that the final element is OE *hōh* 'hill-spur', later confused with *cnoll* 'round hill'. *Kivern-* is unexplained.

The Mynd (470297)

(La) Munede 1219-34 GloucC, 1300 Ipm; *La Minede* 1314 Swin (p);
  Le Mynde 1448 *ET*; *The Munde* 1459, - *Meend* 1637 Duncumb.

In the Forest of Dean, which is not far away, ME *munede*, from Welsh *mynydd* 'mountain', was used in the specialised sense 'forest-clearing', which would be appropriate here: see PNGl, ii, 218 and also 'Wormington', below.

Ridby Court Farm (466311)

Rydeby 1334 SR; *Rydley* 1540 HT.
Over Rudbie 1448 *ET*.

OE *bēag* 'ring' is very well attested in Devon place-names in the sense 'river-bend'. Ridby may be 'reed bend'. The farm occupies a hill-spur between two brooks, one of which makes a right-angle bend east of the site.

(lost)

Tregois 1290 *ET*; *Tregroys* 1323 Charles.
(campis de) Treggreys et Richardestone 1367 Charles.
Richardson 1448 *ET*; *Richardstowne alias Richardson* 1570 *ET*.

Mr Morgan considers *Tregroys* to be Welsh *Tre(f)groes* 'settlement near a cross or cross-roads'. *Richardestowne* may be named after one of several Richard of Kinnersley's who had lands in 'Wormington' (see below) from the late 12th century onwards. Both this and 'Tregroes' were probably within 'Wormington'.

'Westwood' (lost)

> *Weustaurde* 1067-71 Gallia Christiana; *Westuode, Westeude* 1086 DB;
> *Westwode* pre-1127 GloucC; *Westeorda* 1155 Dugdale.

DB *Westuode* was a composite manor covering Dewsall and eastern Much Dewchurch. It may have acquired its name through being the 'western wood' (or *wardine*?) within a large estate called *Mainaure* in 1086, for which see Much and Little Birch, page 42.

'Wormington' (DMV at 486313)

> *Wrmenton, Wrmoton* 1160-70 HDB; *Wirmeton(e)* 1175/6-82 *StGC*, 1200
> Cur; *Wriminton* c1179-86 Barrow; *Worme(n)ton(e)* 1243 Fees, 1292 Ipm,
> 1541 HT; *Wormyntone* 1367 Charl.

> *Dormyntone* c1340 GloucC; *Donyntone* 14th GloucC.

'Estate associated with the Worm Brook'. The stream name is derived in ERN from the word which became Welsh *gwrm* 'dusky, dun'. The spellings suggest an *–ingtūn* compound.

Two townships within the large DB manor of 'Westwood' are called 'Wormington' in HDB. Information from the late Mrs Elizabeth Taylor, who has studied local deeds, makes it certain that they were centred on the DMV at this location. It lies very close to the church of Much Dewchurch, which is occasionally called 'the church of Wormington', the change from 'W' to 'D' in the above examples probably being influenced by Dormington, a few miles to the north-west. Geographically, the estate called 'Wormington' spread south from the vicinity of the church to include Gloucester Abbey's lands at Bryngwyn/'Ashminton' and north as far as to include Dewsall.

༼༻ DEWSALL ༼༻

Dewsall (486335)

> *Fonte Dauid* 1148-9 Foliot, - *David* 1174-86 Barrow, 1269 Capes.
> *Dewiswell(e)* 1160-70 HDB, c1185 CMAD (p); *Deuswelle* c1174 CMAD (p);
> *Doweswelle* 1230 P; *Dewyas Well* 1243 Fees; *Dewyswelle* 1300 Swin;
> *Deweswell'* 1334 SR; *Deweswall* 1341 NonInq; *Dewshall* 1625 BM.

'St David's spring', with *Dew-, Deu-* derived from Welsh *Dewi*, and so echoing the dedication of the church of neighbouring Dewchurch.

Dilwyn (415546)

> *Diluen* 1086 DB; *Dile* c1130 OseneyC; *Dilu(i)n* 1137 AC, 1176 P (p),
> c1200IrishC (p), 1222 Ch, 1243 Fees, 1250 Ipm, 1275 RH; *Dilum* 1193 P;
> *Dilon(e)* 1205 ClR, 1212 Fees; *Dylon(iam)* 1217 ClR, 1251-2 Fees; *Dylum*
> 1272 Orig; *Delewe* 1295 Ipm, 1372 QD; *Dil(u)we* 13th KPC (p), 1372 QD;
> *Dilewa* 1322 Orig; *Dylewe* 1334 SR; *Dylywe* 1431 FA; *Dyllewyn* 1535 VE;
> *Dilwin* 1654 BM.
> *Diliga Prima* 1123 LeomC.
> *Magna Dilun* 1137-9 HDB.
> *Chirchedylue* 1303 FA; *Chirchedlewe* 1346 FA; *Church Dylwyn* 1535 VE.

DEPN's suggestion that Dilwyn represents the dative plural *dīglum*, OE *dīgol* 'secret place', with metathesis of *–gl-*, has been generally accepted, and it must continue to be accepted *faut de mieux*. It is, however, the only instance noted of this word in place-names, and *dīglum* would be the only clear instance of a dative plural formation in Herefordshire.

Little Dilwyn (438540)

> *Dilge* 1086 DB.
> *Diliga Secunda* 1123 LeomC.
> *Parva Dilun* 1137-9 HDB, 1221 Cur; *Parva Dilum* 1204 RotNorm;
> *P'va Dylwyn* 1535 VE.

Dilwyn Sollers (428555)

> *Dilge* 1086 DB, *Dilewe* 1303 FA.

> *Solersdylewe* 1344 Ipm; *Dylwesolers* 1345 Ipm, *Diluesolers* 14th AD.

For the Sollers family, see Bridge Sollers.

Alton Court (426535)

> *Pletune* 1086 DB.
> *Aleton(e)* c1200 IrishC (p), 1317 Ipm; *Alleton* c1220-41 LostC (p), 1272
> Ipm (p), 1303 FA; *Alton* 1428 FA.

Probably 'Ælla's estate'. As pointed out in Thorn, *Pletune* is best interpreted as a scribal error for *Aletone*.

Bagley Head (396545)

Baggel(egh) 1214 Cur, 1361 Ipm (p).

Probably 'badger wood'. Identical with Bagley in Berkshire, Somerset and Yorkshire, and Baguley in Cheshire.

Chadnor Court (432528)

C(h)ab(b)enor(e) 1086 DB, c1130 Gallia Christiana, 1219 SalopFF (p), 1328 Banco, 1353 AD (p), 1392 QD; *Chebenoura* 1160-70 HDB; *Cabenova* 1165-73 Delisle; *C(h)abbenour'* 1174-86 Fr, c1180-6 Barrow; *Chabnor* 1431 FA.
Chalbenore 1210-12 RBE (p).

'Ceabba's ridge', second element OE *ofer*, generally used in place-names to denote a striking topographical feature. In this case the feature is probably the hill south of Upper Chadnor (428517).

Dewell (386537)

Dyswall 1341 NonInq; *Dysch(e)wall(e)* 1259-60 KinRR, 1398 AD (p); *Douwall'*, *Diswall* 1379 PT (p); *Dyssewalle* 1389 AD (p).
(Home) Dewall 1546 HT.

Possibly 'ditch spring', with Norman-French treatment of OE *dīc* which is seen in Diss, Norfolk, and Dishford, Yorkshire. The 'Home' part of the 1765 form refers to The Homme, below.

(probably the moated site at 419538)

Fæliglæh 1016-35 ASCh; *Falle(y)* 1303, 1428 FA.

-*læh* is the Anglian form of OE *lēah* 'wood, clearing'. *Fælig-* is unexplained.

There are various Fawleys (including one in Fownhope), with first elements *fœlithe* 'hay', *fealg* 'clearing' and *fealu* 'fallow coloured', but the spelling *Fæliglæh* indicates a different origin for these. *Falle* was held with Alton Court in 1303 and so probably lay not far from it. The moated site indicated seems appropriate.

Field's Place (415535)

La Felde 1394 QD (p).

'Open land'.

The Homme (413530)

> *Heume* 1243 Fees; *Homma* 1247-72 AD; *Homme* 1265 Cl (p), 1303 FA,
>   1334 Ch; *Le Home* 1535 VE.
> *Home (Dewsall)* 1765 Duncumb.

OE *hamm*, here 'meadow'.

Luntley (393558)

> *Lutelei* 1086 DB.
> *Lunthelega* 1123 *LeomC*; *Luntelee* 1216-28 *LeomC*; *Luntlegh'* 1243 Fees;
>   *Lountele* 1326 Ipm; *Lunteley(e)* 1361 Ipm (p), 1389 AD, 1392 QD;
>   *Lountley* 1372 QD (p).
> *Luntlenlena, Lutlenene* 1158-64 *LeomC*; *Luntlena* c1170 *LeomC*.

This place-name has been cited as evidence for an OE personal name Lunta. The two spellings with Lount- suggest that the first element had a long vowel (**Lūnta*). The second element is *lēah*, here probably 'clearing', but there has been some confusion with the District Name Leen.

Newton Court (398533)

> *Neutone* 1086 DB.
> *Nethere Newton* 1328 Banco.
> *Nyweton Sarmavyll* 1349 Orig.

'New settlement'. *Sarmaville* may be the manorial name Somerville.

Swanstone Court (441531)

> *Svenestun* 1086 DB; *Suinestona* 1160-70 HDB; *Swenestune* 1243 Fees;
>   *Sueynestan'* 1249 Fees; *Sweyneston* 1293 Ipm, 1334 SR; *Swayneston* 1431 FA.

'Sveinn's estate', identical with Swainstone in the Isle of Wight. The personal name is of Old Norse origin, but it was in use all over England at the time of *Domesday Book*.

Dinedor (533367)

> *Dur(r)a* 1067-71, c1130 Gallia Christiana; *Dunre* 1086 DB, 1176 P (p),
> 1189 P, 1206 Cur (p), 1243 Fees, 1291 Tax, 1334 SR, 1357 Trill *Dunre alias*
> *Dyndure* 1453 Bothe; *Dovra* 1166 RBE (p); *Dinra* 1170 P (p); *Dewre* 1302
> RH; *D(u)ynre* 1356 Trill, 1474 Myllyng.
> *Duyndre* 1350 Trill; *Dyndre* 1432 Spofford; *Dyndore* 1489 Myllyng.

A Welsh name, probably 'hill with a fort', *bre* 'hill' being qualified by *din*
'fort'. Dinedor Hill is crowned by a hillfort. The order of the elements suggests a
name going back at least to the Roman period. The *–d–* which appears from 1350
is a parasite, similar to that in *thunder* (OE *thunor*).

Raven (517362)

> *Reveshull* 1194 Abbr; *Ravenhull'* 1230 P (p), 1387 Ipm; *Ravenehul* 1304 Ipm;
> *Ravenhyll* 1547 HT (p).

This place is by Dinedor Hill, and it may be an instance of the association of
ravens with hillforts which elsewhere gives rise to the name Ramsbury.

Rotherwas (536382)

> *Retrowas* 1086 DB; *Rotherwas* 1216 ClR, 1316 FA; *Rudrewas* 1243 Fees;
> *Retherwas* 1322 Ipm; *Rutherwas* 1328 Banco; *Ruderwas* 1330 CRCG (p).

The second element is OE *wæsse*, used in west-midland place-names of land
by a major river which is the subject of sudden flooding and draining. The first
element is OE *hrȳther* 'cattle'.

Dinmore (486503)

> *Dunemor(e)* 1189 Capes, 1212 Fees, 1219 Capes, 1272 Ipm; *Dinnemor* 1291
> Tax; *Donmore* 1292 QW; *Dynemore* 1338 Larking.

This has been interpreted as a Welsh name, *din-mawr*, which would mean
'great fort', and could refer to the hillfort on Dinmore Hill. But this would be
a post-Roman formation, and the earlier type of Celtic compound might be

Your Name (required)

Comment   Photo   Link

What's on your mind?

Post

All Posts   Newest First

There are no posts yet.
Be the first to chime in!

Marriage Coat of Arms

Hand Painted Heraldic Anniversary Family Crest Hand Stitched Tapestry

● ○

The Internet
Surname Database

Home   Index   About Us

LAST NAME SEARCH

🔍

f Log in

Be the first of your friends to use SurnameDatabase.

Cover Funeral Costs

Request Our Free Brochure & Find a Prepaid Funeral Plan That Suits You

⌃

History   **Statistics**   Links (1)

f Like   2 people like this. Sign Up to see what your friends like.

Last name: *Nendick*

0
🐦 Tweet

This interesting and unusual surname is of Anglo-Saxon origin, and is a locational name from some minor unrecorded place, perhaps a "lost" village. There are an estimated seven to ten thousand villages and hamlets that have now disappeared from Britain since the 12th Century; the prime cause of these "disappearances" was the enforced "clearing" and dispersal of the former inhabitants to make way for sheep pastures at the height of the wool trade in the 15th Century, and natural causes such as the Black Death of 1348, in which an eighth of the population perished. The place is believed to have been in Yorkshire, with the component elements being the Olde English pre 7th Century "neowe, niwe", new, with "dic", ditch, moat, dike, wall of earth; hence "new ditch". The placenames Ninfield and Ninham are also derived from the Olde English "neowe", new, with "feld", open country, and "ham", settlement, respectively. Recordings of the surname from English Church Registers include: the christening of Mary, daughter of Anthonie Nendick, on

amazon.co.uk

Gabor Womens Tove Med S Boots
£72.73 - £135.00
(plus delivery)

Gabor Womens Tove Slirr S Boots
£68.53 - £135.00
(plus delivery)

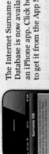

The Internet Surname Database is now available as an iPhone app. Click below to get it from the App Store:

Search over 2 Billion

Historic News Articles

Search Now!

Nendick, on April 6th 1616, at Holy Trinity, Goodramgate, York; and the christening of Humphr, son of Humphr and Izzard Nendick, on November 27th 1676, at St. Gregory by St. Paul, London. The Coat of Arms most associated with the family is a silver shield with a black pale between two black crosses pattee, the Crest being a demi griffin, wings endorsed silver, supporting a black spear headed silver. The first recorded spelling of the family name is shown to be that of Jane Nandicke, which was dated June 1st 1591, marriage to William Toes, at Great Edstone, Yorkshire, during the reign of Queen Elizabeth 1, known as "Good Queen Bess", 1558 - 1603. Surnames became necessary when governments introduced personal taxation. In England this was known as Poll Tax. Throughout the centuries, surnames in every country have continued to "develop" often leading to astonishing variants of the original spelling.

© Copyright: Name Origin Research www.surnamedb.com 1980 - 2015

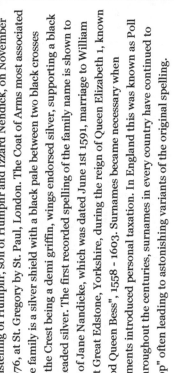

Surname Scroll

Enjoy this name printed onto our colourful scroll, printed in Olde English script. **An ideal gift.** View Details.

expected. The spellings are better suited to an English name 'Dynna's marsh', with OE *mōr*, which would refer to the flood-plain of the river Lugg.

(lost)

> *Futgare* 1185-90 Rees; *Flitgare* 1200-13 *LeomC.*

The final element is OE *gāra* 'wedge-shaped piece of land'.

❧ DOCKLOW ❧

Docklow (564575)

> *Dochelowe* 1277-92 ReadingC; *Dockelawe* 1291 Tax; *Doclue* 1316 FA; *Dok(k)lowe* 1341 NonInq, 1397 VR; *Doclowe* 1535 VE.

'Tumulus where docks grow', OE **docce-hlāw.*

Uphamton Farm and Camp (570580 and 570584)

> See Hampton Wafre.

❧ DONNINGTON ❧

Donnington (708342)

> *Dunninctune* 1086 DB; *Dunintona* c1155 Foliot (p); *Dunington* 1231 Cur; *Doninton* 1264 AD; *Donyn(g)ton(e)* 1341 NonInq, 1297 VR, 1354 St Katherine.
> *Dunituna, -e* 1132 (p), 1140-8 (p), 1163-9 Capes (p); *Duniton'* 1186-98 Barrow; *Dunnitone* 1219 Capes.

'Estate associated with Dunna'. There are more than twenty instances of this name, three of them in Shropshire. The personal name *Dunna* perhaps had a period of popularity which coincided with the period when the *–ingtūn* formula was in use. See also Dingwood Park in Ledbury.

Hatfield (724337)

> *Hadfeld* 1191-9 Capes; *Hatf(i)eld* 1219 InqMisc, 1663 MA; *Halpheld* c1225 Capes (p).

'Open heathland', Bromsberrow Heath lying to the south. The compound of *hæth* and *feld* has become Hadfield, Hatfield (as in the parish in north Herefordshire) and Heathfield in other instances.

❧ DORMINGTON ☙

Dormington (583412)

'Estate associated with Deormod or Deormund', see DEPN.

Hen Hope (582394)

Hinehop' c1138-c58 *StGC*.

'Secluded valley of the monastic community'. The valley was part of the adjacent estate of Prior's Frome (now in Mordiford), which had been in the hands of St Guthlac's Priory since before the Conquest.

Wootton (594392)

Wdeton' 1179-1205 *StGC*.

'Settlement near a wood'.

❧ DORSTONE ☙

Dorstone (314418)

Dodintune 1086 DB; *Dodintona id est Dorsington* 1160-70 HDB.
Dorsin(g)ton 1137-9 HDB, 1243 Fees, 1272 Eyton, 1273 AD, 1309-24 BM;
    Orsinton' 1230 P; *Dorsynton* 1292 QW.
Dorsitone 1219 InqMisc; *Dorsutton* 1291 Tax; *Dorstone* 1250 AD, 1327
    Banco, 1334 SR, 1388 Ipm; *Durston* 1577 BM.

The DB name is 'estate associated with Doda'. This (like Donnington, above) is a recurrent place-name, particularly well evidenced in Shropshire. A note in Thorn suggests that **Dodingtūn* was replaced by **Deorsigeingtūn*, from a different personal name. It is, however, unlikely that a new *–ingtūn* formation would be coined as late as c1100, and the position of Dorstone makes it highly probable that the name contains a reference to the river Dore. Perhaps this is a fanciful creation, in which the *–ingtūn* of the original has been added to a ME genitive of the river-name.

Another name that has been connected with this land-unit is:

Cumbarruc (ynis stratdour) c575; *(agri) Cum Barruc* c595 (c1130) LL.
Cum Barruc id est Cenubia… c745(c1130) LL.

The bounds (incomplete) of *agri Cumbarruc* c595 (c1130) are given in LL: '… *a ualle usque adlech, longitudo latitudo delech usque ad petram crita …*'. 'In length from the valley as far as the stone, in breadth from the stone as far as the stone of (?)Creoda.'

LL places *Cum Barruc* at Dorstone in the Golden Valley and this has been followed by every subsequent authority; *yn is stratdour* means 'in Ystrad Dour' or the Golden Valley, so this far at least it is probably right. Another reference to it in LL seems to reach the same conclusion. Lands at *Tir Conloc* 'on the bank of the Wye (*super ripam Gui*)', which is thought to be Preston on Wye, are said there to reach as far as *Cumbarruc yn Istratdour*. If Preston on Wye is correct for *Tir Conloc*, for an estate based in the Golden Valley to have lands that bordered onto it, it must have been located in the upper part of that valley. The first element of its name is Welsh *cwm* 'valley' and the second a reference to St Barrog or Barrwg (Harris), 'St Barrwg's valley'.

The reference is to the valley of the Pont-y-Weston brook (which has Cwm Farm at 292416), at the mouth of which Dorstone lies. Mr Morgan notes Nant-y-Bar (280409), at the head of the Nant-y-Bar Dingle (a side-valley of the 'cwm' containing Pont-y-Weston Brook), with Welsh *bar* 'hill, top, summit' the likeliest second element, but just possibly a truncated form of 'Barrwg'. It may also be the *ualle* mentioned in the bounds. From there the 'length' of the estate went as far as 'the stone' (*ad lech*), by which is probably meant Arthur's Stone (319431), across the valley of the Dore in the direction of Preston on Wye. Its 'breadth' seems to have been measured from the same stone (*ad lech*) across to the 'stone of (?)Creoda', a conspicuous landmark that may once have existed on the hills to the south of Dorstone.

The deed of king Ithel noted under Abbey Dore says that *Cum Barruc* is *Cenubia* … but does not then give its full name. However, *Cum Barruc* is probably the site of a monastery of St Barrwg, with *cenubia* representing Latin *coenobium* 'monastery', as at Abbey Dore.

The Bage (298432)

Becce 1086 DB; *Becchen* 1127 EpActs; *Le Bache* 1537 Dugdale.
La Heche 1271 Swin.

'Small stream-valley', OE *bæce*.

Mynyddbrydd (281415)

>Ruuenore 1086 DB; Rogenoura 1137-9 HDB.

>Fagemeneda 1160-70 HDB; La Fowemunede 1250 Year Book;
>   La Fowenemind' 1256 Ex (p); Fowemenedene 1317 Pat; La Fowemenede
>   1328 Banco; Sowemyn 1537 Dugdale; Wowminge 1558 Old Rectories.

DB *Ruuenore* is annotated *Fegemeneda* in HDB, suggesting that they were the same place, or at least very close to each other. The DB name is 'at the rough ridge', OE **ruwan ofre*. *Fagemeneda* is a hybrid English/Welsh name, 'variegated mountain'. Modern Mynyddbrydd (properly Mynydd-brith) 'speckled mountain' is the wholly Welsh rendering of this.

(lost)

>Burcstanestune 1086 DB; Buchstanestona 1137-9 HDB; Burstanestona
>   1160-70 HDB.

'Burgstān's estate'.

❧ DOWNTON ON THE ROCK ☙

Downton (428734)

>Duntune 1086 DB; Dontona c1100 WorcC (p); Dunton(a) 1232 Cur (p),
>   1292 QW, 1527 Court; Dounton(e) 1328 Banco (p), 1397 VR, 1535 VE.

'Hill settlement', a recurrent name which sometimes becomes Dunton.

❧ DULAS ☙

Dulas (371296)

>Diveles 1100 GloucC; Duneleis 1137-9 Painswick; Dewlas 1542 HT.
>Dene Layston 1219 InqMisc.

The village is named from the brook on which it stands, Welsh *du-glas* 'black, dark stream'.

An English name for this location may have been:

>Lecche c1115-c25 GloucC (p); (terram de) Leghe juxta ecclesiam Sancti
>   Michaelis de Ewias) 1137-9 Painswick, c1163-86 WalkerReg.

The bounds (incomplete) of *terram de Leghe* 1137-9 Painswick: '... *de fumam usque ad pistil et Duneleis et de fumam usque ad summitatem montis de Maischoit, ex utraque parte de Duneleis.*' Probably OE *lēah* (here 'wood') in spite of the *Lecche* spelling. The land of *Leghe* lay in the southern part of Dulas parish, the only church in the valley of the Dulas Brook dedicated to St Michael before c1150 being Dulas church. Its bounds are too vague to be traced on the ground, but it seems to have had the brook on its northern border. Its southern boundary lay 'at the top of Maescoed Hill' (*ad summitatem montis de Maischoit*), which is probably the high ground by Ball's Cross (364285).

An earlier name for this place may have been *Villa Ellcon super Dubleis* 'Ellcun's estate on the Dulas' c748 (c1130) LL.

Cefn (Upper 360309, Lower 367304)

> *Cheuenerounem* 1232 Dugdale.
> *Cefnbach* 1527 Williams; *Kavenbauch (in Dora)* 1537 Dugdale; *Kevenbeche* 1558 Old Rectories.

Welsh *cefn-y-onnen* 'ash-tree ridge'. Later forms shorten this to *cefn* and add *bach* 'little'.

❧ EARDISLAND ❧

Eardisland (420585)

> *Werlesluna* 1067-71 Gallia Christiana; *Orleslen(a)* 1137-9 HDB, 1174-86 Barrow; *Orlesleu(a)* c1140-55 Dugdale, c1250-63 AcornC; *Urselane* 1243 Fees; *Erleslane* 1285 QD; *Wewislan'*, *Erleslen* 1291 Tax; *Er(le)slon*, 1302 BM 1303 FA; *Ersleone* 1334 SR; *Ereslond* 1529-30 Court; *Erislonde* 1535 VE.
> *Lene* 1086 DB; *Le(e)na* 1148-9 Foliot, 1155 Dugdale.
> *Horlesdone* 1226-30 Capes; *Erlesdene* 1269 Capes.

'Earl's Leen', see District Name Leen. The earl is Morcar, son of earl Ælfgar of East Anglia, who had the estate before 1066 (DB).

(lost)

> *La Barwe* c1250 AcornC (p); *Barewe* c1250-63 AcornC; *Barewa* 13th AD (p); *Bar(r)ow(e)* 1514 Court, 1535 VE, 1542 Dugdale.

'Grove', OE *bearu*.

Burton Court (423572)

> *Bur(e)ton* 1137-9 HDB, 1226-35 ReadingC (p), 1291 Tax; *Burcht'* 1226-34 Barrow; *Burthune* 1243 Fees; *Bourton* 1303 FA, 1305 Ipm.

'Fort settlement', OE *burhtūn*. There are other Burtons in Linton-by-Ross and Weobley.

Hardwick House (405575)

> *Herdynch* 1334 SR.

Probably 'dairy farm', OE *heordewīc*, with a corrupt early spelling.

Nun House (417590)

> *Nonne House* 1542 Dugdale.

Named from the nuns of Limebrook.

(lost)

> *Roslen'* 1542 Dugdale.

Probably Welsh 'marsh in Leen', with 'marsh' one of the meanings of *rhos*. See District Name Leen.

<h1 style="text-align:center">⁂ EARDISLEY ⁂</h1>

Eardisley (312491)

> *Herdeslege* 1086 DB; *Eirdesleg'* 1137-9 HDB; *Ardesle* 1142 Holtzmann, 1222 Cur (p); *Erdesley(e)* 1219 InqMisc, 1269 Ipm, 1275 RH; *Irdesle(y)* 1250 Berks Eyre, 1375 Ipm; *Erdisley* 1292 Year Book, 1535 VE.
> *Ardelai* 1183 P; *Hardelais* 1195 FF; *Erdelegh* 1233 Cl.
> *Erdisley le Englishrie*; *Jerdisley le Walshery* 1413 Ipm.

'Ægheard's clearing', as suggested in DEPN.

The extent of the Englishry and Welshry is unknown, although the latter presumably included Welson (below).

Bollingham House (301527)

Burardestune 1086 DB.

Bollingeshulla 1137-9 HDB; *Bolynghull(e)* 1375 Ipm, 1397 VR.
Ballingham 1373 Ipm.

DB *Burardestune* is annotated *Bollingeshulla* in HDB, so they would seem to be the same place. The DB name is one of a series of names in the Welsh Marches which contain OE *burhward* 'fort guardian'. *Bollingeshulla* may be 'hill of the pollarded tree'. The alteration to –ham may be due to association with Ballingham near Hereford.

Parton (318483)

Parketon 1377 Ipm; *Parton* 1377 Orig.

'Park farm'; Eardisley Park is nearby.

Welson (**Upper** 295513, **Lower** 294503)

Walston(e) 1262 Abbr, 1327 Dugdale; *Welston(e)* 1393 Capes (p), 1545 HT (p),
    1663 MA;
Whelston 1831 Murray's Map.

Walstone could be 'Welshman's estate', OE *Walestūn*, but the change to *Welstone* is puzzling. There may have been influence from the standard English form of the adjective *Welsh*. An alternative etymology would be 'stone at a spring' from OE *welle* (west midlands *wælle*) and *stān*. However, a Welshman paid a customary due of three shillings per annum in Eardisley in 1086 (DB) and if his lands lay here this may well decide the matter in favour of 'Welshman's estate'. A *Wotheloch* of Eardisley (evidently a Welshman) was living in 1220 (Cur).

Woods Eaves Farm (292495)

Wodeseves 1377 Ipm.

'Edge of the wood'. The OE name *wudes efese* occurs in Gloucestershire charter-boundaries, and there is another modern instance in Market Drayton, Shropshire.

Eardisley Wootton (308505)

> *(Hamelantes) Wotton* 1262 Abbr.

Wootton is 'settlement near a wood', as at Wooton in Almeley. *Hamelantes* is more difficult to explain. In 1262 Roger de Mortimer of Wigmore and Radnor came against Walter de Baskerville of Eardisley in curia regis in respect of the manors of *Hamelantes* Wootton and Welson that he held of him by knight's service (Abbr). As lord of Radnor Roger was heir to Hugh Donkey for the manor he had at Woods Eaves in Eardisley in 1086 (DB) and which in 1374/5 Richard Baskerville held of Edmund Mortimer (Ipm). These three places (or two, there is no punctuation mark in Abbr to separate *Hamelantes* from Wootton) are evidently townships within this manor. Wootton and Welson can easily be recognised, but *Hamelantes* cannot. It could represent a garbled form of the place-name Eardisley or something else – possibly Welsh *hen-llan* 'old church'.

❧ EASTNOR ☙

Eastnor (731372)

> *Astenofre* 1086 DB; *Est(e)nover(e)* 1140-8 Capes, 1166 RBE (p), c1317
> St Katherine; *Estenouria* c1153-5 Capes; *Estenouera* c1155 Foliot (p);
> *Esteno(u)r(e)* 1241 Capes, 1291 Tax, 1368 BM.

'Place east of the ridge'. The spur now called Eastnor Hill was perhaps called *Ofer* in pre-Conquest times.

Bronsil (749373)

> *Brankeswellesiche* c1240; *Brankes-walles-siche* c1317, 1361.
> *Brankeswallefeld(e)*, c1240, 1322, 1361 St Katherine.

'Brannog's spring'. To the spring-name have been added *sīc* 'small stream' and *feld* 'open land'. Brannog is a Welsh personal name.

Clencher's Mill (731351)

> *Clenchford's Myll* 1577 AncWood.

The mill is on Glynch Brook, which is *Glench* in 1219 (InqMisc); see ERN.

'Gatleys End' (728377)

> *Gat(e)ley(e)* 12th HRO *Eastnor Deeds* (p), c1240 (p), 1329 St Katherine;
> *Gatesleg* 1230 P (p).
> *Gatelithe* c1240 (p); *Gatelyth(e)* 1345 (p), 1369 (p) St Katherine.

'Goat's slope, with OE *hlith* in the Shropshire and Herefordshire sense of 'concave hill-slope'. There is a Gatley in Aymestrey with the same meaning.

(lost)

> *Geldepire* early 13th St Katherine; *Geldespirie* c1240 St Katherine; *Keldeperie* 13th HRO Eastnor Deeds.

Perhaps 'golden pear tree', with OE *gylden* as first element.

Gold Hill Farm (736364)

> *Goldull* 12th HRO *Eastnor Deeds* (p); *Goldhulle* 1276 Cant (p), c1285 Red Book, 1397 VR; *Geldhulle* 13th HRO Eastnor Deeds; *Goldshulle* 1303 Swin (p).

This is likely to be a reference to golden flowers or to yellow soil.

Ridgeway (740386, etc.)

> *Elfledelega juxta Levithe Rugga* early 13th St Katherine.

Elfledelega is 'Ælfǣd's wood or clearing'. The ridge could also be named from a feminine owner, perhaps *Lēofgȳth*, but more spellings are desirable, as it is likely that this marked topographical feature had a topographical name.

(county boundary at 760369)

> *Shakellyate* 1577-8 AncWood.

'Shackle gate', referring to the pass through which the A438 runs. The meaning of 'shackle' in place-names has not been determined.

(county boundary at 762380)

> *Swyneyate* 1577-8 AncWood.

This is another 'gate' through which a road crosses the Malvern Hills. Swine were presumably pastured on this stretch of the hills. It lies south of Swineyard Hill (761385).

Eaton Bishop (442391)

> *Etune* 1086 DB; *Eton(e)* 1241 Capes, 1291 Tax, 1506 BM.
> *Eton Episcopi* 1341 NonInq.

'River estate'; see DEPN. This was the only one of four Eatons in Hereford-shire that was in episcopal hands.

This is possibly the site of *Lann Guorboe* c615 and of *Lannguoruoe in Campo Malochu* c745 (c1130) LL. It has been equated with Garway (LL), but that is not within Mawfield (*Campo Malochu*). See District Name Mawfield. Abbots of *Lannguorboe* are mentioned in c620 and c745.

Ruckhall Farm (452390)

> *Rughall* 1381 KPC (p); *Ruyhale* 1420 Capes.

More spellings are needed for this place-name.

Warlow Farm (434397)

> *Werlawe* c1210-36; *Warlawe* 1251 *StGC*.

The first element is possibly a bird name, cf. ME *wer-cok*; the second element is *hlāw* 'tumulus'.

Edvin Loach (662584), **Edwyn Ralph** (646575)

> *Edevent, Gedeuen(na)* 1086 DB, 1163-7 *StGC*; *Yedeuen(na)* 1148-63, 1256
>   *StGC*; *Gedefen, Jedefen* 1160-70 HDB; *Yed(d)efen(n)* 1176 P (p), 1211-12
>   RBE, 1265 Cl (p); 1324 ReadingC (p), 1393 QD; *Hedeven* 1210 P (p).
> *Gedesfenna* 1123 LeomC.

> *Yedefen Loges* 1286 Swin; *Edven Loche* 1576 KPC.

> *Gedeuen Maro* 1137-9 HDB.
> *Yeddefen(n)e Radh* 1291 Tax, - *Rauf* 1349 Trill; *Edefen Rad'i* 1341 NonInq;
>   *Edvyn' Radulph'* 1535 VE; *Edvyn Rauf* 1562 KPC.

'Gedda's fen', one of a small class of place-names which have OE *fenn* as the final element of a compound. The area does not look marshy on modern maps, but Saltmarshe is the adjacent parish to the east.

Gerwy de Loges gave the church at Edvin *Loges* to St Guthlac's Priory, Hereford (*StGC*). Loges or Les Loges is a fairly common place-name in Normandy.

A Ralph of *Yedefen* (one of many with the same name) was lord of Edwyn Ralph in 1176 (P) and this part of Edvin may have taken its suffix from him. '*Maro*' may be a reference to the family of *de Mara* (de la Mare) who the held nearby manor of Tedstone Delamere.

Upper Horton (631585)

> *Hortone* 1268-75 *Red Book MS* (p), 1304 Swin; *Herton'* 1334 SR, 1547 HT; *Harton* 1567 KPC, 1663 MA; *Hurton* n.d. KPC (p).

'Dirt farm', OE **horu-tūn*, a fairly common name, usually referring to wet ground. This is another reference to the 'fen'.

❧ EGGLETON ❧

Eggleton (Upper 638451, **Lower** 626451)

> *Eglinton(e)* 1189 P (p), 1285 Red Book, 1304 Swin; *Eglintune* 1219 Capes; *Eglyntone* 1273 Capes, 1292 QW.
> *Eglingtone* 1210-12 RBE.
> *Egluit'* v1250, *Eglutton* c1260 Early Deeds; *Egliton* 1291 Tax; *Egleton(e)* 1334 SR, 1581 KPC.
> *Eglantune* 1262 AD.

A number of place-names which have Eggle- or Eagle- in their modern forms have been explained as containing OE personal names such as Eogwulf, Ecga or Ecgel, but the development to Egg- instead of Edge- has not been explained. Eggleton, therefore, is one of a group of place-names which require further study.

❧ ELTON ❧

Elton (458710)

> *Elintune* 1086 DB; *El(l)eton* 1175-9 (14th) Chronicle, 1199 P (p), 1333 Ipm; *Elton(e)* 1397 VR, 1535 VR; *Elyton* 1434 KPC.

Perhaps 'estate with an eel-fishery'. A place-name element *æling* 'eel-place', is believed to occur in Berkshire and Gloucestershire and this may be another example.

Evesbatch (686482)

> *Sbech* 1086 DB; *Esbec(he)* 1160-70 HDB, 1195-9 BreconC; *Esebak* 1200 P;
> *Asebech* 1201 Pleas; *Es(se)bach(e)* 1268-75 *Red Book MS* (p), 1291 Tax,
> 1313 Ipm, 1316 FA, 1330 St Katherine, 1341 NonInq.
> *Eseberg'* 1199 Pleas (p); *Esebege* 1243 Fees.
> *Estbech* 1199 StGC.

'Esa's stream Valley'. A collection of spellings from later sources, such as parish registers, might throw light on the corruption to Eves-.

Ewyas Harold (388287)

> (*... in wasto*) *Haraldi* 1162 P.
> *Euuiasharold'* 1176 P; *Ewias Castelli Haraldi* 1213/14-36 Walker Reg;
> *Dewyas Haraldi* c1220 DiversAccs; *Euwyas Harold* 1300 Ipm;
> *Ewys Harold* c1540 Leland.
> *Haraldesewyas* 1371 Ipm; *Harolde Ewias* 1543 HT.
> *Mapelart alias Ewisharneis*; *Maperalt alias Maperart, Mapheralt* c1540 Leland.

This was the part of the commote of Ewyas that Harold, son of earl Ralph of Hereford (died 1057) and nephew of Edward the Confessor, gained on the death or forfeiture of Alfred 'of Marlborough', who held it in 1086. In 1162 the sheriff was quit of danegeld on several lands in Herefordshire that were considered to be 'waste' or unproductive (perhaps as a result of civil war in king Stephen's reign), including 'the wastes of Harold'. Leland seems to record a much earlier name for this land-unit, as he does for Lye in Aymestrey. For 'Ewyas-harness', see District Name Lugharness.

'**Monnington**' (lost, but probably an earlier name for Ewyas Harold)

> *Manitone* 1086 DB; *Mamintone* 1166 RBE (p); *Maninton* 1206 Cur (p).

This name and the two Monningtons are probably OE *gemǣnan tūne* 'communal estate', with assimilation of –*an*- to –*ing*- by influence of the -*ingtūn* names which are well-evidenced in south Herefordshire. Manton in Nottinghamshire, Rutland, and Wiltshire, and Manton in Devon, are similar names. Not all of them show influence from –*ing*-, but Manton in Wiltshire has very similar early spellings to the Herefordshire names, except for the development of *Man*- to *Mon*- (which is a west midlands dialect feature).

Associated with this place-name in medieval records is:

Mulstoneston 1300 Ipm; *Molteston* 1344, 1372 AD; *Multeston* 1352 InqMisc.

Perhaps 'settlement with a mill-stone.'

Manitone, entered under Ewyas in DB, is not Monnington Straddle in Vowchurch (cf. VCH, Thorn) but a separate place in Ewyas Harold. In 1166 Godfrey *de Mamintone* held one knight's fee in the castlery of Ewyas Harold and in 1300 the service of half this fee was owed on lands in *Multstoneston* and the other half on lands in Ewyas Harold. There was therefore a close connection between *Mamintone*, *Mulstoneston* and Ewyas Harold, but none with Monnington Straddle in Vowchurch, which was, in any case, held by a different family. In fact, *Mamintone* and *Mulstoneston* were probably two English estates either side of the Dulas Brook in Ewyas Harold. The first of these became the site of the castle and the second the site of the church and town established by Robert, son of Harold.

Callow Hill Wood (395281)

Calowe 1300 Ipm (p).
Caluhull 1334 SR; *Calewehull* 1360 Ipm (p).

'Bare hill'. A derivative of the OE adjective *calu* is used as a noun in hill-names.

Elm Green Farm (401291) and Elm House (403301)

(terram de) Heaume 1215 Dugdale, 1219 PatR; *la Helme* 1300 Ipm (p).

This is the rather rare place-name element *helm* 'shelter'.

❧ EYE, MORETON AND ASHTON ☙

Ashton (516644)

Estune 1086 DB; *Eston'* 1212 Fees; *Aston* 1535 VE.
Esscetun' 1123 LeomC; *Ayshton* 1308 Ipm; *Ascheton* 1367 BM;
    Assheton 1431 FA.
Eyston 1216-c40 BM; *Ays(s)ton* 1219/34-c50 LeomC, 1295 Ipm, 1305 Ipm,
    1316 FA.
Aleston 1303, 1347, 1428 FA.

There are sufficient spellings in the second and third categories to establish the etymology 'ash-tree settlement'. The FA forms are presumably erroneous.

Eye (496638)

> *Heya* 1123 *LeomC*; *Eia* c1150 Capes, c1173-80 BM; *Eya(m)* c1150-4 Foliot, 1213-16 Kemp, c1242-9 *LeomC*; *Eye* 1431 FA, 1535 VE.

'Raised ground in a marsh', OE ēg, a description that exactly fits the situation of Eye Church.

Moreton (502641)

> *Mortun(a)* 1219/34-c50 *LeomC*, 1243 Fees; *Moreton'* 1535 VE.

'Marsh settlement'.

Castle Ground Farm (517655)

> *Castleton* 1219-34-c50 *LeomC*.

There are two castle sites in Ashton, a motte-and-bailey at 514650 and one of an indeterminate nature at 518642. The latter site was excavated in 1958 and found to be the stump of a round tower of mid-13th century date (TWNFC). The reference, therefore, could be to either of these sites.

Merryvale Farm (516663)

> *Murival* 1300 Ipm; *Muryvale* 1437 Ipm; *Morevele* 1535 VE.

See Merryvale in Aconbury.

❧ EYTON ☙

Eyton (475616)

> *Eiton(e)* 1186-99 *LeomC*, 1308 ReadingC; *Eytune* 1238-58 ReadingC (p); *Eytone* 1326 Orl.

'Island settlement'. As in the parish name Eye, OE ēg here has the sense 'raised ground in a marsh'. Old Hall, west of Eyton village, looks an appropriate site. (VCH and Thorn say that DB *Ettone* in Leominster is Eyton, but its tenurial history shows that it was Eaton by Leominster.)

❧ FELTON ☙

Felton (579485)

> *Feltone* 1086 DB, c1230 *StGC*, 1291 Tax; *Feltona* 1148-63 Foliot, c1179-86 Barrow.

> OE **feld-tūn*, 'settlement in open country'.

Hinton (574473)

> *Hinetune* 1086 DB; *Hyneton'* 1249 *StGC*; *Hyniton* 1291 Tax; *Henton* 1346 AD. *Kinetonestowe* c1230 *StGC*.

> 'Estate belonging to a monastic establishment' (in this case St Guthlac's at Hereford), a fairly common name. The c1230 affix is OE *stow* 'holy place'.

Rosemaund (565480)

> *Magge* 1086 DB; *Maga* 1160-70 HDB.
> *Mawene* 1256 Salop Eyre (p).
> *Rous Maune* 1373 Ipm.

> See District Name Maund. The affix is from the Rus or Rous family, subtenants of the manor in the Middle Ages.

(lost)

> *Westelet* 1086 DB; *Westeleg'* 1137-9 HDB.

> Probably '(place) west of the wood'.

❧ FORD ☙

Ford (512552)

> 'Ford over the river (Lugg)', see DEPN.

Fownhope (581343)

> *Hopa* 1067-71 Gallia Christiana, 1142-7 Barrow; *Hope* 1086 DB, 1142
>   Holtzmann.
> *Faghehop, Fauue Hope* 1243 Fees; *Fawehope* 1269 Capes; *Fowehope* 1303 FA,
>   1318 Capes, 1341 NonInq.
> *Fon(e)hop(e)* 1291 Tax, 1334 SR; *Fow(e)n(e)hop(e)* 1315 Orig, 1535 VE;
>   *Founhope* 1429 Cl, 1431 FA.

OE *hop* 'remote place' is the term commonly used in Herefordshire and
south Shropshire for settlements in the type of valley characteristic of this coun-
tryside. The affix is OE *fāg* (dative *fāgan*), 'variegated multi-coloured'.

Little Hope (578368)

> *Chittelhope* c1225 Capes; *Lytylhope* 1429 Cl.

'Little' to distinguish it from Fownhope.

Foy (598283)

> *Lann Timoi* c866 (c1130); *Lanntiuoi* 1056-1104 (c1130), 1063-6 (c1130) LL.
> *Sancte Fidis (de Eton')* 1139-48 Capes.
> *Sancta Foa (de Etton)* c1187-98 Barrow, 1205-16 Capes; *Sanctae Foe* 1195
>   GloucC.
>
> *Foy(e)* 1148-61 GloucC, 1186-9 EHC, 1242 GloucC, 1252 Capes, 1291 Tax,
>   1334 SR, 1428 FA, 1535 VE; *Fo(y)a* 1205-16 Early Deeds, 1233 GloucC;
>   *Le Foy* 1443 Ipm.

Moi or Moe, the Welsh saint's name, has survived, without the hypocoristic
Ti-, as modern Foy. In the 12th century the church was also known as St Faith,
presumably because of confusion between the saint's name and French *foi* (Latin
fides). Its dedication today is to St Mary. For *Et(t)one* sea Eaton, below.

Hill of Eaton or **Eaton Tregoz** (605277)

> *Edtune* 1086 DB.

Et(t)on(e) 1139-48 Barrow, 1186-9 EHC, 1222 GloucC, 1281 AD, 1283 Swin,
  1292 GW, 1303 FA, 1357 Ipm; *Ethone* 1195 GlouC, 1284-1316 GloucC.
Eton(e) Tregoz 1300 EHC, 1310 Orig; - *Tregos* 1316 FA, 1375 BM.
Eton(e) super Wayam 1283 Swin; - *Suway* 1301 InqMisc.

'River settlement', OE **ēa-tūn*, perhaps referring to some specialised function performed by this place in relation to the river. The road through the settlement from the south leads to the only crossing place on a great loop in the Wye. The suffix is from the family of Tregoz, who were from Troisgots, between St-Lô and Tessy-sur-Vire, dépt. Manche (Loyd).

(**Carthage** 599284)

The Homme 1410 Ipm.

Duncumb says that Carthage was once called Hom House. The earliest sense of *hamm* in place-names is 'land enclosed by a river bend'. This may be the earliest English name of the whole Foy peninsular.

Ingestone Farm (609292)

Enche(s)tone 1283, 1305 Swin (p); *Yngeston* 1410, 1422 Ipm.
Ivestone, Iverston 1443 Ipm.

Probably 'settlement of the manorial servants'. ME *enche* 'manorial servant' is fairly well preserved in place-names.

Lyndor Wood and Cottages (617296)

Lyndonere 1357 Ipm; *Lyndorr Wood* 1410 Ipm.

'Lime-tree ridge', OE **lind-ofer.*

(**Hole-in-the-Wall** 611286)

Turlestane 1086 DB.

Hole-in-the-Wall (which appears on the 19th century OS map, so has some antiquity) is a modern rendering of DB *Turlestane* 'hole stone'. Another instance of the DB name occurs in Thurlestone, Devon, where the reference is to a coastal rock pierced by a natural hole. Stanthorne, Cheshire, was earlier *Stanthirle*, with the same elements in reverse order; it has been suggested that this referred to a megalithic tomb with a port-hole entrance.

Snogsash (622297)

> *Fnogesesse (-hundredum)* 1180 P; *Fuoggesshassh* 1376 Ipm; *Fucogeaishe* 1422 Ipm.
> *Snogeiasshe* 1422 Ipm.

The OE form of Snogsash was apparently **Fnogesæsc*. The second element is *æsc* 'ash-tree', and it would be reasonable to assume a personal name as the first element. Nothing like **Fnog* is on record as a personal name or significant word. The initial consonant combination *Fn-* only occurs in OE in a group of words – *fnæran, finæs, fnæst, fnæstian, fneosan, fnesan, fnore* – all referring to sneezing and snorting. Modern *sneeze* is an alteration of *fnese*, apparently due to misreading of *f-* as *s-* in the 15th century. There is no reason to assume that the first element of **Fnogesæsc* is related to these words. It is clear, however, that *Fn-* is a possible initial consonant combination in OE, and the development of the name to Snogsash is a parallel to *sneeze* from *fnese*.

In Henry I's reorganisation of the Herefordshire hundreds, Bromsash and Greytree Hundreds were combined to form a larger hundred that seems at first to have been called Snogsash Hundred. It had become (or reverted to) Greytree Hundred by 1243 (Fees)

✂ BISHOP'S FROME ✂

Bishop's Frome (663483)

> *Frome* 1086 DB.
> *F(f)rom(e) Epi(scopi)* c1285 Red Book, 1291 Tax, 1397 VR.
> *Byschopusfrome* 1428 FA.

Stands on the river Frome, for which, see ERN. The estate belonged to the bishop of Hereford.

Halmond's Frome (673483)

> *Nerefrum* 1086 DB; *Nederefroma* 1160-70 HDB.
> *Frome Hamunde* 1205-16 StGC; *- Heymund* 1243 Fees.
> *Haymondsfrome* 1399 Ipm.

'Nether' Frome was annotated *Hamonis* in HDB, and he may be the man from whom it took its affix.

Leadon Court (684466)

> *Lede* 1086 DB.
> *Leden(e)* 1147-8 GloucC, 1243 Fees, 1291 Tax, 1334 SR.
> *Leden-frome* c1250-c75 St Katherine.
> *Ledon infra p(ar)ochia de Ledbury* 1524 HT.
> *Priors Fromeledon* 1542 PNHe.
> *Ledons Holywater* 1547 HT.

Named from the river Frome. The *Frome* affix was perhaps added to distinguish it from Upleadon in Bosbury, four miles to the south. The manor belonged to St Guthlac's Priory, Hereford. 'Holywater' tithes were payable to the minster within whose *parochia* the place lies, in this case Ledbury church.

Paunton Court (670500)

> *Panton'* 1239-66 BeauchampC (p), 1265 Cl (p); *Paunton* 1277 Cant.

Apparently a manorial name, derived from the family of Paunton who held land here within the manor of 'Stanford Regis' in the 13th century.

Rhea Farm (671505)

> *Atthere* 1266 Ipm (p); *(La) Ree* c1285 Red Book, 1301 Ipm (p), 1318 Ipm (p), 1341 NonInq, 1345 Ipm (p).

'At the river'.

'Stanford Regis' (DMV at 667500)

> *Stanford* 1086 DB.
> *King(e)Stanford(e)* 1243 Fees, 1296 Ipm; *Stanford Regis* c1273 Ipm, 1316 FA.

'Stone ford', a common name. Other parts of 'Stanford' were at Stanford Bishop and 'Stanford Faucon'.

Lower Walton Farm (655473)

> *Walton'* 1230, 1231 cur.

Probably 'spring settlement', with the west midlands form of *welle*.

CANON FROME

Canon Frome (645434)

> *Frome* 1086 DB; *Froma* 1107-15 *StGC*, 1136 Barrow, c1230-56 BM.
> *Parva Frome* 1131 Holtzmann, 13th KPC; *Frome Minor* c1132 Regesta;
> *Parvam Fromam* 1155-c63 *StGC*.
> *Froma Canonicorum* 1160-70 HDB, 1205-15 *StGC*, 1243 Fees, *Frome*
> *Canonicor'* 1291 Tax; *Canonffrome* 1397 VR.

Both this and Castle Frome were in Lacy hands in 1086, this being the smaller of the estates. Hugh de Lacy (died c1115) gave it to the canons of Llanthony Prima, his own foundation.

CASTLE FROME

Castle Frome (668459)

> *Bricmarifrome* 1074-85 GloucC; *Brismerfrum* 1086 DB; *Bricdmeri Froma*
> 1107-15 *StGC*.
> *Majoris Frome* 1101-2 *StGC*.
> *Frome Herberti* 1201, 1205 ClR.
> *Froma Castri* 1243 Fees; *From' Castelli* 1291 Tax; *Castel Frome* 1342 Ipm;
> *Castyl Frome* 1428 FA.

Brictmer held this estate from earl Harold Godwineson before 1066. Afterwards, this and Canon Frome were in Lacy hands, this being the larger of the estates. It was the only one of several 'Frome' estates to acquire a castle. In HDB (1160-70) *Brismerfrum* is annotated *Castelli*, but this may refer to Herbert *de Castello*, of Castle Holdgate, Shropshire, its current subtenant, rather than to the castle. The 1201 and 1205 forms arose from Herbert's subtenancy.

GANAREW

Ganarew (529163)

> *Genoreu* c1135 Geoffrey; *Genoire* c1155 Wace, c1190 Layamon; *Generu*
> 1291 Tax; *Genre* 1293 Swin; *Genereu* 1325 Ipm; *Generew* 1345 Ipm;
> *Generrywe* 1397 VR.

DEPN explains this name as 'hill pass', Welsh *genau rhiw*.

As the church stands close to the hillfort on Little Doward Hill it may be the site of:

Lanndougarth c620 (c1130) LL.

See Little Doward, below. The reference is to an abbot of *Lanndougarth*.

Possibly it was also either *Lann Celinni* ('church of St Celynin': LBS) or *Lann Tisauuc*, churches which existed in Archenfield in 1045-1104 (LL), but whose locations are unknown. See also St Wolstan's in Welsh Newton.

Little Doward (540160)

Cloartius c1135 Geoffrey; *Droare* c1155 Wace; *Cloward* c1190 Layamon; *Denard* 1292 QW; *Douwarth* 1327 Ipm.
Lytledowarth 1413 Ipm.

This is a Welsh name *dwy-garth*, 'two heights': the settlements of Little and Great Doward lie on the lower slopes of two neighbouring hills. Geoffrey's fabulous 'History of the Britons' has king Vortigern burnt to death in his castle (*oppidum*) of *Genoreu*, on a hill called *Cloartius* beside the Wye in 'the land of *Herging*'. Layamon copied Geoffrey in mistaking 'd' for 'cl'.

Wyastone Leys (534156)

Lay in Geney Rue 1645 Duncumb.
Wyeston Leys 1665 Duncum.

Lay is probably OE *lēah* 'clearing' and Wyeston 'rock on the river Wye', but earlier forms are needed for safe etymologies.

❧ GARWAY ❧

Garway (455225)

Licat Amr c820 HB; *Lagademar* 1086; *Landmore* 1505 Rees.

Garou 1137 AC; *Gar(e)wi* 1160-70 HDB, 1185-9 Lees; *Garwy* 1230 Cl, 1312 Orig; *Garew(a)y* c1230 Capes, 1297 Duncumb, 1300 Ipm (p), 1334 SR, 1338 Larking; *Gorewy* 1320 Capes (p).

Langarewi 1189 Lees.

Lagademar is the DB name for the estate that is called Garway in HDB and is thus, probably, an earlier or alternative name for it. *Llygad Amr*, Welsh 'source of the Gamber' (Gamber being called *Amhyr* or *Humir* in the 7th to 10th centuries: LL), seems to have been the semi-legendary source somewhere on Garway Hill of the Gamber/Garren watercourse. In HB, however, *Amr* is called a son of 'the warrior Arthur', and he passes into Welsh myth as 'Amhar son of Arthur' (AW). A similar process must have been involved in the appearance in Welsh legend of *Lochou* (see District Name Mawfield) as another son of Arthur's.

Even though there is no connection (etymological or otherwise) between Garway and *Lannguorboe* (?Eaton Bishop, see above), the personal name *Guoruoe* (Gwrfwy) involved in the place-name *Lannguorboe* could also be the origin of this place-name. Garway is not the location of *Lannguorboe*, as has been alleged (LL), because that was in Mawfield and not Archenfield. A lost church or chapel called *Lann Mihacgel supra Mingui* 'church of St Michael above the Mynywy' (1045-1104 (c1130): LL), which has also been connected with Garway (LL), was also not here, but at a site one mile south, on a tongue of land surrounded on three sides by the Mynwy (*Mingui*) (c462207) and, although east of that river, it is now within the parish of Skenfrith in Monmouthshire. This chapel of St Michael was still extant in the 16th century (AD).

When king Richard I gave Garway to the Templars he gave it under the title of 'the land of *Langarewi*' and included with it 'the castlery that had been Herman's' (Lees), Herman (de Dreux) being the DB holder of Garway.

❧ GOODRICH ❧

Goodrich (572190)

> *Hulla* 1086 DB.

> *Castelli Godrici* 1101 MonC, *Castello Godrici* 1146 Fr; *Cast' Godr'* 1160-70 HDB, 1230 Divers Accs, *Castrum Godrici* 1219-29 Capes, 1302 BM, *Castrum de Godrhe* 1249-50 Fees; *Goderih* 1322-6 BM.

The DB estate called *Hulla*, OE *hyll* 'hill', is annotated *Castr' Godr* in 1160-70 showing that they were different names for the same land-unit. Godric Mapson, the DB holder of *Hulla*, founded the castle named after him that eventually became the name for the whole estate. The eponymous 'hill' is likely to be Huntsham Hill (see Hentland, below) and not Howle Hill (cf. VCH; Thorn), which is in Walford.

Coppet Hill (c572175)

Coppyngwode 1372; *Coppodewoode* 1413 Duncumb.

Coppet is a reduced form of *Coppodewoode*, probably 'pollarded wood', though 'wood rising on a peak' is also possible. *Coppyngwode* may contain an unrecorded noun *copping*, either 'something pollarded' or 'something peaked'.

Hentland (567163)

Hentland 1831 OS.

By analogy with the parish name Hentland, this should be Welsh *henllan* 'old church'. As such, it is likely to be the site of:

Mainaur Garth Benni c575 (c1130); *Gurit Penni* c625 (c1130) LL.
Lann Custenhinngarthbenni c575 (c1130), *Lann Custenhin* 1045-1104
   (c1130) LL.
Lanngarthbenni c620 (c1130); *Ecclesia Garthbenni* c700 and c743 (c1130) LL.

The bounds of *Mainaur Garth Benni* c575 (c1130) LL: (under the title of *Lann Custenhinngarthbenni in Ercicg*, king Peibio gave) '*Mainaur Garth Benni usque ad paludem nigrum inter siluam et campum et aquam et iaculum Constantini Regis...trans Guy amnem.*' '*Mainaur Garth Benni* as far as the Black Bog and the ford of king Constantine across the river Wye, in wood, field and water'.

These very brief bounds take in an area roughly corresponding to the present civil parish of Goodrich. Watkins (in TWNFC (1966)) gives reasons for believing that the 'Black Bog' stood west of Huntsham Court, between Huntsham Pool (561173) and the Wye, in an area that is still liable to flood. This will mark its southern extremity. Its northern was at 'king Constantine's ford', which is the ford on the Wye that still exists below Goodrich castle (576202) and which was the reason for the castle's existence. This was a major crossing of the Wye between Hereford and Monmouth and was important enough to be retained in royal hands by being excluded from the grant. The ford itself and a small amount of land on either bank remained separate from all other estates around it (including Goodrich) from the time of this grant (and probably before) until 1846, when it and they were finally brought within the county of Hereford (TWNFC (1962)). *Mainaur Garth Benni* was therefore an earlier name for the estate called *Hulla* by the English and Goodrich by the Normans. The chief topographical feature of this estate was Huntsham Hill, on top of which is a hillfort and below which a Roman villa once stood (at 564176). This hill gave it its English name *Hulla*. The ecclesiastical centre of the estate was at Hentland, where there was a church of St Constantine that became ruined in the 11th century and was combined with

105

a 'church of the Twelve Saints' in the cemetery at Welsh Bicknor (which see). *Mainaur Garth Benni* was the seat of a bishop from c575.

An abbot of *Lanngarthbenni* is mentioned c620 and a grant of lands on the river Wye (location not given) was made in *ecclesia Garthbenni* c743 (LL).

Huntsham Court (563172)

Hentham 1075-87 AD.
Hondsum 1179-1205 GloucC, 1275-6 CRCG (p); *Handsum* c1290 CRCG (p); *Hontsum* 1302 CRCG (p).
Houson 1186 Fr, 1454 Ipm; *Honsom* 1304 CRCG (p), 1318 Orl (p); *Housom* 1396 Ipm (p), 1399 Ipm; *Hunsom* 1660 Duncumb.
Honsham 1397 VR; *Housham* 1413 Ipm.

In view of the situation of Huntsham, it is reasonable to interpret the second element as 'land in a river-bend', from OE *hamm*. The *–um, -om* spellings show west midlands rounding of â before a nasal. Perhaps 'Hun's river-bend', OE **Huneshamm,* identical with Huntsham, Devon, or 'Hund's river-bend', with the early loss of *–d-* which is found in Hounslow in Middlesex.

(at 565157, **where the B4432 crosses a short stretch of Offa's Dyke**)

Jetelynde 1300 Hart; *Getelynde* 1300 Swin; *Jutelinde* 1300 Trill.

'Lime-tree in a gap', from OE *geat* 'gate' and *lind.*

✤ GRAFTON ✤

Grafton (496370)

'Estate by a grove', see DEPN.

Bullinghope (510370)

Bollynghope Superior 1316 FA; *Bullyngeshop Superioris* 1341 NonInq; *Bollinghope Sup'ior* 1535 VE.

See also parish name Lower Bullingham ('Bullinghope Inferior').

GRENDON BISHOP

Grendon Bishop (598563)

> *Gren(e)den(e), (-a)* 1086 DB, 1241 Capes, 1275-82 Swin (p), c1285 Red Book,
> *Grendon* 1269 Ipm; *Greyndon* 1291 Tax.
> *(Gr)endon' Sancti Michaelis* 1249 Fees.
> *Grendon(e) Episcopi* 1316 FA, 1334 SR.

'Green valley', the final element is *denu-*, later confused with *dūn* 'hill'. Another part of Grendon (Grendon Warren) is in Pencombe. This part came to the bishop of Hereford in 1241. Its church is now dedicated to St John the Baptist.

Batchley Farm (601574)

> *Bacheleye* 1268-75 *Red Book MS* (p).

'Wood or clearing by a stream-valley', from OE *bæce* and *leah*.

Horsnett Farm (605554)

> *Horsnede(n)* c1250 St Katherine, 1275 Cant (p), 1312 Swin (p).

'Horsa's valley'; the *denu* could be the small side-valley which branches off from the main valley of Grendon at this point.

Westington Court (589567)

> *Wetinton'* 1207 Pleas; *Westintone* 1261-91 ReadingC.

'(Place) west in the estate'.

HAMPTON BISHOP

Hampton Bishop (559380)

> *Hantune* 1086 DB; *Hamtona* 1186-1200 Capes; *Hanton'* 1195 P (p); *Hamtuna*
> c1200 Capes; *Hampton(e)* 1246 Capes, 1292 Swin, 1316 FA, 1341 NonInq,
> 1535 VE; *Hompton(e)* 1334 SR, 1376 BM.
> *Hampton Episcopi* 1592 BM.

'Estate in a river bend', OE *hamm-tūn*. This was the only 'Hampton' (of which there are six in Herefordshire, not all of them with the same etymology) that belonged to the bishop of Hereford.

Colcombe House (548375)

> *Calecumbe* 1200-15 Barrow; *Col(e)cumbe* 1234 Cur, 1296 KPC, 1299 Swin, *Calcombe* 1268-75 *Red Book MS* (p); *Colcome* 1524 HT (p).

'Cola's valley'. The name is not applicable to the site of Colcombe House, and the settlement for which it was coined must have lain elsewhere.

Tupsley (533401)

> *Topeslage* 1086 DB; *Topesle* 1241 Capes, 1265 InqMisc; *T(h)opesley(e)* 1292 Swin, 1316 FA, 1506 BM.

DEPN translates Tupsley as 'pasture for rams'. OE *lēah* could mean 'wood' here, as this and Litley are the only *lēah* names in quite a wide area. The first element could be a personal name.

❧ HAMPTON CHARLES ☙

Hampton Charles (at Manor Farm 608605)

> *Hanton'* 1204 Cur; *Hampton(e)* 1223 Cur, 1269-75 *Red Book MS*, 1334 SR; *Hompton(e)* 1269-75 *Red Book MS* (p), 1283 Swin, 1341 NonInq. *Hamptone Colde* 1304 Swin; *Coldehampton* 1402 Ipm.

This is probably OE *hēantune* 'at the high settlement' as at Hampton Wafre (below). The origin of the two affixes is unknown, though 'Charles' is presumably manorial.

❧ HAMPTON WAFRE ☙

Hampton Wafre (576570)

> *Hantone* 1086 DB; *Hantune* 1103-7 BreconC; *Heentun'* 1123, 1186-90
>   LeomC; *Heamt'* 1126-36 LeomC; *He(a)nt'* 1136-70, 1186-99 LeomC;
>   *Hamptone* 1271 Swin.
> *Hompton(e) Wafr(e)* 1275-82 Cant, 1341 NonInq.

Heantune 'at the high settlement', as in Wolverhampton. This looks appropriate geographically. There may have been a large upland estate called *Hēantune*, lying on the higher ground between Leominster and Bromyard, of which this place, Hampton Charles, New Hampton, Uphampton in Docklow and Dunhamton in Hatfield are remnants. See District Name Leen.

The affix is from the family of *le Wafre*: in 1103-7 Hugh *cognomina Guafre* ('wafer, waferer') gave tithes here to Brecon Priory.

❧ HAREWOOD ☙

Harewood Park (530280)

> *Harewuda* 1137 AC, 1160-70 HDB, 1188 P; *Harew(o)d(e)* 1215 AD, 1251 Ch, 1265 Cl, 1292 QW, 1338 Larking.

Probably 'hare wood', identical with Harewood, Yorkshire, and several instances of Harwood. See also Hentland. There is another Harewood in Clifford.

Elvastone (524283)

> *Elvareston* 1334 SR; *Elvastone* 1540 HT.

PNHe gives Elverstone as an alternative modern form for this name. Perhaps 'Ælfhere's estate', but more spellings are needed.

❧ LOWER HARPTON ☙

Lower Harpton (278601)

> *Hercope* 1086 DB; *Herchopa* 1160-70 HDB.
> *Herecopton* 15th Rodd.
> *Herton* 1307 Ipm, 1479-80 Rodd; *Harton* 1508 Ipm, 1546 BM.
> *Lower Heracton* 17th Rodd.

Much fuller documentation is needed, but *Hercope, Herchopa* might be 'valley by Herrock Hill' (278597). *hop* is appropriate to the site, and well-evidenced in this area. Thorn suggests that *tūn* was added to *Herchope*, and the name then reduced to Harpton. Harpton in Radnorshire (now Powys), to which this place, by the 16th century, was being compared to as 'Lower', is *Hortone* (OE *horu-tūn*, 'dirt farm') in DB, and so is a different name. Furthermore, in 1546 this was *Harton infra dominium de Lugharney* 'Harpton in the lordship of Lugharness [or Stapleton]' (see District Name Lugharness) whereas the other Harpton was in the lordship of Radnor.

Middleton Barn (277592)

> *Mildetune* 1086 DB; *Midletona* 1160-70 HDB.

'Middle settlement'.

❧ HATFIELD ☙

Hatfield (585594)

> *Het(h)feld(a)* 1086 DB, 1123, 1131-48 *LeomC*; *Hedfeld* 1137-9 HDB; *Hattefeld* 1341 NonInq.
> *Hatfeud Maiori* 1277-82 ReadingC; *Hatfeld Magna* 1291 Tax.

'Heathland', a common name. Hatfield 'Parva' was at Hatfield Court (below).

Bilfield (598578)

> *Billefeld'* c1200 *LeomC* (p), c1250-c75 St Katherine (p); *Billefield* 1202 *LeomC*; *Belfild* 1545 HT.

Perhaps 'open land by the pointed hill'. The word *bill* occurs in place-names with a topographical sense.

Hatfield Court (576592)

> *Parva Hetfeud* 1243 Fees (p); *Hatfeud Minori* 1277-82 Reading C; *Hat(te)feld Parva* 1291 Tax, 1341 NonInq; *Parva Hatfeld* 1303 FA.

Dunhampton Farm (584603)

> *Dunhamtona* 1243 Fees (p).

'Lower Hampton', *dūne* 'down' is for distinction from Uphampton in Docklow. See also Hampton Wafre.

Fencote Abbey (594591)

> *Fencot(e)* 1086 DB, 1291 Tax.

'Marsh cottage(s)'. 'Abbey' because it belonged to Reading Abbey, mother-house of Leominster Priory.

❧ HAYWOOD ☙

Haywood (486348)

'Wood containing enclosure', see DEPN. Haywood or the 'Hay of Hereford' was a royal forest that covered an area much larger than the present parish of Haywood. See Map 6, page 24.

Hentland (543264)

> *Hennlan (dibric et lann teliau in uno cimiterio)* 1045-1104 (c1130) LL.
> *Hentlan* 1291 Tax, 1320 Orl; *Henthelau* 1302-3 LWE; *Hent(h)(e)lan* 1330
>   Capes, 1341 NonInq, 1356 Capes, 1535 VE; *Hent(l)lane* 1525 HT, 1581
>   Owen.

> *Meiner Reau* 1160-70 HDB.

Welsh *henllan* 'old church'. The first church on the site was dedicated to
St Teilo (*Teliau*). Later a church of Dyfrig (*Dibric*) was established in the same
cemetery, having been moved there in 1045-1104, possibly from Llanfrother (see
below) and possibly after it had become ruined.

In 1086 a certain Waerstan had an estate and a wood in Archenfield, neither
of which are given names. The estate is annotated *Meiner Reau* in HDB (probably
Hentland) and the wood *Harewuda* or Harewood. Jones suggests (see Much and
Little Birch) that *Meiner Reau* is a *maenor fro* or 'lowland *maenor*' of Archenfield
corresponding to a *maenor wrthir* or 'upland *maenor*' centred on Aconbury
hillfort. Owing to a misreading of HDB, however, he attaches *maenor fro* to
Ballingham rather than to Waerstan's nameless estate, Hentland.

Aberhall (529242)

> *Abrehal(e)* 1255 Duncumb (p), 1557 AD (p); *Abrahale* 1296 Ipm (p), 1443
>   Duncumb (p), 1488 Ipm (p); *Aberhale* 1334 SR, 1386 AD, c1420
>   Duncumb (p); *Aburhale* 1429 KPC (p).
> *Alberhal(e)* 1256 Salop Eyre (p), 1300 Swin (p).

'Eadburg's nook', with a feminine personal name. Aberford, Yorkshire, has
similar 13th century spellings, but also 12th century ones such as *Ædburgford*
1177 which demonstrates that this personal name is the first element. Second
element *halh*.

Altbough (546300)

> *Echlebuch* c1250 StGC (p); *Achelbogh* 1302-3 LWE; *Altebo(u)gh* 1419 Owen,
>   1474 Charles; *Halt(e)bough(e)* 1534 Owen, 1548, 1565 BM; *Adlebuch*
>   16th AD.

The main elements are Welsh *allt* 'hill-slope and *bwch* 'buck'. Mr Morgan
points out that the medial –e- of some of the spellings may indicate a lost definite
article, the name being *Allt-y-bwch*.

Dason Farm (538268)

> *Davidston* 1302-3 LWE; *Davyston(e)* 1308 Ipm (p), 1349 Trill; *Damston*
> 1334 SR; *Davynston* 1362 QD; *Danyeston* 1370 Duncumb (p); *Deyewaston*
> 1543 HT.

'David's settlement', a ME name.

Gillow Manor (532253)

> *Cil Luch* 1045-1104 (c1130) LL; *Gilhou* 1228 Ex, 1350 Trill; *Kilho* 1280 Ipm;
> *Gyllouch* 1296 Ipm; *Gwillon* 1325 Orl; *Gyllough* 1334 SR, 1540 HT.

A Welsh name, 'lake nook'. See also Michaelchurch (in Tretire with
Michaelchurch).

Hoarwithy (546295)

> *La Horewythy* 1272-1307 Owen; *Horewethye* 1519 Owen.

'Whitebeam', a tree-name.

Kynaston (543272)

> *Kynnadeston* 1302-3 LWE; *Kynyatestoune* 1308 Ipm (p); *Kynyoceston'* 1334
> SR; *Kynarston* 1525 HT; *Kynnason* 1581 Owen.

The spellings are a little inconsistent for etymology. 'Cyneweard's estate', as at
Kinnersley, Shropshire, is not out of the question.

Llanfrother (542287)

> *Hendresroudre* 1334 SR; *Hendre Frother* 1540 HT; *Henfrowther* 1546 Owen.

Perhaps *hendref-brodyr*, 'old place of the brethren'. This may have been the
site of:

> *Hennlan (super ripam Gui)* 6th (c1130) LL.

Working from the place-name, local tradition places St Dyfrig's first church
in Archenfield at Llanfrother rather than Hentland, and this site certainly suits
the description *super ripam Gui* better. Only in the 11th century, perhaps after
it had become ruined, was it transferred to a site within the same cemetery as a

Teilo-church at Hentland, the Dyfrig dedication eventually replacing the earlier one to St Teilo.

Treaddow (at Chapel Tump 539244)

> *Trairat* 1136-42 Holtzmann; *Trerado(u)* 1272-1307 Owen, 1334 SR, 1525 HT; *Traradon* 1278 Abbr; *Treradow(e)* 1519, 1625 Owen; *Trevered* 1540 HT.

Charles suggests *Tre'r-adwy*, 'settlement at a gap'.

Egerton Phillimore (LL) thought that *villa Iudbiu* or *Iuduiu*, 'Idfwy's estate' (c738 (c1130) LL), may have been situated here, although there can be no etymological connection with it of course. The grant was made 'in the midst of Ergyng' and 'in the presence of all the better men of the whole of Ergyng.

Treseck (542297)

> *Treisac'* 1220 Cur; *Trayhac* 1249-50 Fees; *Treissak'* 1334 SR; *Treysac(ke)* 1419, 1475 Owen; *Treswek* 1540 HT; *Treshack* 1546 Owen; *Hessek* 1534 Owen.

Perhaps Welsh *tre* + Isaac.

❧ HEREFORD ☙

Hereford (510398)

'Army ford', see DEPN.

An earlier name for Hereford seems to have been:

Fernlage c800 (early 12th), *Fernlega* c800 (c1200) Two Lives.

'Ferny clearing'.

Aylestone Hill (521407)

> *Ægelnoðes stane* 1016-35 ASCh; *Aylnadestan* c1205-16 StGC; *Eilnethestan* 1233 Barrow; *Aylmeston* 1265 InqMisc, 1352 AD; *Ailueston* c1285 Red Book; *Aylymston* 1291 Tax; *Aylestone* 1385 Capes; *Eyleston', Hellyston'* 1379 PT (p).

'Ægelnōth's stone', i.e. probably 'stone on the boundary of Ægelnōth's estate'.

Barton (504397)

> *Bertune* 1086 DB; *Bert(h)on(am)* c1148, c1150-63 Foliot, 1291 Tax, 1476 BM; *Bertone* 1241, 1356 Capes.

'Grange', OE *beretūn*.

Bartonsham (514392)

> *Bertanesham* 1219 Capes; *Berstanesham* 1221 Pat; *Berchomesham* 1291 Tax; *Berthonesham* 1294 Swin; *Bertonesham* 1294 Staffs Pleas; *Bartoneshome* 1356 Trill.

Second element *hamm*, referring to the loop of the river. First element perhaps the personal name *Beorhstān*, but there has been association with the place-name Barton.

Hinton (510390)

> *Hyneton* 1265 InqMisc; *Hineton* 1290 Swin; *Hinitone* 1290 Capes, 1300 Swin; *Hynyton* 1291 Tax.

In most instances the modern name Hinton derives from OE *higna-tūn* 'estate of the monastic community'. The Hereford name, however, shares with Little Hinton in Wiltshire some spellings like *Hinitone*, *Hynyton* which may indicate a different origin. Perhaps 'estate associated with Higa', from *–ingtūn* and a personal name.

Huntington Court Farm (485418)

> *Huntenetune* 1086 DB; *Hunti(n)ton(e)* 1219 Capes, 1328 Banco; *Huntynton* 1265 InqMisc.
> *Huntidune* c1215 Capes; *Hontidon* 1291 Tax.

'Estate or settlement of the huntsmen'. There is another Huntington near Kington.

Litley Court (523391)

> *Lutelei* 1086 DB; *Lut(te)ley(a)* 1144-8, 1355 Capes; *Luttelege, -a* 1231-4 Capes, 1256 Salop Eyre (p); *Lytteley* 1535 VE.

The consistent *–u-* and occasional *–tt-* of the early forms are against a derivation from *lȳtel* 'small'. Perhaps 'Lutta's clearing'.

Moor Park (494413), **Prior's Moor** (506409) and **Moor Barn** (498412)

> *(La) Mora, -e* 1131-48 Dugdale, 1158 Holtzmann; 1265 InqMisc, 1291 Tax; *La Mare* 1291 Tax.
> *Mora (canonicorum Lantonie prime)* 1219 Capes; *Mara Canonicorum* 1308 Capes.
> *Moram de Wydemar* 1291 Tax; *Widemarshmore* 1562-3 Court.

OE *mōr* 'low-lying, wet ground'. Prior's Moor (no old forms) is named from the prior of St Guthlac's, who, like the canons of Llanthony Prima, had rights in the bishop's manor of Moor. See also Allensmore, page 31.

Newton House (498385) and **Newton Farm** (497383)

> *Neuwetone* 1273 Capes (p); *(Wynestone juxta) Newtone*

'New settlement'. See 'Winstone', below.

Putson (514386)

> *Put(t)eston(e)* 1265 InqMisc, 1291 Tax, 1294 Swin; *Potestone* 1300 Swin; *Putston* 1831 OS.

Probably 'Putt's estate'.

'Straddle' (c505382)

> *(Wyneston et) Stradel* 1263 AcornC; *(… apud) Straddele (in Blakemonstone)* 1294 Swin.

Gifts to Acornbury Priory of lands in *Wyneston et Stradel* and at *Straddele* in *Blackmarstone* locate a place called 'Straddle' in the southern suburbs of Hereford at about the location given. The hundred-court of the DB hundred of *Stradel* may have met here, where a Roman road (now the A49) crosses the now culverted Bailey Brook; see District Name Straddle.

Walney Farm (527413)

> *Waleneya* c1166-87; *Waleineie* 1183-5 StGC; *Walneye* 1275 Cant, c1285 Red Book.

'Island of the spring', OE *wællan-ēg*.

'**Winstone**' (c502388)

> *Wingestone, Wimeston* 1224 Cur; *Wynestune* c1225 Capes; *Wyneston (et Stradel)* 1263 AcornC; *Wymgeton* 1291 Tax.
> *Wynestone juxta Newtone* 1324 Orl.

The first element could be a derivative of the personal name *Wine*, such as **Winic*.

✤ LITTLE HEREFORD ✤

Little Hereford (553680)

> Another 'army ford', see DEPN.

Bleathwood Manor Farm (560597)

> *Blethewode* n.d. BM.

OE *blēath* 'weak, gentle, timid' is not perhaps impossible as a term applied to a wood; but a personal name derived from the adjective seems more likely.

Easton Farm (562687) and **Easton Court** (559685)

> *Estetone* 1348 BM.

> 'East settlement'.

Lower Upton (546662)

> *Upeton(e)* 1086 DB, 1220 Cur, 1291 Tax; *Uptuna* 1158-61 Foliot; *Huptun* 1243 Fees.

The original 'higher settlement' is presumably Upton Court (in Middleton-on-the-Hill) on a low ridge between two stream-valleys.

✤ HOLME LACY ✤

Holme Lacy (569348)

> *Hammæ* 1085 Galbraith; *Hamme* 1086 DB, 1210-12 RBE, 1216-c40 BM, 1253 Capes, 1264-72 BM, 1320 Capes; *Ham(m)a* 1101-2 Regesta, 1146 Holtzmann.

Homme ultra Waiam 1134-9 Barrow; *Hamme ultra Wayam* 1186-98 *StGC*.
Homme Lacy 1221 Capes, 1334 SR; *Hamme Lacy* 1243 Fees, *Hum' Lacy* 1291
    Tax.

OE *hamm* 'land in a river-bend', referring to the great loop in the Wye here.
The west midland form *Homme* has been associated with *holm*, a ME term with
overlapping terms. The family of Lacy were from Lassy, 17 kilometres north-east
of Vire, dépt. Calvados (Loyd).

Billingsley (535332)

Bylgeslege 1055 ASC.

An element *bylig* occurs also in a Suffolk name, Balsdon (*Byligesdynæ*,
Byliesdyne in OE sources). It is a variant of *belg* 'bag', and these terms are used in
place-names for distinctively shaped hollows. 'Clearing in a bag-shaped hollow'.

Gannah Farm (547334)

Gamma, Gannon c1225 Capes (p); *Gannou* 1336 Ipm; *Gannowe* 1344 Ipm.
Glannah 1831 OS.

Gannah Farm lies under the tip of a hill-spur, so it is reasonable to assume
that *hōh* is the second element of the name. This is one of six names, apparently
of identical origin, which are discussed in PNWo. The only available suggestion
for the first element is OE *gamen* 'game, play', the suggestion being that these
hill-spurs were the venue for sports or contests. The spelling *Gamma* lends some
support to this derivation; objection has been made to it on the grounds that hitherto available spellings included none with *Gam*.

Hollington Farm (562338)

Hol(l)ampton 1489 Ipm, 1501 BM.

Probably 'settlement in a hollow', OE *holh-hāmtūn*.

❧ HOLMER ☙

Holmer (505423)

Holemer(e) 1086 DB, 1272 Capes, 1291 Tax; *Holemore* 1273 Capes;
    Hol(e)mare 1309 Capes, 1334 SR, 1328 Banco.

'Pond in a hollow'.

The Burcott (522421)

> *(La) Burcota, -e* 1163-72 Capes, 1247 Ipm, 1334 SR.
>
> *Kentis(she)burcote* 1330 QD, 1485 Ipm; *Kentsburcott* 1543 HT.

OE *bur* is used for an inner chamber in a house, and a **burcot* may have been a cottage with an extra room. The name occurs also in Buckinghamshire and Somerset. *Kentisshe-* is named from Richard 'of Kent' (*de Cantia*) who was given lands in Burcott c1185.

Shelwick (524431) and **Shelwick Green** (528430)

> *Scelwicke* 1086 DB; *Sceldwica* early 12th Two Lives; *Shelwick* 1241 Capes;
> *Schelwyk* 1291 Tax; *Sceldwyke* 1292 Swin; *Shel(l)(e)wyk(e)* 1316 FA, 1334
> SR, 1361 Ipm (p); *Shellewicke* 1506 BM.
> *Scelfwica* 1160-70 HDB.

'Dairy farm on a shelf of land'.

❧ HOPE MANSELL ❧

Hope Mansell (625196)

> *Hope* 1086 DB, - *Gingen(e)i* c1140-5 MonC, 1157 Fr.
> *Hoppe Maloisel* 1160-c80 MonC, 1214 Cur; *Hope Mal Oysel* 1243 Fees,
> - *Malosel'* 1291 Tax.

'Remote valley'. *Gingenei* is the Breton personal name Ginguené. The lords of Monmouth, who owned Hope Mansell, were Bretons. Ginguené was succeeded c1160 by Henry *Maloisel* 'bad bird' and his nick-name has stuck as an affix.

❧ HOPE UNDER DINMORE ❧

Hope-under-Dinmore (511528)

> *Hope* 1086 DB, 1179 P (p), 1203 *LeomC*; - *sub' Dinnemor* 1291 Tax.

'Remote valley'. '-under-Dinmore' to distinguish it from Miles Hope in Leysters, both of these 'Hopes' belonging to Leominster Priory.

Gattertop (480539)

> *Gadredhope* 1086 DB; *Gatred(e)(h)ope* 1087-96 Regesta, 1123 *LeomC*;
> *Gaterildehope* 1101-2 *StGC*; *Gedredhop'* 1137-9 HDB; *Guterildeopa*
> 1169-76 *StGC*; *Gaderildehope* 1303 FA; *Gaderesdhope* 1346 FA;
> *Gaterildishope* 1428 FA.

hop means 'secluded valley'. For the first part of the name, it seems necessary
to postulate another place-name, meaning either 'goat clearing' or 'goat slope'.

Hampton Court (520524)

> *Hanton(e)* 1086 DB, c1170 *StGC*, 1210 P; *Hamt(ona)* 1123 *LeomC*, 1148-63
>   Foliot, 1173-86 *LeomC*; *Hemton* 1212 P; *Homptun'* 1249 Fees (p);
>   *Hompton(e)* 1304 Swin, 1324 ReadingC, 1355 Capes; *Hampton* 1317 Ipm.
> *Hamtona Gilberti* 1173-4 ReadingC.
> *Homtona Ricardi* 1243 Fees; *Hampton Richard* 1431 FA.
> *Homtona Mappenor'* 1243 Fees.

'Settlement in a river-bend', OE *hamm-tūn*. The place is enclosed on three
sides by the Humber Brook and the river Lugg. It was held in two moieties in
1086, one of which came into the family of Gilbert of Bacton, who had it in 1160-
70 (HDB) and he had a grandson, Richard of Hampton. The other moiety was in
the hands of Adam *de Mapenour'* in 1160-70. His family were from Mapnors in
Knightwick, Worcestershire.

Upper Hill (470532)

> *(La) Hull(e)* 1200-13 *LeomC*, 1332 QD.
> *Hill Hide* 1765 Duncumb.

'Hill'.

Pervin (497547)

> *Pirebunn* c1250 Croft; *Pyrbyn* 14th ReesMap; *Penvyn* 1553 QD; *Purbyn*
>   1599 KPC.

The early spellings demonstrate that –b-, not –v-, is the genuine form. The
name is unexplained.

Winsley House (484527)

> *Wlfenesle* c1150 Capes; *Elfwinslege* c1189 Capes.
> *Winesblava* 1158-64 *LeomC*; *Winsleg'* 1200-13 *LeomC*; *Wynesleye* 1247 Ipm;
> *Windesley* 1327 Price.

Apparently 'Ælfwine's clearing', shortened by dropping the first syllable.

The Yoke (469529)

> *La Yoke* 1200-13 *LeomC*; *La Rok(e)* 1334 Ch, 1345 Ipm; *Le Roke by Burleye* 1361 Ipm.

Apparently the word 'yoke', perhaps used of a natural feature thought to resemble this implement. Cf. Cwmyoy (Cwmiou), Monmouthshire (PNGw). The *Roke* spellings may be due to misreading of *Y*. 'by Birley' to distinguish it from The Rock in Mordiford.

❧ HOW CAPLE ☙

See page 63.

❧ HUMBER ☙

Humber (536563)

A pre-English river-name used as the name for a settlement on the banks of the Humber Brook; see DEPN.

Priddleton (547572)

> *Portlinton'* 1148-54 ReadingC; *Purtlint'* c1150-4 Foliot; *Purtleton* c1250
> *LeomC*, 1309 QD; *Prytelton* 1546 HT; *Prittleton* 1654 BM.
> *Puclinton* c1250 *LeomC*; *Pokelintun* 1253 InqMisc (p).

Probably an *-ingtūn* formation with a personal name, perhaps **Purtel*.

Risbury (548551)

> *Riseberia* 1086 DB, 1177 P (p); *Risebir(ia)* 1123 *LeomC*, 1217-18 ReadingC;
> *Russebur'* 1143-8 StGC; *Risebergh* 1148-54 Foliot; *Risebur(y)* 1212 Fees,
> 1292 Subs (p), 1303 FA; *Eisebur'* 1272 *LeomC*; *Rysebury* 1547-53 Court.

'Brushwood fort', referring to Risbury Camp.

❧ HUNTINGTON ☙

Huntington (249534)

> *Hantinetune* 1086 DB; *Huntin(g)ton(e)* 1137-9 HDB, 1275 RH; *Huntynton*
> 1322 Orig.
> *Huntindon(e)* c1280 *StGC*, 1316 FA; *Hontyngdone* 1333 Capes.
> *Huntington Welshe* 1567 BM.

Another 'huntsmen's estate', identical with Huntington in Hereford. The part
of Huntington manor around Penllan and Hengoed was known as the 'Welshry'.

❧ KENCHESTER ☙

Kenchester (438429)

> *Chenecestre* 1086 DB; *Kenecestram* 1137-48 Barrow; *Kenecestria* c1153-5
> Capes; *Ken(n)ecestr(e)* 1166 RBE, 1243 Fees; 1334 SR; *Kenchestre* 1397
> VR, 1428 FA.
> *Kentestre* 1291 Tax.
> *Chylchestre* 1373 Ipm.

'Cēna's Roman town'.

The Weir (435420)

> *La Wer(r)e* 1214 OblR, 1219 P, 1243 Fees (p), 1265 Cl (p), 1296 Ipm (p);
> - *juxta Sugwas* 1450 BM.

'Weir'.

❧ KENDERCHURCH ☙

Kenderchurch (402284)

> *Lann Cruc* 1045-1104 (c1130) LL; *Lanncinitir lann icruc* 1066-87 (c1130) LL.
> *Sancti Kenedri* c1200 WalkerReg, 1291 Tax; *S'ti Keindri* 1341 NonInq.
> *Kend(er)church(e)* 1397 VR, 1535 VE.

> *Stane* 1086 DB.

In the first of these forms, *Cruc* probably refers to Mount Hill, for which Old Welsh *cruc* 'hill shaped like a tumulus' would be an appropriate term. 'Church of St Cynidr' is and was an alternative name for the church and land-unit.

The equivalent English name for the estate seems to have been *Stane* 'stone', perhaps from some prominent stone, now gone, similar to The Wergins stone by the Lugg in Sutton. *Stane* and Didley (in St Devereux) were two adjacent manors along the line of the Worm Brook from Hereford to Ewyas Harold that the bishop of Hereford had once had in his possession. By the time of DB, however, the current bishop had only a small part of Didley in his hands (the part nearest to Hereford containing the motte-and-bailey castle at 451320), the rest of it, represented today by Wormbridge, together with *Stane*, was now waste and in either the royal forest of Treville or the castlery of Ewyas Harold. The bishop retained his moiety of Didley, but the other moiety only returned to the Church when king Richard gave Wormbridge to the Hospitallers of St John of Jerusalem. The adjacent estate of *Stane* lay at Kenderchurch, further down the Worm Brook, and had been acquired by the lord of Ewyas Harold by 1086. It returned to the bishop shortly after that, but was given by him to Hugh de Lacy (died c1115) in exchange for Much and Little Birch.

It is possible that the episcopal manors of *Stane* and Didley represent part of the twelve hides of land 'next to the river Mynwy' that king Merewalh gave to Wenlock Abbey in the 7th century (ECWM). Kenderchurch/*Stane* does not quite touch the Mynwy, but beyond it lay English settlements at *Elwistone* (now Pontrilas) and 'Hardwick', both now in Kentchurch, which, if they had been included, would have extended Merewalh's gift to the Mynwy. As noted under the District Name Lyde, Hereford's bishop seems to have been the inheritor of Wenlock's lands in Herefordshire.

Howton (415294)

> *Hug(g)ton(e)* 1163-7 StGC, c1179-86 Barrow, 1243 Fees, *Huetune* c1182-86 StGC; *Hut(t)on* 1216-72 Owen, 1244-6 StGC, 1290 Ipm, 1311 QD; *Hou(gh)ton* 1324 Ipm, 1327 Banco, 1407 Ipm, 1540 Dugdale.

Possibly a post-Conquest name, 'Hugh's estate', named after Hugh de Lacy (who acquired Kenderchurch from the bishop, see above) or a subtenant of that name, but an OE formation with a personal name **Huhha* is also possible. This last is considered to occur in two instances of Houghton in Devon. The references to this name in DEPN all refer to Houghton in Bodenham.

Kentchurch (419257)

> *Lan Cein* 1045-1104 (c1130) LL.
> *Sancta Kaenæ* 1100(?) GloucC; *Sancta Keynæ* 1195 GloucC; *Sancta Keina*
>   1217-29 WalkerReg; *Sancta Keyn(a)*, -(e) 1222, 1280 GloucC, 1291 Tax;
>   *Sancto Keyna* 1353 Trill.
> *(ecclesia de) Keme* 1194 Cur, - *Kein* 1194 Abbr.
> *Kemschirch* 1300 EH (p); *Keyn(e)churche* 1339 BM, c1380 GloucC;
>   *Keynchirche* 1341 NonInq; *Keynecherche* 1349 Trill; *Kynchurche* 1397 VR;
>   *Kenchurch* 1535 VE.

From a female saint, *Cain*, who is also celebrated at Keynsham in Somerset
and near Liskeard in Cornwall (LBS).

Bradley Farm (402270)

> *Bradlegh* 1233 LostC (p); *Bradele(e)* 1258-65 LostC (p), 1265-1300 EHC;
>   *Bradley* 1274 Owen.

'Broad clearing', a common name.

Great Corras (420249)

> *Caneros* 1100(?) GloucC, 1296 Swin, 1334 SR, *Canelros* 1217-29 WalkerReg;
>   *Candoris* 1349 Duncumb; *Canos* 1540 HT.
> *Kaveros* 1100-35 Skidmore; *Kaueros* 1234-44 Skidmore; *Cauros* 1247 Cl;
>   *Caweros* 1409 AD (p).

Second element, Welsh *rhos* in the sense 'promontory' would suit the site, at
the neck of a narrow ridge jutting into a sharp curve of the Mynwy. It is uncertain
whether the first element had –*n*- or –*u*-.

(at or near Pontrilas 396275)

> *Elwistone* 1086 DB; *Heliston(a)* c1180-96; c1206 WalkerReg; *E(y)lston* 1300
>   Ipm (p), 1300 EH (p); *Ailstone* c1540 Leland.

Perhaps 'Ælfwīg's estate'. See WalkerReg for the probable location of this
lost place.

'Hardwick' (411258)

> *Herdewica(-iuxta-Ewias)* c1174-9 WalkerReg; *Hordewika* c1206 WalkerReg; *Hardwick* 1300 Ipm (p).

'Dairy farm'. The field-name 'The Hardwick' at 412258 suggests that 'Hardwick' is the present hamlet called Kentchurch, on the banks of the Monnow. '*-iuxta-Ewias*' to distinguish it from Hardwicke in Clifford. In the 12th century Ruald Maubanc built a chapel at 'Hardwick'. This chapel was in the castlery or lordship of Ewyas Harold throughout the Middle Ages, so it is probably the chapel of *Dewias* attached to Kentchurch in 1194 (Cur).

Llanithog Farm (435268)

> *Lanherthoc* 1225 Pat; *Lenheydock* 1325 Ipm; *Llanheydock* 1334 SR; *Llanhaythocke* 1546 HT; *L(l)anhithock* 1637 Duncumb, 1663 MA.

This was another chapelry of Kentchurch parish. The first element is probably Welsh *llan* 'church enclosure', though Mr Morgan points out that it might be *glan* 'river-bank, hill-side'. The qualifying element is *heiddog* 'barley place'.

KILPECK

Kilpeck (445305)

Welsh *cil* 'nook', retreat' with an unidentified qualifier: see DEPN.

KIMBOLTON

Kimbolton (526615)

> *Kinebalt'* 1186-99 *LeomC*, *Kimbalton* 1216-72 BM; *Kimbolton* 1200-59 *LeomC*; *Kynbolton* late 13th BM; *Kynebalton* 1329 InqMisc; *Kymbaltone* 1397 VR.

'Cynebald's estate'.

Bach (**Upper** 539603, **Lower** 544612)

> *(La) Bache* 1269-90 ReadingC, 1431 KPC.
> *Coubache (in Kynbolton)* late 13th BM.
> *Overbach* 1558 Old Rectories.

> OE *bæce* 'stream valley', with 'cow' and 'over' prefixed.

(lost)

> *Gramanton* 1263 AD, 13th KPC (p).

> More material is needed.

Hamnish Clifford (533593)

> *Hamenes(se)* 1086 DB, c1135-c70 ReadingC, 1243 Fees; *Hamenesca*
>   1190-1221 *LeomC*; *Hamenass(ch)e* 13th KPC (p), 1303 FA, 1360 KPC,
>   1361 Ipm (p); *Hampnasshe* 1409 AD; *Hamonasshe* 1431 AD.
> *Homenesse* 1263 AD (p).
> *Hamnashe Clifford* 1548 KPC.

> 'Hāma's ash-tree', perhaps originally a boundary marker. The Clifford family
> were overlords of the estate.

The Lea (538622)

> *Lege* 1086 DB; *La Le(e)* 1200-50 *LeomC*, 1216-72 BM; *Lea* c1220 *LeomC*.

> 'Clearing'. As there is no subsequent record of his family having lands there,
> William fitzNorman of Kilpeck's DB manor of *Lege* in the manor of Leominster
> was not at Lye in Aymestrey (cf. VCH; Thorn). This seems the only other possible
> site for it within the boundariy of Leominster as it then was.

Pateshall (523621)

> *Paolnshale* 13th KPC (p).
> *Paccheshale* 1324 ReadingC (p).
> *Patssale* 1547 HT (p); *Pateshall* 1577 KPC (p).

> 'Peatta's nook', second element *halh*.

Stockton (519612)

>*Stoctune* 1086 DB; *Stoc(k)tuna* 1123 *LeomC*, 1186-98 ReadingC; *Stocton(e)* 1291 Tax, 13th KPC (p); 1326 Orl; *Stok(es)ton(e)* 1324 ReadingC (p), 1332 QD.

These spellings suggest OE *stocc-tūn*, perhaps 'farm built of logs'.

⚜ KING'S CAPLE ⚜

See page 64.

⚜ KINGSLAND ⚜

Kingsland (447613)

>*Lene* 1086 DB; *Lenes* 1278 Cant.
>*Kingeslen(a)* 1137-9 HDB, 1195 Barrow; *Kingeslone* early 13th *StGC*;
>   *Kingeslane* 1243 Fees, 1381 QD; *Kyngeslane* 1317 Ipm, c1433 BM;
>   *Kyngesleone* 1334 SR; *Kynguslone* 1368 CRCG (p); *Kyngylane* 1535 VE.

'Royal estate in Leen', see District Name Leen.

Aston (462625)

>*Estintun* early 13th *LeomC*; *Aston(e)* 1334 SR.

'Place east in the estate'. The forms given in PNHe for this place belong to Aston in Eye, Moreton and Ashton.

Lawton (445594)

>*Lautune* 1086 DB, 1243 Fees; *Lawtone* 1397 VR.
>*Over-, Nethir Lauton* 1431 FA.

'Settlement by a tumulus', first element OE *hlāw*. There is another instance in Cheshire.

Street Court (424602)

>*Lestreet* 1086 DB; *Streta, -e* 1086DB, 1101-2 Regesta, 1143-8 *StGC*, 1243 Fees, 1317 Ipm, 1347 KPC (p), 1361 QD; *Streate* 1585 BM.

'Roman road'; the Roman road called Watling Street passes close by.

See page 189.

ᛥᚥ KINGSTONE ᚥᛥ

Kingstone (424357)

> *Chingestone* 1086 Db; *Kingestuna, -e* 1148-55 Foliot, 1173 Capes; *Kingestone*
> c1218 Capes (p); *Kyngeston* 1291 Tax, 1307 Orig.
> *Westkyngestonam* 1155 (1291) Swin.
> *Kyngeston in Malghfeld* 1306 AD; *Kingstone in Malefeld* 1371 Ipm.

'Royal estate'. *West-* to distinguish it from Kingstone in Weston under
Penyard. For the last two forms, see District Name Mawfield.

Arkstone Court (436361)

> *Archeteleston'* 1160-70 HDB; *Archelestun'* c1179-82 Patterson; *Erchetelstun*
> c1182-c86 StGC; *Ark(ete)leston* 1211 Cur, 1289 Ipm; *Arclestun'* 1243 Fees;
> *Arkelesdune* 1243 Fees (p); *Arcleston(e)* 1303 FA, 1334 FA, 1356 Capes,
> 1437 Ipm; *Arkston* 1316 FA.

'Arnketill's estate', probably a post-Conquest name, since the personal name
is ultimately Old Norse. The estate was part of Cobhall in 1086 and is identified
as Arkstone in HDB.

Coldwell (415360)

> *Caldewell* 1300 Ipm; *Caldewall'* 1379 PT (p).

'Cold spring'.

(at or near Kingstone Grange 422345)

> *Wapleford* 1086 DB.

> *Terra Laur' in Kingest'* 1160-70 HDB.

> *(Grava de) Kiperlegh* 1232 Dugdale.

Wapleford contains the rare element *wapol*, recorded in the sense 'bubble,
froth', which is a credible qualifier for *ford*. The first element of *Kiperlegh* might be
a personal name. *-legh* probably means 'wood' in this name.

DB says Ralph de Bernay the sheriff placed *Wapleford* in Kingstone in earl William's day (1067-71). The manor is annotated *terra Laur' in Kingstone* in HDB, *Laur'* perhaps being a short form of the Christian name of Laurence of Kingstone. Laurence gave to Dore Abbey land *à grava de Kiperlegh* which seems to have formed the nucleus of its Kingstone grange.

❧ KINGTON ☙

Kington (Old 291567, New 298566)

> (Old) *Chingtune* 1086 Db; *Chinton* 1121-2 Fr; *Kintone* c1174 *StGC*; *Cyninton* 1216-72 BM.
> (New) *Kinton' (in Wallia)* 1203 P, 1267 Ipm; *Kyngtone* 1333 Capes; *Kynton* 1341 NonInq.

'Royal estate'. OE *cyning-tūn*, an alternative formation to Kingstone, from *cyninges-tūn*. 'New' after a new town was laid out by the Braose family sometime after 1175.

Barton (299575)

> *Beuretone* 1086 Db; *Beverton* 1121-2 Fr; *Bauerton* 1267 Ipm, 1292 Subs (p); *Baverton* c1280 *StGC*, 1341 NonInq; *Barton* 1553 Court.

'Beaver farm'.

Bradnor Green (292576)

> *Brademare* 1216-72 BM.
> *Brad(e)nor(e)* 1335 Supplement, 1339 Ipm, 1553 Court.
> *Bradenorsence* 1372 Banks.

Probably 'broad flat-topped ridge', with OE *ofer* as second element. More spellings are needed, however. The second element could be *ōra* 'bank, slope'. Pershore in Worcestershire has been considered the furthest north instance of *ōra*, which is a Jutish and West Saxon word; but Bradnor is not significantly further north than Pershore.

Breadward (282551)

> *Brudeford(e)* 1086 DB, c1280 *StGC*, 1372 Banks.

'Brides' ford', identical with Bridford, Devon, and Birdforth, Yorkshire.

Chickward (283532)

> *Cicuurdine* 1086 DB; *Chicwordin* 1137-9 HDB; *Chicwurdine* 1160-70 HDB; *Chickwardin* 1267 Ipm; *Chyckwardyn* 1553 Court.

> *Stiuingeurdin* 1086 DB.

Chickward is 'chicken farm'. *Stiuingeurdin* is said in HDB to be part of Chickward. This is perhaps a compound of *worthign* 'settlement', with a place-name based on *styfic* 'tree-stump'.

Empton (273533)

> *Ulfelmstune* 1086 DB; *Ulfhemeston* 1137-9 HDB.

'Wulfhelm's estate'. DB *Ulfelmstune* is not Welson in Eardisley (cf. VCH; Thorn), as this place-name has a different origin. The estate had passed to Roger de Port by 1137-9 (HDB) and his lands in this area formed the marcher lordship of Kington, within which Empton lay.

Hergest (**Upper** 262548, **Lower** 276555)

> *Heregest(h)* 1086 DB, 1340 Ipm; *Heregast* 1251 FA; *Heregeste* 1546 HT.

This name is assumed to be Welsh, but no suggestions are available concerning the etymology. Upper Hergest was *Westheregest* in 1340 (Ipm).

Kingswood Common (293541)

> *Kynges Wode* 1268 *StGC*; *Kingwode* 1335 Supplement; *Kyngwodd* 1337 Ipm.

'Royal wood'.

Lilwall (301545)

> *Lollewall(e)* 1355 Supplement, 1372 Banks; *Lulewale* 1397 VR; *Lillwall* 1598 AD (p).

'Lulla's spring'.

Rushock (307584)

> *Ruiscop* 1086 DB.
> *Ru(i)ssoc* 1137-9 HDB, 1148-63 Foliot, 1164 *StGC*, 1203 (p); 1229 Cur (p),
>   c1280 *StGC*; *Russchok* 1349 Trill; *Rushoock* 1598 AD.
> *Risset* 1204 P (p); *Russet* 1291 Tax.

The modern forms and most of the spellings suggest this is the same name
as Rushock in Worcestershire, a stream-name meaning 'rushy brook'.

ꙮ   KINNERSLEY   ꙮ

Kinnersley (345497)

> *Chinardeslege* 1123 *LeomC*; *Kinardesl(e)(g)* 1148-63 Foliot, 1208 Cur (p),
>   1229 Cur (p), 1243 Fees 1256 Ipm (p); *Kynardele* 1211-12 RBE (p);
>   *Kynard(e)sl(eye)* c1200 Lost C (p), 1291 Tax, 1311 BM; *Kenardesleye*
>   1277-82 ReadingC.

'Cyneheard's clearing'; the same name occurs in Shropshire (modern
Kinnerley) and in Worcestershire. There was another *Kenardesl'* in How Caple in
1230 (CRCG).

(at or near Kinnersley)

> *Elburgelega* 1086 DB; *Edburgelega* 1160-70 HDB.

The first element is probably a female personal name, possible Æthelburh,
the change to *Edburgelega* in HDB most likely being a scribal error. The estate is
annotated 'Kinnersley' in HDB, suggesting that it lay close to that place. However,
in 1316 Newchurch (see below) was held jointly with Kinnersley (FA), and this
makes it possible that *Elburgelega* is an older or alternative name for it.

Ailey (341484)

> *Ayling'* 1267 Supplement (p); *Aylyuele* 1297 Coram Rege (p); *Ailliveleye* 13th
>   AD (p); *Aylineleye* 1310 Swin (p); *Alynleye* 1312 Swin; *Aylueleye* 1359-60
>   KinRR.
> *Ayley* 1335 Charl, 1359-60 *KinRR*, 1429 Ipm, 1638 KPC; *Ailley* 1400-1 *KinRR*.
> *Adeley* 1575 Robinson.

Probably 'Æthelgifu's wood or clearing', with the same feminine personal
name as Aylton.

Newchurch (252506)

Neuchurche 1316 FA; *Newechirche* 1395 AD (p).

'New church'. There is no church here today. See *Elburgelega*, above.

Newton (334497)

(La) Neuton' 1359-60; *Newton'* 1400-1 *KinRR*.

'New settlement'.

Sallies (356501)

Selleye 1359-60 *KinRR*; *Salas* 1546 HT.
Selleygrene 1400-1 *KinRR*.

Probably 'willow wood', from OE *sele* and *lēah*.

꒰ꙮ   **KINSHAM**   ꙮ꒱

Kinsham (**Upper** 364649, **Lower** 360646)

Kingesmede 1210-12 RBE (p), 1276 Cant (p).
Kingeshemede 1216 PatR, 1272-1307 AD (p); *Kingeshamet, Kingishemed*
   1263 Pat; *Kyngeshemeda* 1287 Swin (p); *Kyngesheinde* 1292 Year Book,
   1307 Ipm; *Kynggeshemede* 1355 Ipm, 1390 KPC.
Kinsam 1522 BM.
Overkyngesheinde 1349 Ipm.
Netherkyngesheinde 1349 Ipm; *Nether Keynsham* 1397 VR.

This name contains an element, *humede*, also present in early forms of the name Presteigne (for which see DPNW), which appears as *Humet* in DB and *Prestehemed* in 1137-9 (HDB). It is probably a contracted version of OE *hemm-mæd* 'meadow on a boundary'. Between Presteigne and Kinsham lies a triangle of flat ground in the confluence of the river Lugg and a tributary. There are steep hills all round, which makes this a notable feature, and it is on the Radnorshire (Powys)/ Herefordshire boundary. One part of this feature came into the hands of certain priests (a religious community? Connected with the pre-Conquest architectural elements in Presteigne church?) and the other into the hands of (or was retained by) the king. The medieval ecclesiastical parish of Presteigne included Discoed (Radnorshire; now Powys) as well as Willey, Stapleton, Kinsham, Combe and Rodd, Nash and Little Brampton and this may give some indication of the extent of the territory dependant on the *hemm-mæd* feature in pre-Conquest times.

KNILL

Knill (291604)

> *Chenille* 1086 DB; *Chunulla* 1160-70 HDB; *Kennell'* 1243 Fees; *Kinille* 1275-82 Cant.
> *Cnulla* 1158-64 *LeomC*, 1243 Fees (p); *Cnille* 1220 Cur (p); *Knolle* 1225 Cur (p); *Knelle* 1292 Subs; *Knulle* 1292 Swin, 1307 Capes.

OE **cnyll(e)*, a variant of *cnoll* 'small hill'. The spellings with *Chen-*, *Chun-*, *Ken-* and *Kin-* are due to the Norman-French tendency to insert a vowel in the consonant cluster *Cn-* (as seen also in *Canute*, from *Cnut*).

LEA

Lea (657217)

> *Lecce* 1086DB; *Leche* 1160-70 HDB; *Lacu* 1201 P.
> *La Le(e)* 1219 InqMisc, 1275 Ipm (p), 1280 Grundy, 1370 Ipm; *Lay* c1250 LostC, 1275 Ipm (p).
> *Netherle* 1300 Swin.
> *Overle* 1300 Swin.

'Clearing', OE *lēah*. The *–cce, -che* spellings can be paralleled. *Lacu*, however, is erratic and presumably erroneous.

LEDBURY

Ledbury (713377)

> *Liedeberga* 1086 DB.
> *Ledburia* 1135-48 Capes; *Ledbury sub Malverna* 1232 Capes.
> *Ledb(ury)* 1150-4 Capes, 1230 Swin, 1291 Tax, 1316 FA, 1320 Capes, 1327 Banco, 1364 Charl.
> *Lideberi(a)* 1162 Capes, 1173-4 Foliot, 1200 Cur; *Lidebirie* 1163 Foliot; *Lydebury* 1280 Cant.
> *Lindeberia* 1167 P.
> *Leddeberi* 1200 Cur; *Leddibire* 1200 ChR.

'Settlement on the river Leadon'. – *sub Malverna* is to distinguish it from 'Ledbury' (Lydbury) North in Shropshire, both places being in episcopal hands. Spelling of both in medieval documents is erratic and can easily be confused.

Dingwood Park (721352)

    Dulingwode 1276 Cant; *Donngewode* 1344 PNHe.

'Donnington wood', the name has been shortened by dropping *–ton-*; cf. Bringwood in Burrington. The wood is on the boundary between Ledbury and Donnington.

Dunbridge Farm (718363)

    Dunebruge c1240 St Katherine (p); *Donebrugge* 1322 St Katherine.

Probably 'bridge by a hill', with OE *dūn* as first element.

(hill at 722373)

    La Dune 1174-83 Capes (p); *Dona* c1240 St Katherine.

OE *dūn*, probably the massif from which Dunbridge is named.

Hazle Farm (704364)

    Hasles 1086 DB; *Hesela* 1141 WalkerCh (p); *Hesla* 1143-55 BreconC (p); *Esele* 1148-54 Capes (p); *(La) Hesele* 1159-60 WalkerCh (p), c1174-86 Capes; *(La) Hasele(g')* 1210-12 RBE, 1224 Cur (p), c1285 Red Book, 1303 FA, 1304 Swin.
    Haselor 1428 FA.

'Hazel wood'.

Hill House Farm (691364)

    (La) Hulle 1313, 1363 St Katherine.

OE *hyll*, often used of a spiky eminence.

Kilbury (722388)(?)

    (villa de) Berehe 1274, *(villa de) Berga* c1285; *La Berwy* 1376 St Katherine (p).

The forms suggest *beorg* 'barrow, hill', though *burh* 'fort' would be appropriate for the earthwork.

Massington Farm (740396)

> *Mefflituna* c1155 Foliot (p).
> *Mesinton* c1174 CMAD (p); *Mesendun* c1185 CMAD (p); *Me(i)sintun* c1200
>   CMAD (p), c1243 St Katherine (p); *Messyntone* 1276 Cant.
> *Mas(s)ing(e)ton(e)* 1201 Pleas (p), 1242 Cur, 1276 Cant; *Masintone* c1250
>   St Katherine; *Masyntone* 1316 Swin.
> *Masyngton Halywat'* 1545 HT.

'Settlement associated with Mæssa'. 'Holywater' tithes were payable to the minster within whose *parochia* the place lies, in this case Ledbury church.

Netherton Farm (748393)

> *Northinton* 1200-15 Dugdale, c1240 St Katherine (p); *Nordintune* earl 13th
>   St Katherine (p); *Northyntone* 1304 Swin.

'(Place) in the northern part of the estate', OE *north in tūne* would suit the position. A corresponding 'Southington' is now Siddington (below). There was another 'Northington' (now Lower Norton) in Brockhampton-by-Bromyard.

Ockeridge Farm (750399)

> *Alk(e)rugg(e)* c1155 Foliot (p), 1234 Capes (p), 1275 WorcsSR, c1285 Red
>   Book; *Alchurges* 1166 RBE (p); *Alcrig'* 1204 Cur (p).
> *Altrugio* 1174-86 Capes (p).
> *Alberugge* 1304 Swin (p).

'Alca's ridge', OE *hrycg*.

Orlham Farm (694359)

> *(H)erlingh(e)ham* 1193-8 WalkerSC, c1225 Capes (p), 1291 Tax; *Olham* 1316
>   Swin; *Orl(h)am* 1362 St Katherine, 1505 AD.

Probably 'enclosure associated with Eorla', OE **Eorlinghamm*. This is a very unlikely situation for an *–ingahām* name. Upham in Dymock, a mile south in Gloucestershire, is *Uphome* in 1550). *hamm* in the sense 'enclosure in marginal ground' is suitable.

Siddington Farm (699356)

> *Suchyntone* 1307 Swin (p); *Sothintone* 1338 AD; *Sechinton* 1352 St Katherine (p).

'Place in the south of the estate', OE *sūth in tūne*. There is a Southington in Linton-by-Bromyard.

Underdown (715370)

> *Underdune* 1231 Cur; *Underdon(a)* c1240 St Katherine, c1285 Red Book, 1304 Swin (p); *Underton'* 1379 PT (p).

'Place under the hill'.

'Winster' (703393)

> *Wimestruil, Wimundestreu* 1086 DB; *Wymondestre* c1285 Red Book; *Winsters (Elm Copse)* 1832 OS.

'Wīgmund's tree'. The site of one of the DB hundred courts, this is a common type of hundred-name.

LEINTHALL STARKES

Leinthall Starkes (452700)

'Corner of land or retired place on the river Lent', see DEPN. 'Starkes' is a manorial name. 'Lent' may formerly have been the name of the stream system about this place and Leinthall Earls (in Aymestrey), tributary to the river Teme.

LEINTWARDINE

Leintwardine (404741)

'Enclosure on the river Lent', see DEPN.

'Lent' may formerly have been the name of the lower Clun.

Kinton (409748)

> *Kynton(e)* 1249 Inspeximus, 1292 QW, 1305 Ipm, 1316 BM, 1535 VE, 1631 KPC; *Kyntun* c1250-72 BM.
> *Kinteton* 1283 Palgrave.

'Royal estate', OE *Cynetūn*.

Marlow (400765)

> *Marlow(e)* 1249 Inspeximus, 1535 VE, 1631 KPC; *Markelowe* 1292 QW;
> *Merlawe* 1361 Ipm (p).

'Boundary tumulus', with *gemǣre* and *mearc* alternating as the qualifying element for *hlāw*. Marlow is in an angle formed by the county boundary.

Mocktree Farm (420758)

> *Moctro* 1154-89 GloucC; *Moktre* 1301 Pat.
> *Trowehers* 1292 QW.

Probably an English (as opposed to Welsh, e.g. Mochdre in Denbighshire and Montgomeryshire) name, with *trēow* 'tree' and an obscure first element. There is a personal name *Mocca*, but forms such as **Mocketre* might have been expected from that. The 1292 form may be a shortened version of the place-name with *hyrst* 'wooded hill' added.

Trippleton (411735)

> *Turplinton'* 1221 Rolls.
> *Turpleton(e)* 1244 Inspeximus, 1305 Ipm, 1358 BM, 1424 Ipm, 1479 Court,
>   *Turpelton* 1395 AD (p).
> *Turpitton* 1249 Inspeximus.
> *Turpeton* 1357 Ipm (p).
> *Tripulton* 1467 KPC; *Tripleton* 1535 VE, 1631 KPC.

This name is unexplained. The forms suggest the ME word *turpel* 'broil, encounter, tumult', but this is of French origin, not recorded till c1330, and most unlikely as a qualifier for *tūn*.

(lost, but close to Leintwardine)

> *Walton* 1535 VE.

Earlier spellings are needed. This may be 'wall settlement' referring to the Roman defences.

Whitton (412741)

> *Witton* 1242 Inspeximus, 1359 Ipm; *Wytton* 1292 QW, 1529-30 Court, 1535
>   VE; *Wycketon* 1547 HT.

Probably 'white settlement'.

Leominster (498593)

The English name is perhaps a translation of its Welsh name Llanllieni 'church in the district of streams'. See District Name Leen.

Aulden (463549)

> *Elvitheduna* 1158-64 *LeomC*; *Aldon* 1547-53 Court.

'Ælfgȳth's hill'. The personal name is feminine.

Brierley (496560)

> *Bredege* 1086 DB.
> *Bradelega* 1160-70 HDB.
> *Brerel(e)y* 1553 AD, 1599 KPC.

See Freeman's note in Thorn for a full discussion of the problems posed by these spellings.

Broadward (497572)

> *Brad(e)ford(e)* 1086 DB, 1123 *LeomC*, 1159-60 Regesta, 1212 Fees, 1216-28 *LeomC*, 1292 Orig, 1356 Trill, 1485 Ipm.
> *Brod(e)ward* 1291 Tax, 1663 MA.

'Broad ford'.

Cholstrey (466596)

> *Cerlestreu* 1086 DB; *Scholestre* 1397 VR; *Charlester* 1547 HT; *Cholstrey* 1599 KPC.

'Ceorl's tree'. Position on the parish boundary is frequent in names of this type.

Dishley Court (484581)

> *Dustel(e)* 1186-99, 1213-26 *LeomC*.

lēah may be 'wood' rather than 'clearing' in this name. The first element is probably *dūst* 'dust'.

Eaton (509583) and **Westeaton** (509586)

> *Et(t)on(e)* 1086 DB, 1186-99 *LeomC*, 1270 Ch, 1272 *LeomC* (p), 1325 Ipm;
>   *Eatuna* 1123 *LeomC*; *Eaton(a)* 1204-1239/40 *LeomC* (p).
> *Eton by Leominstre* 1307 Ipm.
> *Etone villa* 1397 VR.
> *Eton Gamage* 1485 Ipm, 1564 KPC; - *Grange* 1578 KPC.

'River settlement', OE *ēa-tūn*. There were two estates at this location in DB and a third Eaton at Eaton Hennor (see below). One of the estates here was held by Godfrey de Gamages in 1137-9: his family were from Gamaches-en-Vexin, between Les Andelys and Gisore, dépt. Eure (Loyd). VCH and Thorn say DB *Ettone* is Eyton, two miles north-west of Leominster, but its tenurial history shows that it was Eaton at 509583.

Eaton Hennor (525588)

> *Iatton* 1243 Fees.
> *Eton Bedford* 1485 Ipm.

See Eaton (above). In 1243 it was held from the honour of Bedford (Fees). See also Hennor (below).

Hennor (539586)

> *Heanoura* 1123 *LeomC*; *Henor(e)* 1279 Cant, 1334 SR, 1360 KPC; *Honor* 1547-53 Court.

'High flat-topped ridge', second element *ofer. Henorfolde* occurs in 1564 (KPC).

Hyde (**Upper** 453351, **Lower** 457551), **Hyde Marsh** (453548), **Hyde Ash** (449555)

> *La Hyde* 1230 Cur, 1332 QD.
> *West Hide* 1309 QD.

'Estate assessed at one hide'.

Ivington (474566)

> *Lumtune* 1086 DB.
> *Ivent'* 1130-5, 1200-13 *LeomC*; *Iuentonia* 1135-54 OxfordFacs; *Iuinton(e)* 1160-70 HDB, c1250 *StGC*; *Inynton* 1291 Tax; *Ivynton* 1328 Banco.

'Estate associated with Ifa'. Thorn points out that *Lumtune* is one of Farley's few transcriptional errors; the DB MS has *Iuintune*.

Knoakes Court (456555)

> *Alac* 1086 DB; *Ach(is)* 1123, 1213-26 *LeomC*, 1126-36 ReadingC; *Akes* late
> 12th *LeomC*; *Le Oake* 14th ReesMap.

'Oak tree'. ReesMap places *Le Oake* at Knoakes Court. The lands Gruffudd ap Maredudd had at *Alac* in 1086 passed, with other estates of his, to the Blez family, and in the late 12th century William de Blez was disputing his rights in *Ach* or *Akes* with Reading Abbey (*LeomC*). There is a Noakes Farm in Bredenbury (see above) and a Court of Noke in Pembridge (see below).

Stagbatch (464584)

> *Stakebache* 1276 Cant (p).
> *Stag(ge)bach(e)* 1397 VR, 1599 KPC.

'Stag stream'. OE *bæce* usually denotes a well-marked stream-valley, so this name is atypical.

Wharton (509556)

> *Wavertune* 1086 DB; *Wavertona* 1103/4-c30 OseneyC, 1243 Fees;
> *Wauerton(a)* 1137-9 HDB, 1401 OseneyC; *Wauertuna* 1158-64 Foliot;
> *Warton* 1599 KPC.

There are two instances of this name in Cheshire, Waverton and Wharton. It means 'settlement by something wavering', but the precise significance has not been ascertained.

Upper Wintercott (471547)

> *Wintercote* 1200-13 *LeomC*, 1243 Fees (p), 1256 Salop Eyre (p); *Wyntercote*
> 1357 Ipm.

'Winter cottages'.

❧ LETTON ❧

Letton (335464)

> *Letune* 1086 DB; *Leitun* 1159-64 *LeomC* (p); *Lettun'* 1243 Fees; *Letton* 1535 VE.
> *Lecten* c1130 Dugdale; *Lectun* 1174-86 *LeomC* (p); *Lecton(e)* 1219 InqMisc,
> 1220 Cur, 1230 P (p), 1246 OseneyC (p), 1291 Tax, 1464 AD.
> *Nether Letton* 1431 FA, 1492 Ipm.

OE *lēactūn* 'leek enclosure' or 'herb garden', a fairly common name which usually has the modern form Leighton, as at Leighton in Much Cowarne. 'Over' Letton was at Letton Court Farm in Staunton on Wye.

Hurstley (349490)

> *Lege* 1086 DB, 1148-63 HDB.
> *Hurt(h)esleg(e)* 1158-64 *LeomC*, 1243 Fees (p), late 13th *LeomC* (p);
>   *Hurtesle(y)* 1292 Subs (p), 1350 Trill, 1547-53 Court.
> *Horcesley* 1316 FA (p).

'Stag's wood or clearing', first element *heorotes-*, perhaps confused in fairly recent times with *hurst*. The tenurial history of Hugh Donkey's DB manor of *Lege* makes it fairly certain that it is Hurstley in Letton and, if this identification is accepted, the name was originally a simplex.

Kinley (329477)

> *Kynley(e)* 1359-60 *KinRR*, 1379 PT (p).

Perhaps 'Cyna's wood or clearing'.

❧ LETTON, WALFORD AND NEWTON ❧

Letton (380704)

> *Lectune* 1086 DB; *Lect(h)on(e)* late 12th BM, 1243 Fees, 1535 VE.
> *Letten* 1263 Pat; *Letton* 1292 Subs (p), 1359 Ipm.

Another 'leek enclosure'.

Newton (373694)

> *New(e)ton(e)* 1249 Inspeximus, 1292 QW, 1397 VR, 1535 VE.
> *La Newton* 1291 Tax.

'New settlement'.

Walford (380725)

> *Waliforde* 1086 DB; *Walfor(d)* 1249 Inspeximus; *Wal(l)eford* 1292 QW, 1305 Ipm.

Possibly 'ford of the Welshmen', but a fuller collection of spellings is needed.

Leysters (568632), **Leysters Pole** (559638), **Little Leysters** (**Leysters Lodge Farm** 566629), **Great Leysters** (Leysters 568625)

> *Last* 1086 DB; *Lastes* 1160-70 HDB, 1226 SalopFF, 1243 Fees; *Lastr(es)* 1220 Cur, 1243 Fees, 1303 FA, 1354 Ipm; *Lasters* 1346, 1432 FA; *Lasetres* 1420 Ipm; *Laysters* 1575 KPC.

This name is unexplained.

Great Heath (556627)

> *Hed* 1086 DB; *Heth(e)* 1160-70 HDB, 1243 Fees; *La Hadhe* 1230 P (p); *Heuhe* 1316 FA.

'Heath'.

Woonton (548623)

> *Wenetone, Winetune* 1086 DB; *Winestona* 1160-70 HDB; *Wunetun'* 1222 BreconC; *Woneton* 1316 AD; *Wyneton'* 1334 SR.

'Wynna's settlement'. There is another Woonton in Almeley.

❧ **LINGEN** ❧

Lingen (365672)

> *Lingen* 704-9 ECWM, c1150 Capes; *Lingein(e)* 1190 P (p), 1221 Cur; *Lingayn(e)* 1243 Fees (p), 1292 Subs (p), 1346 FA, 1535 VE; *Lingeyn* 1331 AD (p).
> *Lingham* 1086 DB.
> *Lingieura* 1176 P (p).

It is reasonable to assume that this is a pre-English stream-name, but no satisfactory etymology has yet been proposed for it. The form from ECWM may be a good deal later than 704-9 as some of the names in the Much Wenlock charters are ME in form. See also Upper and Lower Lye in Aymestrey, page 38.

Birtley (367694)

> *Britleia, Birdleia* c1183 PNHe.
> *Brerehelde* 1292 QW.
> *Berkley* 1833 OS.

The forms are too inconsistent for etymology.

Limebrook (373661)

> *Logebrok* 1292 QW; *Lyngebrok(e)* 1292 QW, 1316 FA, 1527 Court; *Lingbrok*
> 1320 Capes; *Lymebroke* 1535 VE; *Lynebroke* c1540 Leleand.

The first part is the same as Lingen, shortened in the compound with *brōc* 'brook'.

🙦 LINTON-BY-BROMYARD 🙤

Linton (680535)

> *Lintoun* 1199 *StGC* (p); *Linton'* 1268-75 *Red Book MS* (p); *Lynton* 1575-80
> Bromyard.
> *Lynton Holywat'* 1524 HT.

Probably 'flax enclosure'. 'Holywater' tithes were payable to the minster within whose *parochia* the place lies, in this case Bromyard church.

Ashminton (675532)

> *Asmentone, Esmentone* 1268-75 *Red Book MS* (p).

Possibly 'Æscmann's estate'. There was another 'Ashminton' in Much Dewchurch. See Bryngwyn in Much Dewchurch, page 76.

Burley (668533)

> *Burley* 1294 Swin.

Probably 'wood by a fort', OE *burh-lēah*. There is a tradition of a fortification on the high ground to the south-east (*Wms*).

Clater (685543)

> *Cletera* 1166 RBE (p); *Cletere* 1256 Salop Eyre.
> *Clatere* 1256 Salop Eyre (p); 1269 Ipm.
> *Clade* 1268-75 *Red Book MS* (p).
> *Clatre* n.d. KPC (p).

There is a place-name element *clater* (Mercian form *cleter*) which is believed to mean 'loose stones, heap of boulders': cf. *Clatretune* (now Clatterbrune) in Presteigne (DB), which stands on the Clatter Brook.

Hodgbatch (662543)

> *Hodebach(e)* 1268-75 *Red Book MS* (p); 1269 Ipm (p); *Hod(d)esbach(e)*
> 1268-75 *Red Book MS* (p), 1296 KPC, 1575-80 Bromyard; *Hoesbache*
> 13th KPC.

'Hod's stream-valley'. The house overlooks a small valley containing Hodgwall Brook.

Southington Farm (684531)

> *Sothintone* 1268-75 *Red Book MS* (p); *Suttintone* c1310 *StGC* (p).

'Place in the southern part of the estate'. There is another 'Southington' (now Siddington) in Ledbury, and this type of name is well-evidenced in the adjacent parts of Worcestershire. The 'Northington' that corresponds to this Southington is now Lower Norton in Brockhampton-by-Bromyard.

Yearsett Court (706535)

> *Ersete* 1268-75 *Red Book MS* (p).
> *Over Ersett* 1575-80 Bromyard.

Second element apparently *(ge)set*, one of the meanings of which is 'fold for animals'. The first element may be *ēar* 'gravel'.

❦ LINTON-BY-ROSS ❧

Linton (660254)

> Probably 'flax enclosure', see DEPN.

Bromsash (649242)

> *Bromesais* 1086 DB; *Bromesheff* 1228 Hart; *Bromesasse* 1282 Grundy.

> 'Brēme's ash-tree'. This was the site of one of the DB hundred courts.

Burton Court (661240)

> *Beritone* 1277 Cant (p); *Biriton* 1280 Hart; *Buriton* 1282 Hart.

> OE *byrig-tūn*, 'settlement with a fort'.

Eccleswall Court (652233)

> *Egleswalle* 1274 Ipm; *Ecleswelle* 1275 RH; *Ekelewell* 1280 Hart; *Ec(c)les(e)wall(e)* 1286 Swin, 1292 QW, 1346 FA; *Ekleswall* 1303 FA, *Eckeluswall* 1306 Ipm; *Eggleswell* 1541 HT.

> 'Spring at a Celtic Christian centre', OE **ecles*.

⚜ LITTLE BIRCH ⚜

See page 42.

⚜ LITTLE COWARNE ⚜

See page 71.

⚜ LITTLE DEWCHURCH ⚜

See page 74.

⚜ LITTLE HEREFORD ⚜

See page 116.

⚜ LITTLE MARCLE ⚜

See page 157.

Llancillo (366256)

> *Lann Sulbiu*; *podum Lann Suluiu* c620 (c1130) LL; *Lansilion* 1311 QD;
> *Llancello* 1399 Ipm; *Llancellie* 1432 Ipm; *Llancillo* c1540 Leland.

'Church of (St) Sulfyw'.

The bounds of *Lann Sulbiu* c620 (c1130) LL: '*Opennclaud ismael arnant igalles iclaud nihit trui icoit betimais dilicat finnanaun guualon, guualon inhit bet nant greitiaul, arihit bet mingui, mingui nihit bet aper nant igalles, nant igalles nihit bet pennclaud ismael ubi incepit.*' 'From the head of Ismael's Dyke on the *Galles* Brook, along the dyke through the wood to the open, to the *Gwvalon* Brook. Along the *Gwvalon* as far as the Greidol Brook, along it to the Mynwy. Along the Mynwy as far as the mouth of the *Galles*. Along *Galles* Brook as far as the head of Ismael's Dyke, where it began'.

These bounds are among the clearest and easiest to work out on the ground today. It is bounded by the *Galles* Brook (*Nant y Galles*) on the west, the Greidol Brook (*Nant Greitiaul*) on the east (ReesMap has these reversed, with *Galles* to the east and Greidol to the west) and the Mynwy (*Mingui*) on the south. Within it lies the Iron Age hillfort at Walterstone Camp, a Roman villa at Coed-y-grafel, the site of a chapel of the 6th or 7th century saint Eiliwedd (or Ailworth) between them and the church at Llancillo, so it is probably a very old land-unit. *Galles* Brook is probably an old name for the brook that runs down between Walterstone church and Walterstone Camp to meet the Mynwy at Alltyrynys, while Greidol is the name of a farm and Dingle at 349273 and 349275, close to which rises the Cwm Brook (formerly Greidol) which runs down past Rowlstone to the Mynwy at Llangua (Monmouthshire).

Llandinabo (518284)

> *Lann Hunapui* 1045-1104 (c1130) LL; *Landinab(ou)* 1214 Cur (p), 1334 SR;
> *Laund'* 1249-50 Fees; *Landynabo* 1280 Cant; *Llanndenabe* 1540 HT.

The identity of the saint involved in this name is not known.

Blewhenstone (526298)

Blowhenston 1458; *Bluehenstone* 1480, *Blewhenston* 1481 Owen.

This might be 'blowing stone', but from *blowen*, obsolete past participle of the verb *blow*, rather than the present participle. There is a Blowing Stone in Kingstone Lisle, Berkshire, a perforated block of sandstone which can be made to emit a loud noise.

❧ LLANGARRON ❧

Llangarron (532212)

Lan(n) Garan(n) c745 (c1130), 1045-1104 (c1130) LL; *Lagara* 1137-42 Holtzmann; *Langara(n)* 1148-63 MonC, c1163 Filiot, 1291 Tax, 1330 Capes, 1334 SR, 1341 NonInq, 1356 Capes; *Langare(n)* 1160-c80 MonC, 1535 VE.

'Church on the river Garren'.

Bernithan Court (541215)

Brenythyn 1302-3 LWE, 1334 SR; *Brineithyn* 1386 AD; *Bernythen* 1499 AD; *Trynythen* 1523 Owen; *Brenythen* 1526 AD.

A Welsh name *bryn-eithin* 'gorse hill'.

Biddlestone (543230)

Byddelston 1386 AD; *Byddylston* 1533 AD; Bydilston 1543 HT; *Byddleston* 1583 AD; *Bedilston* n.d. AD.

'Beadle's estate', perhaps referring to an owner with a special administrative function.

Kilreague Farm (512212)

Kilre(y)k 1302-3 LWE, 1334 SR; *Kilreck* 1525 HT; *Kilrege* 1540 HT.

Mr Morgan suggests this is Welsh *cil* 'nook' with *rhyg* 'rye'.

Langstone Court (534221)

> *Langareston'* 1221 P (p); *Langeston(e)* 1305 Orig, 1397 VR; *Lankeston* 1334
> SR, 1540 HT; *Llanghton* 1582 AD; *Llangeston alias Langeston* 1599 BM.

Perhaps 'farm by the long ridge', in which case the first element would be the genitive of a place-name **Langgāra*. This has become Langar in Nottinghamshire. There is a tongue of land between two brooks here, which might have been called 'The Long Gore'.

Llancloudy (497208)

> *Podum Loudeu* c620(c1130) LL.
> *Lann Loudeu* c620, c745 (c1130) LL; *Lontlendi* 1267 Ipm; *Lancleudy* 1313
> Duncumb; *Lancloudy* 1334 SR; *Lantloudy* 1540 HT.

Again, the identity of the saint involved in this name is not known. The 1267 form is probably a mistake for *Loncleudi*.

Llangrove (527192)

> *Longegroue* 1372 Duncumb; *Langrove* 1831 OS.

'Long grove', with modern confusion of the first element with Welsh *llan*.

Llangunnock (504229)

> *Lann Cinauc* 1045-1104 (c1130) LL; *Llangennock* 1302-3 LWE; *Langhenok*
> 1334 SR; *Llannock* 1587 AD; *Llangunnocke* 1599 BM.

The saint involved is possibly Cynog, an alleged son of Brychan Brycheiniog. LBS says he has six dedications in Breconshire and one in Radnorshire. (Mr Morgan discounts the Montgomeryshire dedication given in LBS).

Trebumfrey (527225)

> *Humfreston* 1224 Cur; *Humfrayston* 1247 Ipm; *Hunfreyeston* 1292 Ipm;
> *Hunfrayeston* 1327 Ipm; *Houmfreyston* 1331 Ipm.

A ME name 'Humphrey's estate', translated into Welsh. There is another Humphreston in Donnington, Shropshire. The *–b-* of Trebumfrey is probably an inorganic consonant, that is, a consonant added over time and in common speech to ease the passage from one consonant to the next.

Trecilla Farm (534213)

> *Tresele* 1302-3 LWE; *Tretillee* 1500, *Tretylle* 1507; *Trecelle* 1524 AD;
> *Teselley* 1525 HT; *Tretyllay* 1542; *Trecelly* 1558 AD.

Mr Morgan suggests Welsh *tref* + personal name *Selyf*, colloquially Sely.

Treduchan Farm (520196)

> *Tradraghaun* 1499 Ipm; *Tredroughan alias Tredroughan Waylod* 1588 AD.

Mr Morgan suggests *tref* + personal name *Trychan*, which occurs in LL. *Waylod* is Welsh *gwaelod* 'bottom, base'.

Tredunnock (521210)

> *Treredennock* 1302-3 LWE; *Tredono(c)k* 1504, 1582 AD.

Mr Morgan suggests *tref* + *rhedynog* 'ferny', identical to Tredunnock near Caerleon, Monmouthshire (Gwent).

Tre-Essey (504220)

> *Treosseth* 1334 SR; *Cresseth* 1540 HT.

Mr Morgan suggests *tref* + personal name *Esni*.

Lower Tre-Evan (522223)

> *Trezevan* 1334 SR; *Tre eavan* 1486 Owen; *Creghevan* 1540 HT; *Treyevan alias*
> *Treevan* 1599 BM.

Mr Morgan suggests *tref* + personal name *Ieuan*, *Ifan*.

Trereece (528206)

> *Trerease* 1587 AD; *Trereers* 1663 MA.

Tref + personal name Rhys.

Treribble (516228)

> *Trerevel* 1207 Cur; *Trerrybil* 1302-3 LWE.

Mr Morgan suggests *Tre'r-efail* 'farm of the smithy'.

Trewarne (526180)

> *Trawern* 1137 AC; *Trewene* 1211 Fees; *Trawenn'* 1225 DiversAccts;
>   *Trewar(e)n* 1255 Orig, 1663 MA.
> *Trawent* 1159, 1172 P; - *Regis* 1167 P.
> *Tramayr* 1337 Ipm.
> *Hendrew(r)en* 1221 Cur, 1302-3 LWE.

'Alder-swamp settlement', *tref* + *gwern*. *Hendrew(r)en* is 'Old Trewarne', Welsh *Hen Drewern*.

'Wallingstones' (moated site at 503222, now gone)

> *Waldygston* 1385 AD; *Waldyng(e)ston* 1499 AD; *Wallyngston* 1523 Owen.

A ME name 'Walding's settlement'. Probably named from Walding, father of Roger fitzWalding (fl. 1147-9), whom Payn fitzJohn, sheriff of Herefordshire, settled here. Excavations at the moated site in the 1960s (prior to its levelling) produced pottery of the 12th century (TWNFC (1960), etc.).

ᏽ   LLANROTHAL   Ꮽ

Llanrothal (471186)

> *Lann Ridol* 1045-1104 (c1130) LL; *Lanraut'* c1163 Foliot; *Lanrothal* 1278
>   Cant; *Lanrochal* 1291 Tax; *Lantrothall* 1313 Duncumb; *Lanrothel* 1341
>   NonInq; *Llanrithalle* 1397 VR.
> *Ecclesiam Beati Rualdi* 1131-44 MonC; *Ecclesia Sancti Roaldi* 1160-c80
>   MonC.

The identity of the Welsh saint involved in this name is unknown. In the cartulary of Monmouth Priory his or her name is replaced by Roald or Ruald (ON Hróaldr) to create a fictitious saint, probably because it sounded like the Welsh saint's name.

The Cwm (489176)

> *Combotlyn, Comboglyn* 1292 Duncumb; *Cabotheloun* 1327 Banco.

Mr Morgan suggests the qualifying term may be *boglyn*, *bogelyn* 'knob, buckle, bunch', applied to some topographical feature.

Llangunville Farm (494166)

> *Merthir Cynfall* c860, - *Chinfall* (c1130) LL.
> *Lann Cinfall* c860, c1030 (c1130); *Lann Cinuil* 1045-1104 (c1130) LL.
> *Ecclesie Cinfall* c1030 (c1130) LL.

'Church of St Cynfall'.

The bounds of *Lann Cinfall* c860 (c1130) LL: *'Cirn cinfall ital irfoss arhit irfoss dilicat finnaun efrdil iguuer nihit bet mingui, mingui nihit bet pull rud diuinid bet tal irbrinn diguairet dilech forch diaper gefiat, gefiat nihit dital iraithnauc ad dextram irall, maliduc iclaud bet cirn cinfall ubi incepit.'* 'Carn Cynfall to the head of the ditch, along the ditch to Efrddyl's Spring, along its course as far as the Mynwy. Along the Mynwy as far as Pwll Rhudd, upwards as far as the end of the hill, downwards to the forked stone, to the mouth of the *Gefiat*. Along the *Gefiat* to the end of the *Aithnog*, to the right of the hill as the dyke leads to Carn Cynfall, where it began.'

Rollason discusses these boundaries. As in the case of Llancillo they are largely delineated by watercourses – 'Efrddyl's Spring' on the south, the Mynwy on the west, an unnamed brook on the north and the *Gefiat* (now Mally) Brook on the east. 'Carn Cynfall' probably stood near the modern A466 road where the present boundary between the counties of Hereford and Monmouth cross it – 505169. From there it followed the county boundary (the line of a dyke) down through Buckholt Wood to 'Efrddyl's Spring' at 495160, whose watercourse it then follows to where it meets the Mynwy at 493153. Following this river it comes to 'Pwll Rhud' ('red pool or pit'), where a small brook meets it at 490163, then along this unnamed brook upwards past Llangunville Wood and Cwm Farm ('as far as the end of the hill') to Moyle's Cross 496175. The boundary then follows approximately the course of the road from Cwm Farm to Welsh Newton until it meets the A466, which it crosses to reach the *Gefiat* or Mally Brook. Somewhere on this road stood the forked stone (*lech forch*), possibly where it reaches the A466. The Mally Brook is then followed south back to 'Carn Cynfall'. There were churches of St Efrddyl at Llanerthil in Monmouthshire, and also at Madley, from whence he or she gave their name to 'Ynys Efrddyl': see District Name Mawfield. The church of Rockville in Monmouthshire (*St Kinephaut of Rokevilla* 1186 Fr) may also be a Cynfall dedication. (ex inf. Mr Morgan).

Tregate Castle Farm (480172)

> *Treg(g)et* 1131-44 MonC, 1176 P (p), 1186 Fr, 1210 Fees, 1256 Salop Eyre
>   (p), 1292 Subs (p), 1346 Ipm, 1370 Ipm.
> *Treket* 1144 MonC.
> *Trejet* 1146 Fr.

DEPN suggests Welsh *tre goed* 'hamlet in the wood'.

Llanwarne (505282)

> *Hen Lenhic Lann Guern (in Ercicg)* c758 (c1130) LL.
> *Ecclesiam hennlennic super ripam amyr, id est lannguern* c758 (c1130) LL.
> *Ladguern* 1086 DB; *Lanwara(n)* 1131 Holtzmann, 1291 Tax, 1334 SR, 1341
>   NonInq; *Landwarnat* 1146 Holtzmann; *Landwar(a)* 1158, 1163
>   Holtzmann; *Lanwaryn* 1325 Ipm, 1383 Capes (p).
> *Lann Guern Teliau ha Dibric* 1045-1104 (c1130) LL.
> *Lann Guern Aperhumur* 1066-87 (c1130) LL.

The church of *Hen Lenhic* was at Lenaston, which is 'on the banks of the Gamber' (*super ripam Amyr*), a mile south of Llanwarne in Pencoyd (see below). It seems to have been amalgamated with Llanwarne (which means 'church by the alder swamp') by bishop Herewald, after many churches in Archenfield had fallen into ruin, to produce a church with a double dedication (as at Hentland and Welsh Bicknor), SS Teilo and Dyfrig. A chapel at Lenaston survived into the Middle Ages (Duncumb).

Little Hill (479273), **Hills Farm** (489276) and **Hill Gate** (497275)

> *Rosnet(h)* 1131, 1146, 1158 Holtzmann.

> *Hulle* 1334 SR; 1540 HT.

Rosnet is probably a Welsh name with *rhos*, in the sense 'promontory' as generic. The qualifier might be *nant* 'valley', and the whole 'promontory by a valley'. See Monkton, below.

Lyston House (496287)

> *Leytheston* 1302-3 LWE; *Lecheston* 1334 SR, 1349 Trill, 1415 Duncumb.
> *Lyiston* 1505 PNHe; *L(e)yston* 1525, 1540; *Lyestyn* 1536 HT.

The first element is likely to be a ME personal name or surname, perhaps *Lece*, modern Leece.

Monkton (**Lower** 490268, **Upper** 491265) and **Monkton Bank** (484266)

> *Moneketon(e)* 1279 Cant, 1291 Tax, 1316 FA, 1334 SR; *Munketon* 1292 QW,
>   1297 Duncumb.

'Estate of the monks'. Hugh de Lacy gave lands here to the canons of Llanthony Prima. In 12th century documents they are described as lying at *Rosnet* and Pendigott (below), with the first of these places apparently becoming the canons' estate called 'Hill'.

Pendigott (487261, partly in St Weonard's)

Pendagoit 1146 Holtzmann

Mr Morgan suggests 'end of the black wood', from Welsh words *pen*, *du* and *coed*. Dugoed occurs as a place-name in Merioneth (now Gwynedd).

(lost)

Penebecdoc 1086 DB; *Penebredoc* 1160-70 HDB.

Mr Morgan suggests *pen* 'headland' with an unknown qualifier.

❧ LONGTOWN ☙

See Clodock, page 67.

❧ LOWER BULLINGHAM ☙

See page 60.

❧ LOWER HARPTON ☙

See page 109.

❧ LUCTON ☙

Lucton (437642)

'Estate on the river Lugg', see DEPN.

❧ LUGWARDINE ☙

Lugwardine (551410)

> *Lagordin* 1067-71 Gallia Christiana; *Lucuordine* 1086 DB; *Lugwerdine*
>   1125-25 HDB; *Lugwardin* 1143-8 *StGC*, 1275 RH; *Lugwurdin* 1168 P;
>   *Lugwardyn* 1316 FA, 1327 Banco (p), 1327 Capes; *Logwordyn* 1332 BM;
>   *Logwardyne* 1412 Capes.
> *Ladeo* 1146-63 Foliot.

'Settlement by the river Lugg', from OE *worthign*.

Longworth (563393)

> *Langesfort* 1148-54 CathDign; *Langueford* 1158 Holtzmann; *Langeford*
>   1243 Fees, 1306 Ipm, 1327 Banco, 1330 Capes; *Longeford(e)* 1183-5 *StGC*,
>   1217-18 Barrow.
> *Longeuorde* 1334 SR; *Longeward* 1572 KPC.

'Long ford'. The corruption of –*ford* to –*worth* is found in a number of places.

Tidnor (555398)

> *Tudinoverem* c1240 Duncumb; *Tudenore* 1327 Capes (p), 1354 Trill.
> *Tudnourshirous* 1517 AD.
> *Tudnoursmylles* 1517 AD.
> *Tidnor Forge* 1831 OS.

'Tudda's flat-topped ridge'. The farm called Sheepcotes is in a position appropriate to the place-name element *ofer*.

❧ LUSTON ☙

Luston (486630)

> *Luston(e)* 1086 DB, 1291 Tax; *Lustun(e)* 1123 ReadingC, 1173-86 Kemp,
>   1206 P (p); *Lussetone* c1285 Red Book.

The c1285 form suggests a personal name **Lussa* as first element, perhaps a shortened version of *Lustwine*.

Lyonshall (331563)

> *Lenehalle* 1086 DB; *Line(s)halla* 1096 Regesta (p), 1103-7 BreconC (p);
> *Lenhal(es)* 1173-4 Foliot, 1213-16 *LeomC* (p), 1243 Fees, 1256 BM, 1291
> Tax; *Lenhaul* 1209 Robinson; *Leyhales* 1263 AncCorr; *Leonhales* 1271
> Swin, 1303 FA, 1341 NonInq, 1371 BM, 1535 VE; *Leenhales* 1331 Ipm;
> *Leomhales* 1338 Larking.

'Nook in the district called Leen', see District Name Leen. There is a Lyons-hall in Peterchurch that has a different derivation.

Holme Marsh (341548)

> *Hulmo* 1229 Cur; *Hom alias Leonhales* 1547-53 Court.

Probably, in spite of the earliest spelling, OE *hamm* in the sense 'dry ground in a marsh'. There has been influence from ME *holm*, of similar meaning.

Hope (337568, and **Sheriff's Farm** 348580)

> *Hope* 1086 DB, 1567 *Faraday*, 1833 OS.
> (land in) *Hope* (and) *Hopeswood* (called) *Sheriffs* 1588 BM.

hop 'secluded valley'. The farm marked Hope on the OS 1" map overlooks a narrow valley. VCH and Thorn are incorrect in identifying DB *Hope* as Hopleys Green in Almeley.

(Lynhales 325552)

> *Moor* 1216-28 Dugdale, 1833 OS.

'Marsh', OE *mōr*. There seems to have been a fairly recent change of name here, with the modern name echoing early spellings for Lyonshall.

Madley (420387)

> *Lann Ebrdil* c745 (c1130) LL.

> *Medelagie* 1086 DB.
> *Matle* c1130 LL.
> *Maddele(ia)* c1200, 1272 Capes; *Maddeley(e)* c1220, 1308 Capes, 1287
>   Swin, 1341 NonInq; *-in Straddel* 1360 Ipm.
> *Madele(ye)* c1200, 1246 Capes, 1291 Tax, 1327 Banco; *Madeley(a)* 1252
>   Capes, 1411 QD; *Madley* 1428 FA.
> *Magdale* 1219 Capes.
> *Maudel* 1280 Ch.

The forms closely resemble those for Madeley in Shropshire. The early and
frequent *–dd-* suggests a personal name *Madda*, hence 'Madda's wood or clearing'.
Magdale 1219, which is unexplained, curiously echoes the spelling *Magdalee*,
which occurs in the 'Testament of St Mildburg' for Madeley, Shropshire.

Davies places the *Lann Ebrdil* ('church of St Efrddyl') given by king Ithel
ap Morgan to bishop Berthwyn c745 at Llanerthil in Monmouthshire because
she assumes an earlier grant of a *Lann Efrdil in Brehes* by king Ithel ap Arthrwys
to bishop Euddogwy c685 is the same place. However, it is clear that, because
the later grant is included in a grant of eleven places in Ergyng (or between that
district and the Wye) restored to the church after their devastation by the English,
it is very unlikely to be Llanerthil in Monmouthshire. Egerton Phillimore (in
Owen's Pembrokeshire) suggests that the later *Lann Ebrdil* is Madley, and this
identification has been accepted by most authorities (e.g. LBS, LWSS). That there
was a *Lann Efrdil in Brehes* at Llanerthil, on the Olwy (*Ilgui*) in Monmouthshire,
is not in doubt (see PNGw).

Ebrdil or Efrddyl figures in the 'Life of St Dubricius (Dyfrig)' contained in
LL as the mother of Dyfrig, to whom she gives birth at *Matle*, a name for which
the author gives the ingenious derivation (from the Latin) of *mat* 'good' and *le*
'place', that is, 'good place', thus providing his subject with a suitable birth-place.
Efrddyl was the dedicatee of the first church at Madley and she also gave her
name to *Insulam Ebrdil* or 'Efrdyll's Island', the name of a district around Madley.
By the 12th century, however, she had been replaced by Dyfrig her son, although
today's church is dedicated to the Nativity of the Virgin. The church was rebuilt
in the 14th century on a scale that far outweighed the importance of the village
in which it was (and is) situated. This circumstance may be accounted for by an
underlying popular identification of Efrdyll with the Virgin and by the possibility
that Madley had been a sacred site since before Christianity arrived in Britain. See
District Name Mawfield.

The Bage Farm (416397)

> *(La) Bach(e)* c1220 Capes (p), 1327 Banco, 1334 SR, 1394 QD.
>
> 'Stream-valley', OE *bæce*.

Brampton (Great 410367, **Little** 407372)

> *Bromton* 1274 Owen; *Brompton(e)* 1275 RH, 1318 Capes, 1334 SR; *Brampton*
>   1316 FA.
> *Michelebrompton, Littlebrompton* 1327 Banco.
>
> 'Broom settlement'.

Carwardine Green Farm (403409)

> *Kauendinan'* 1198 CartAntiq; *Canendinam 1199 Dugdale*.
> *Kayrwardin* 1252 Ex (p); *Kerwerthin* 1273 CRCG (p); *Karwardyn* 1290
>   CRCG (p); *Carewardyn(e)* 1334 SR, 1470 AD (p).

Nothing cam be done with forms as inconsistent as these. The name has been interpreted as containing OE *worthign* 'enclosed settlement', but this may be a rationalisation of a Welsh name.

Chilstone (Upper 392395, **Lower** 409398)

> *Childestune* c1200 Capes; *Childeston(e)* 1210-12 RBE, 1242 Cur, 1287 Swin,
>   1303 FA, 1327 Banco, 1346 Capes, 1446 BM.
> *Chil(le)ston* 1437 Ipm, 1440 BM, 1521 Court.
>
> 'Estate of the young nobleman', OE *cild*.

Webton (421366)

> *Web(b)eton(e)* 1086 DB, 1230 P, 1291 Tax, 1316 FA, 1342 BM; *Webbetune*
>   c1200 Capes; *Wibbitone* c1220 Capes.
>
> 'Webba's estate'. The same personal name is found in Webtree in Allensmore.

Wormhill (432392)

> *Wimell'* c1200 BreconC (p); *Worme(le)* 1281 Select Cases (p), 1334 SR;
>   *Wormle* 1291 (p), 1318 Capes (p).
>
> Probably 'reptile wood', from OE *wyrm* and *lēah*. The place is not near Worm Brook.

❧ MANSELL GAMAGE and MANSELL LACY ☙

Mansell Gamage (394445), **Mansell Lacy** (426456)

> *Mælueshylle* 1043-6 ECWM; *Malveselle* 1086 DB; *Maueshulla, Melueshull'*
> 1160-70 HDB; *Maushil* 1169 P; *Maweshull* 1199 P; *Malmeshull(e)* 1292
> Ipm, 1356 Capes; *Malveshulle* 1340 Capes.
> *Mumwell* 1184 Foliot.
> *Mauneshulla* 1195 P.
>
> *Maumeshull' Gamages* 1243 Fees; *Malmeshul(l)(e) Gamage(e)* 1291 Tax,
> 1317 Ipm, 1318 Ipm.
> *Maumeshull' Lacy* 1243 Fees; *Malmeshull(e) Lacy* 1291 Tax, 1294 Swin,
> 1305 Ipm, 1341 NonInq, 1397 VR, c1433 BM.

DEPN's etymology 'hill of gravel' has been generally accepted. The change
of *Malwes-* (genitive of OE **malu-*) to *Malmes-* is ascribed by Ekwall to 'a kind of
assimilation' (presumably meaning that the *M-* is echoed) or to association with
m(e)alm 'sandy soil'. The two settlement names are two miles apart, and separated
by Offa's Dyke. Mansell Gamage has the more imposing hill, now called Garnon's
Hill, with Offa's Dyke running along its crest. If this is the original *Malweshyll*, it
presumably gave name to a district which extended far enough to include Mansell
Lacy. For the families of Gamage and Lacy, see Eaton in Leominster and Holme
Lacy respectively.

Shetton Farm (407449)

> *Schutinton'* 1251 StGC (p); *Schytrincton* 1291 Tax; *Shutynton, Shutinton* 1344
> Ipm; *Schitton* 1359-69 KinRR.

Probably 'estate associated with Scytta'.

❧ MUCH MARCLE and LITTLE MARCLE ☙

Much Marcle (657328), **Little Marcle** (666362)

> *Merchelai* 1086 DB; *Marchelai* 1148-9 Foliot; *Markelai(a)* 1160-70 HDB,
> 1216-c40 BM; *Marcle(ie)* 1163-9, 1356 Capes; *Merclai, Mertlay* 1175 P;
> *Merlai* 1176 P (p); *Markele(ia)* 1230-4, 1269 Capes; *Marklee* 1292 QW;
> *Markeleye* 1317 Ipm.
> *Magna Merkel(e)(y)* 1243 Fees, 1275 RH, 1358 BM; - *Marcle(y)* 1291 Tax,
> 1378 BM; - *Markley* 1334 SR; *Marcle Magna* 1363 BM.
> *Parva Marcle(y)* 1208 Cur, 1334 SR; - *Markel* 1243 Fees; - *Martleye* 1291 Tax;
> *P(ar)va(m) Markeleye* 1299 Orig, 1303 FA.

'Boundary wood', from OE *mearc* and *lēah*. The reference will be to the boundary between the sub-kingdoms of the Magonsæte and the Hwicce.

Bickerton Court (657307)

Bicretune 1086 DB; *Bickertuna* 1160-c80 MonC; *Bickerton(e)* 1211 P, 1326 Ipm; *Bykerthon* 1300 Ipm (p); *Bykerton(e)* 1307 Swin, 1320 Capes (p), 1397 VR.

'Bee-keepers' settlement', one of several instances of this name.

Hellens (661333)

Helyn 1291 Tax.

A manorial name from a family of Helion domiciled in Herefordshire since the 12th century. The Helions of Helion Bumpstead in Essex were from Helléan, between Josselin and Ploërmel, in Brittany (Sanders) and this may be the same family.

Huntleys Farm (656346)

Hundeslawa 1160-70 HDB; *Hundeslawe* 1238 Cur, 1256 Salop Eyre (p);
    Hontelowe 1352 Trill.

The early name, 'tumulus of the hound', is repeated in Hounslow, Middlesex, and in a Berkshire charter-boundary. Huntleys Farm is a likely site for a tumulus, but intermediate forms are needed to confirm the identification.

Kynaston (643358)

Kynewardestone 1294 BM; *Kenewerston* 1306 Ipm; *Kyna(r)ston* 1362
    St Katherine, 1398 BM; *Kynastone* 1397 VR, 1547 Court; *Kynnerston*
    1545-53 Court.

'Cyneweard's estate'. Kynaston in Hentland is a different name; DEPN confuses the forms.

Tyrrel's Frith Farm (683381)

Tirelesfryth (once called) *Roselynes fryth* 1362 St Katherine; *Tyrellesfrith*
    1362 St Katherine.

Frith is OE *fyrhth* 'brushwood, scrub'. The Tyrrels were a family domiciled in Herefordshire since the Conquest. A Rocelin Tyrrel was lord of Little Marcle in 1137-9 (HDB).

Marden (512471)

> *Maurdine* 1086 DB; *Mawerdine* 1125-35 HDB; *Maordine* 1137 AC; *Maurdin(a)*
> 1138 AC, 1148-55 WalkerCh, 1169, 1187 P, 1201 RBE (p), 1247 Ipm,
> c1250 Capes, 1272 Ipm; *Mawerdin(am}* 1141 Regesta, 1275 RH;
> *Mawurd'in* 1173 P; *Mahurdin* 1194 RBE (p), 1203 P (p), 1243 Fees (p);
> *Maurthyn* 1195 Barrow; *Maordin* 1199 RBE (p); *Maurdia* c1200 RATD
> (p); *Mahurthin* c1200 RBE; *Maw(o)rdin* 1204 P (p), 1246 Capes; *Mawrthin*
> 1210-12 RBE (p), 1256 Salop Eyre; *Mauwrdin* c1212-17 (p); *Mawurthyn*
> 1220 Cur; *Maurden(e)* 1252 Capes, 1291 Tax; *Maurdon* 1272 Capes;
> *Maurdyn* 1286 Ipm, 1316 FA, 1328 Banco (p), 1334 SR, 1357 Ipm, 1419
> BM; *Mawardyn* 1291 Tax, c1433 BM; *Mardyn* 1292 Capes; *Marwardyn*
> 1302 Ipm (p); *Mauwardyn* 1309 Ipm, 1328 Banco; *Mawarden* 1667 BM.
> *Magewurdin* 1177 P; *Magwardyn* 1425 Cl.
> *Maiordina* 1212 Fees (p).
> *Machwrthin* 1256 Salop Eyre (p).

'Enclosed settlement in the district called Maund', second element OE
worthign. See also District Name Maund, page 19.

Amberley Court (546478)

> *Amburlege* 1086 DB; *Amberlege* 1200 Cur; *Amberley(e)* 1247, 1327 Ipm,
> 1341 NonInq; *Ambreleye* 1291 Tax; *Aumbresley* 1315 Swin (p); Ambrelegh
> 1316 Ipm; *Aumburley* 1328 Banco.

Probably 'wood frequented by the yellowhammer'. There are two other
Amberleys, in Gloucestershire and Sussex. The OE bird-name *amore* is the second
element of *yellowhammer*; the reference could be to other birds of the bunting
family.

Burmarsh (532469)

> *Burdenesmars* 1247-92; *Burdewardesmers* 1274; *Burmers* 1293 (p);
> *Boremarssche* 1433; *Burmarshe* 1497 AD.

Second element 'marsh'. The spellings are too inconsistent for identification
of the first element.

Fromington (532473)

> *Froremerton* 1247 Ipm; *Froremarton* 1302 Ipm.
> *Fromanton* c1274 AD.
> *Frormanton* 1281 Ipm; *Frormynton* 1307 Ipm.
> *Foremarton* 1302 Orig.

Unexplained; perhaps most likely to be a compound of *tūn* with the name of a post-Conquest owner.

Sutton Lakes (544469)

> *Suttokes* 1219-34 Capes.

Tumpy Lakes and Sutton Lakes are *–Lake* on the 19th century OS map. This is OE *lacu* 'drainage channel', used of canalised portions of the small stream here.

The Vauld (532494)

> *(La) Fald(e)* 13th AD, late 13th AD, 1470-4 Court; *La Felde* 1328 Banco (p); *Le Fald* 1409 AD; *The Valde* 1614 BM; *Vale* 1654 BM.

'Fold'.

Wisteston Court (517488)

> *Wistanestunam* 1132 *StGC*; *Wistaneston(a)* 1148-63 HDB, 1272 Ipm, 1299 Ipm; *Wystaneston* 1198 Fees (p); *Wisteneton'* 1203 P (p); *Westeneston'* 1205 P (p); *Wystanestun* 1247 Ipm; *Westaston* 1247 Ch; *Wistantune* 1270 AD; *Westempston* 1305 Ipm; *Wystanston* 1316, 1327 Ipm; *Westamston* 1361 Ipm; *Wystastone* 1459 BM; *Wistaston* 1614 BM.
> *Wystanestowe* 1185 *StGC*.

'Wigstān's estate'.

❧ MARSTOW ☙

Marstow (554192)

> *Lann Martin* 1045-1104 (c1130) LL.
> *Martinstowe* 1277 AD (p), 1334 SR; *Martenstewe* 1540 HT.

'Church of St Martin'. The site of the church was excavated in 1964 (TWNFC (1964)). This may also be the site of:

agri Guruarch; terram Gurmarch c740 (c1130) LL.

One Rhiadaf bought this 'for twenty-four [objects unspecified], a Saxon woman, a precious sword and a valuable horse' before giving it to the Church (LL).

Brelston Green (559201)

Brokhaleston 1334 SR; *Brokeleston* 1540 HT.

tūn has been added to the genitive of the place-name *Brōchalh*, which describes the position of the hamlet in the junction of the Lyde and Garren Brooks.

(at New Court Farm 558196)

Cachalren 1075-87 AD; *Chachabren* 1101 MonC, *Crakebrun* 1200 Cur; *Kakebrein* 1200 Cur (p); *Cockebrayne* 1558 Old Rectories.

Mr Morgan suggests OE **Crake-burna* 'heron stream', and thus a duplication of the river-name Garron, Welsh *garan* 'heron'. For the location of this lost place, see TWNFC, **55** (2007).

Glewstone (558221)

Gleaustun' 1212 Patterson (p).

'Gleaw's estate', with a personal name derived from OE *gleaw* 'wise'.

Pencraig (564208)

Penncreic (in Ercig super Gui) c860-6 (c1130) LL; *Penkreid* 1334 SR; *Pentreige* 1540 HT.

A Welsh name, 'rocky hill'. Cf. Pencraig (Old Radnor) in Radnorshire (now Powys) (PNRa).

Ruxton Green (542194)

Coroxstone 1663 MA.

Earlier spellings are required.

Mathon (733458)

> *Matham* 1014 ECWM; *Matma, -e* 1086 DB; *Madma, -e* 1137-9, 1160-70
> HDB; *Mathm(a)* 1163-86 Barrow, 1248 AD; *Mademe* 1243 Fees;
> *Machema* 13th AD; *Mathine* 1336-7 CRCG (p).

This is considered to be OE *māthm* 'treasure, gift'. There was a *Mathunleye* in Foy in 1282 (QW).

Bagburrow Wood (749452)

> *Bageberge* 1086 DB.

Bagborough in Somerset, which is *Bacganbeorg* in a charter of 904, was reduced to *Bageberge* in DB. **Bacga* 'bag-shaped' may have been the name for a small hill of the sort denoted by OE *beorg*. This *Bageberge* is identified as Bagborough in Thorn. The DB settlement may have been centred round Ham Green (747446) and its moated site.

❧ **MICHAELCHURCH ESCLEY** ☙

Michaelchurch Escley (317342)

> *Eskelyn* 1232 Dugdale, 1327 ChR.

> *Michaeleschirche* 1265-1300 EHC.

> *Llanvihangelesglye* 1543 HT.

'Church of St Michael'. It is situated on the Escley Brook. The affix is to distinguish it from Michaelchurch in Tretire and Michaelchurch on Arrow in Radnorshire (now Powys), both of which are not far distant.

Cefn-cist Farm (316359)

> *Keistin* 1227 Ch; *Kesty* 1232 Dugdale; *Kesti* 1327 Ch.

Mr Morgan suggests this is 'house of the sergeant of the peace', from Welsh *cais* 'sergeant of the peace' and *tŷ* 'house', noting further that about one mile north-west is Maerdy, which is 'house of the steward'.

Middleton (541646)

> *Miceltune* 1086 DB; *Miclatun'* 1123 *LeomC*; *Michelet(una)* 1143-55 WalkerCh,
> 1178-86 Kemp; *Mucletona* 1160-70 HDB; *Micleton'* c1250 *LeomC*.
> *Mittleton* 1200-50 *LeomC*; *Middleton* 1269-74 Swin (p); *Mydetone* 1397 VR.

'Large settlement', later confused with the very common place-name which means 'middle settlement'.

Miles Hope (573644)

> *Hope* 1186-99 (p), 1200-13 *LeomC*, 1231 Cur.
> *Hope Mililon'* 1200-50 *LeomC*; - *Mile* 1337 QD.
> *Milonis Hoppe* 1231 Cur; *Milleshope* 1332 QD; *Milsoppe* 1535 VE.

'Secluded valley', with the name of an owner prefixed.

Moor Abbey ('Moor Aubin' 544632)

> *Mora* 1291 Tax; *La More* 1303 FA,
> *Moreaubyn* 1547-53 Court.

'Marsh', OE *mōr*. 'Abbey' because it belonged to Reading Abbey, mother-house of Leominster Priory, and to distinguish it from other 'Moors'. John *de Sancto Albino* had this manor in 1243. See Rowberry in Bodenham for the St Aubyn family.

Upton Court (552661)

See Lower Upton in Little Hereford.

❧ **MOCCAS** ❧

Moccas (357433)

> *Mochros* 6th, c620, c745 (c1130) LL; *Mocres* 1115-20 *StGC*, 1137-9 HDB,
> 1186-98 *StGC*, 1243 Fees; *Mocris* 1202 P; *Mocras* 1202 Cur.
> *Moches* 1086 DB; *Mokes* 1224 Cur; *Mockers* 1291 Tax, *Mokkas* 1316 FA, 1341
> NonInq; *Mockas* 1535 VE.

A Welsh name, *Mochros* 'pig marsh'.

Woodbury Farm (352419)

> *Wdebiri* 1185-9 BMFacs; *Wodebur(y)* 1193 P, 1291 Ch; *Wudebir'* c1276 AD.

'Wood fort'. A hillfort on Woodbury Hill has been discovered recently (KR).

〆 MONKLAND ❧

Monkland (460577)

> *Leine* 1086 DB.
> *Monecheslene* 1160-70 HDB; *Monekesleona* 1137 Barrow; *Muneke(s)len'*
>   c1180-8, 1233 Barrow; *Monekeslane* 1193 P; *Munekeslane* 1243 Fees;
>   *Munkenelane* 1277-92 ReadingC; *Monkelene* 1291 Tax, 1328 Banco;
>   *Moneclond* 1316 FA; *Munkeleone* 1334 SR.

'The part of Leen belonging to the monks', see District Name Leen. The monks of St Peter de Castellion at Conches had the manor by grant of Ralph de Tosny (died 1102).

〆 MONNINGTON ON WYE ❧

Monnington (373434)

> *Manitune* 1086 DB; *Manintona* 1160-70 HDB; *Moninton'* 1207 Cur;
>   *Muneton'* 1241 Cur; *Monintun* 1243 Fees; *Moniton* 1265 Ipm, 1322 Orig,
>   1326 Banco; *Monyton'* 1292 QD, 1334 SR.
> *Multon* 1238 Pat.
> *Monitun Mucegros* 1277 InqMisc.
> *Mointon' super Weyam* 1292 QW; *Monynton supra Wyam* 1418 BM.

'Communal estate', see Monnington Straddle in Vowchurch and a lost 'Monnington' in Ewyas Harold.

〆 MORDIFORD ❧

Mordiford (571375)

> *Mordford(e)* 1148-63 Foliot, 1186-98 *StGC*.
> *Mordeford(e)* 1143-8 *StGC*, 1243 Fees, 1275-82 Cant, 1291 Tax, 1535 VE;
>   *Mordiford(e)* c1160 GloucC, c1230, 1332 Capes, 1429 Cl; *Mardeford* 1198
>   CartAntiq; *Mordyford* 1422 AD, 1489 BM.

The first part of this name is unexplained. DEPN tentatively suggests Welsh *mor-dy* 'great house', but this is not a convincing ancient Welsh name.

Backbury Hill and Camp (586387)

Bach(k)ebur' c1138-c58, 1186-8 *StGC*.

'Fort on a back-shaped ridge'.

Checkley (594384)

Chackileg 1252 PNHe; *Chek(k)ley(a)* mid 13th *StGC*, 1485 Ipm, 1525 BM; *Checkeley* 1353 AD.

Probably 'Ceacca's wood or clearing'.

Larport ('Frome Henry' and 'Little Frome' 572389)

Fro(u)me 1086 DB, 1220 Cur.
Froma Henrici 1243 Fees.
Little Froma 1281 Ipm, - *Freme* 1373 Ipm.

Lorteport 1148-63 Foliot, c1205-13 *StGC*, 1303 FA; *Lurteport* 1326 Ipm; *Larpotte* 1525 BM; *Lorpott* 1663 MA.
Lurcepert 1308 Ipm.
Lusteport 1373 Ipm.
Lordford 1148-63 Foliot.

For *Frome*, see ERN. Larport means 'dirty market-place'.
Henry de Ferrers's DB manor of Frome is later found held in two parts, one at Larport belonging to the Monmouth family and one at Mordiford and Checkley held by the Hereford family. In c1160 the Monmouth family's demesnes are described as being at Larport, while their whole manor was located at *Froume* in 1220, at *Froma Henrici* in 1243 and at *Little Froma* in 1281. Henry of Monmouth held it in 1243 and his name seems to have stuck as an affix.

Prior's Frome (576391)

Frome 1086 DB.
From' Prioris 1243 Fees, *Froome Priors* 1663 MA.

This part of *Frome* belonged to St Guthlac's Priory at Hereford.

Old Sufton (575384) and **Sufton Court** (573380)

> *Sulftona* c1200 PNHe; *S(h)uffton* 1332 BM, 1390 Ipm.
> *Suttone* 1221 Pleas (p).

If the c1200 spelling can be trusted this could be 'settlement on a shelf', OE *scylf-tūn*. Elsewhere this compound has become Shelton, Shilton, however, and the loss of –*l*- is perhaps unlikely. More spellings are needed.

MORETON JEFFRIES

Moreton Jeffries (603485)

> *Mortune* 1086 DB; *Mortuna* c1155 Foliot.
> *Morton Jeffrey* 1273 Capes; - *Geffrey* 1316 Ipm; - *Geffray* 1341 NonInq.
> *Morton P'va* 1535 VE.

'Marsh settlement'. A Geoffrey son of Geoffrey of Moreton was living in 1265 (Cl). The affix could be from either of them. 'Parva' to distinguish it from Moreton on Lugg, both manors belonging to the dean and chapter of Hereford Cathedral.

MORETON ON LUGG

Moreton on Lugg (504456)

> 'Marsh settlement', see DEPN.

MUCH BIRCH

See page 42.

MUCH COWARNE

See page 71.

MUCH DEWCHURCH

See page 76.

166

MUCH MARCLE

See page 157.

MUNSLEY

Munsley (663409)

> *Muleslage* 1086 DB; *Mulesle* 1201 Cur (p).
> *Muneslai* 1086 DB; Munesl(e)(ia) 1160-70 HDB, 1166 RBE, 1201 Cur (p),
>   1229 Pat; *Muneslega* c1175 Capes; *Munesleye alias Monesleye* 1317 Ipm.
> *Moneslai(a)* 1086 DB; *Moneslaya* 1133 WalkerSC; *Monesle(y)* 1256 Salop
>   Eyre (p), 1291 Tax, 1317 Ipm.
> *Mimesleia* 1166 RBE (p).
> *Mowsley* 1311 QD; *Mouseley* 1608 KPC.
> *Mounsley* 1428 FA.
> *Moundisley* 1552-4 BM.

Possibly 'Mūl's clearing', transformed by the common Norman-French confusion of –*l*- and –*n*-. DEPN suggests 'Mundel's clearing' for this name and for Mundesley in Norfolk, but neither name has spellings which point clearly to the personal name *Mundel*.

NEWTON-BY-LEOMINSTER

Newton (505538)

> *Newentone* 1086 DB; *Niweton'* 1123 *LeomC*; *Nivet'* 1186-99 *LeomC*; *Newet'*
>   1213 *LeomC*; *Neutona* 1243 Fees; *Newtone* 1347 Trill.

'New settlement'.

NEWTON-IN-EWYAS

Newton (347329)

> *Neuton(e)* 1247-72, 1287, 14th AD.

'New settlement'.

WELSH NEWTON

Welsh Newton (499180)

> *Neweton(e)* 1313 Duncumb, 1334 SR, 1397 VR.
> *Welshnewton* 1505 Duncumb, *Newton Wallia* 1535 VE.

'New settlement'; 'Welsh' to distinguish it from English Newton ('Newton Huntly'), now Newton Court in Monmouth.

Buckholt (507162)

> *Bocholt'* 1199 Pleas (p); *Bokholt, la Bocholte* c1235 (1400) Dugdale; *Bochole* c1306 AncCorr, Dugdale (ex inf. Mr Morgan).

'Beech wood'. There are other examples in Hampshire and Sussex.

'Newland' (now Pembridge Castle 488193)

> *Neuelonde* 1213 ClR; *Nywelonde* 1304 Ipm; *Newelond(e)* 1346 Trill, 1375 InqMisc.

'New land', won by the Templars from waste land after they received Garway from king Henry II. William de Braose acquired 'Newland' from the Templars in 1205-8 and gave it to Henry of Pembridge. Henry built (or re-built) a castle there that his family held until 1375. It was still called 'Newland' in 1429, two generations after it passed out of Pembridge hands, and does not appear as 'Pembridge Castle' until 1505 (Duncumb).

St Wolstan's Farm (518174)

> *Wolestan* 1297 Duncumb.
> *Sentt-, Seint Wolstan* 1313 Duncumb, 1334 SR; *Sanctus Wostanus* 1338 Larking.

The reference is to Wulfstan, bishop of Worcester, who died in 1095 and who was canonised in 1203. Baderon of Monmouth gave lands here to the Knights of St John of Jerusalem (the Hospitallers) in c1150-66 (RBE). In 1175 king Henry II gave Callow near Hereford to Worcester Cathedral Priory, but at the instigation of Richard I (1189-99) the cathedral priory gave it to the Hospitallers in return for certain services (WorcC). These dealings between the Hospitallers and Worcester Cathedral were being made at a time when moves to canonise Wulfstan were well under way, and it may have been this that inspired the Hospitallers to attach his name to the lands in Archenfield given them by Baderon.

St Wolstan's could have been the site of either *Lann Celinni* or *Lann Tisauuc*, churches in Archenfield known to have existed in 1045-1104 (LL), but whose locations are now lost. See also Ganarew (above).

❧ NORTON CANON ❧

Norton Canon (382478)

'North settlement', of the dean and chapter of Hereford, see DEPN.

Eccles Green (378485)

> *Eckeleia* c1280 Robinson; *(H)eckeleye, Heckel* 13th Rawlinson; *Ek(k)eley, Eccles* 1392 QD.

'Ecca's wood or clearing', second element *leah*. The 1392 form is probably aberrant.

Hinton Farm (381457)

> *Hyn(e)ton* 13th, 1353 AD.

'Estate of the religious community'; the reference will be to ownership by Hereford Cathedral.

Hyatt Sarnesfield (380500)

> See Sarnesfield.

❧ NORTON-BY-BROMYARD ❧

Norton (**Upper** 681581, **Middle** 678576)

> *Norton(e)* 1268-75 *Red Book MS* (p), 1269, 1501 Ipm.
> *Nortons Holywatir* 1524 HT.

'North settlement'. 'Holywater' tithes were payable to the minster within whose *parochia* the place lies, in this case Bromyard church. Parts of the settlement of Norton were at 'Vinschurch' (below) and at Saltmarshe, both of which once had 'Norton' prefixed to their names.

Buckenhill (685566)

> *Bucchehulle* c1153-5 Capes; *Bukehull'* 1200-15 Barrow (p).
> *Buckenhull'* 1216-19 Barrow (p), *Buckenell* 1219-27 Barrow (p); *Bokenhull(e)*
> 1268-75 *Red Book MS* (p), 1375 Capes; *Bokynhull* 1431 KPC.

The earliest forms suggest 'hill of the he-goat', from OE *bucca*. If this be the first element, it is in the genitive in later forms. There is another Buckenhill in Woolhope.

Mapletone Barn (662562)

> *Appultone* 1268-75 *Red Book MS* (p).

'Orchard'.

Rhea Farm (660555)

> *(ate)Ee, (del)Ee* 1268-75 *Red Book MS* (p); *(atte) Ree* 1304 Orig (p); *(La, Le)
> Ree* 1328 Banco (p), 1575-80 Bromyard.

'(Place) at the river', OE *æt thǽre īe*. The farm overlooks one of the headwaters of the Frome.

'Vinschurch' (probably the DMV at 682580)

> *(Norton) Fyndeschurche* 1501 Ipm; *ffinchurche* 1575-80 *Wms*.

The DMV is noted in Bromyard; it lies not far from Vinschurch Plantation (688585). If there is not likely to have been an ancient church here, the name is probably a fanciful one coined from the deserted site.

(lost, but possibly at Newhouse Farm 665576)

> *Wetelecha* 1140-8 Capes.
> *Wetebach(e)* 1140-8 Capes, 1240-68 Whitbourne; *Wetebeth'* 1219-27 Barrow;
> *Wed(d)ebache* 1268-75 *Red Book MS* (p), 1304 Swin (p).

'Wet stream-valley'.

Ocle Pychard (595462)

> *Aclea* 1017-41 Dugdale; *Acla, -e* 1086 DB, 1132-3 *St GC*, 1148-63 Foliot;
> *Akleya* c1230 *StGC*; *Ocle* 1232 Pat; *Hocle* 1265 AD.
> *Acle Pichard(i)* c1179-86 Barrow, 1243 Fees; *- Pychard* 1291 Tax; *Achepichard*
> 1317 Ipm; *Oclepichard* 1336 Ipm; *Okel Pychard* 1346 FA; *Okelpyscharde*
> 1397 VR.
> *Pycherd(e)s Ocle* 1545 HT.

OE *āc-lēah* 'oak wood', a recurring compound which frequently becomes Oakley. Roger Picard had the manor in 1243.

Castleton (**Upper** 594458, **Lower** 594455)

> *Castel(l)* 1100-35 Early Deeds (p); 1385, 1447 *Slocombe* (p), 1512 HT;
> *Castylle* 1420 Capes (p).
> *Castelton* 1547 HT; *Castleton* 1637 Duncumb.

Possibly manorial in origin, taking its name from Roger *Castel* who occurs in a deed relating to the adjacent manor of Much Cowarne. The same surname also occurs in deeds of Pencombe. There is no sign of a castle.

Hillhampton (590474)

> *Hul(l)ampton(e)* 1271 Ex, 1409 AD; *Hulhampton* 1280 AD, 1291 Tax;
> *Hullamton(e)* 1333 Ipm, 1379 AD (p).

'Hill settlement'.

Lyvers Ocle (577464)

> *Acle* 1100 Fr; *Acleya* c1215 BreconC.
> *Acla monachorum de Lira* 1160-70 HDB; *Acle Lyre* 1243 Fees, 1299 Swin;
> *Lyre Acle* 1286 Swin; *Ocle Lyre* 1334 SR; *Oclelere* 1341 NonInq;
> *Lyers Oc(c)le* 1346 Trill, 1520 KPC.

Hugh Donkey gave land in Ocle to the abbey of Lyre in Normandy (Fr).

Monkton Farm (Old Monkton 579454)

> *Acle, -e* 1148-63 Foliot, 1186-98 *StGC*, 1291 Tax; *Aclam* 1219-21 *StGC*.
> *Acle Monachorum* 1160-70 HDB.
> *Acla Priore* c1230 *St GC*.
> *Mounton* 1547 HT.

Walter de Lacy (died 1085) gave land in Ocle to the monks of St Peter at Hereford. St Peter's amalgamated with St Guthlac's in 1143.

❧ ORCOP ☙

Orcop (474263)

> *Orcop(pe)* 1137 AC, 1136-42 Holtzmann, 1168, 1210, 1214 P, 1334 SR, 1341 NonInq; *Horcope* 1198 CartAntiq; *Oretop* 1210-12 RBE; *Orkhope* 1280 Cant; *Arcoppe* 1535 VE.

A compound of *ōra* and *copp*, two terms for hills, the precise meaning of which has not yet been determined. *copp* is a rare element in place-names. It is sometimes used (as in Mow Cop, Cheshire) for hills with a long, narrow summit, and the ridge at whose tip Orcop is situated is of this kind. The term is predominantly a southern one, cf. the discussion of Bradnor in Kington.

❧ ORLETON ☙

Orleton (494672)

> *Alretun(e)* 1086 DB, 1243 Fees; *(H)olreton(e)* 1285 Swin (p), 1291 Tax, 1333 Ipm; *Orleton(e)* 1292 QW, 1304 Ipm, 1324 Capes (p), 1357 Ipm; *Erleton* 1431 FA.

'Alder-tree settlement'.

Comberton (495677)

> *Comertown* 1529-30 Court; *Com(er)ton, Cou(er)ton* 1547 HT.

Earlier spellings are needed.

Pembridge (391580)

> *Pen(e)brug(g)e* 1086 DB, 1100 GloucC, 1103 CartAntiq, c1148 (14th)
> Chronicle, 1243 Fees, 1327 Capes, 1328 Banco (p); *Penebrigia* late 12th
> *LeomC*; *Penebrigg(e)* 1275 RH, 1292 QW, 1343 QD, 1346 Capes (p);
> *Pembrug'* 1317 Orig; *Penbregg* 1327 Orog; *Pennebrugge* 1406 BM.
> *Pena Burga* 1096 Fr (p); *Penberge* 1203 P (p).

> Probably 'Pena's bridge'.

Bolton (356536)

> *Boleton* 1292 QW; *Balton* 1591 *Faraday*.

> Probably 'Bola's estate'.

Broxwood, **Court** (360540), **Upper** (365534), **Lower** (366544) and **Nunsland** (in Weobley 379539)

> *Brokeswo(o)de* c1250-72 AcornC, 1339 Ipm; *Brockwoode* 1272 Abbr;
> *Brockeswode* 1304 Ipm; *Brockeswade* 1334 SR.
> *Brokkeswode Power* 1351 Pat.
> *Broxcarworthes* 1540 HT.

> Probably 'badger's wood'. Hugh *le Pouwer* had lands at Broxwood Court in 1304(Ipm). The Mortimers gave lands in Broxwood to the nuns of Limebrook, and these became known as Nunsland.

Leen Farm (383591)

> *Lene* late 12th *LeomC*; *Leone* 1334 SR; *Leoue* 1529-30 Court; *Lean* 1540 HT.
> *Lene juxta Penebrugge* 1310 Swin.

> From the pre-English district name, see District Name Leen.

Marston (365576) and **Upper Marston** (358582)

> *Mer(e)eston(e)* 1086 DB, 1176 P, 1221 Rolls, 1250 Fees; *Merstun(e)* 1250
> Fees(p), 1270 AD; *Mers(c)hton(e)* 1292 QW, 1326 Ipm, 1327 Capes (p);
> *Marshton* 1334 SR.

> 'Marsh settlement'.

Milton House (386610)

> *Mildetune* 1086 DB; *Middetun'* 1243 Fees; *Middelton* 1316 FA; *Myddelton'*
> 1334 SR.

'Middle settlement', perhaps referring to the position halfway between Shobdon and Staunton on Arrow.

Moorcot (356557)

> *Mor(e)cote* 1160-70 HDB, 1334 SR, 1591 *Faraday*; *Mor(e)cott* 1619 *Faraday*.

'Marsh cottage(s)'. *mōr* sometimes refers to less valuable wet land than *mersc* (in Marston) above. Moor Court, nearby, is probably a deliberate corruption of Moorcot.

Court of Noke (372596)

> *Alac* 1086 DB; *Le Aka* 1286 Ch; *Akes* 1334 SR; *(La) Noke* 1334 Ch, 1355,
> 1382 Ipm, 1397 VR, 1529-30 Court, 1591 *Faraday*.

'Oak tree'. The name seems to have gone through the same phonological change as Noakes Farm in Bredenbury and almost the same as Knoakes Court in Leominster.

Nokelane Head (363595)

> *Nokeleon* 1594, 1616; *Nokelene* 1615 *Faraday*.

The early name appears to be the district-name Leen with the name of Noke manor prefixed. The compound was perhaps interpreted as the name of one of the footpaths which meet here.

Rowe Ditch (382580, etc.)

> *Rogedich, Rugedich* 1219 InqMisc.

'Rough ditch'.

Strangworth Farm (343589)

> *Nether -, Overstrangeford* 1442 Land of Leen.

An interesting occurrence of the rare place-name element *strang*, modern *strong*. The reference here will be to the flow of water over the ford, which is at the place called Ford on the OS map (344593) and which is possibly the *Myle ford* of a charter of 958 (BCS). *–ford* is fairly frequently corrupted to *–worth* (as at Longworth in Lugwardine. There is a modern Strangford in Sellack.

Weston (367564) and **Westonbury Farm** (372567)

Weston' et Bury 1334 SR; *Weston and Burie* 1569 *Faraday*; *Bury* 1833 OS.

'West settlement' (i.e. from Pembridge). Westonbury contains *byrig* in its late sense 'manor house'.

The Yeld (345585)

(La) Held 1328 Banco, 1334 SR; *(Le) Held* 1615, 1619 *Faraday*; *Heeld* 1619 *Faraday*.

OE *helde*, 'slope'.

❧ PENCOMBE WITH GRENDON WARREN ❧

Pencombe (600528)

Pencofan 1017-41 Dugdale.
Pencumb(a) c1115-c25 GloucC, 1160-70 HDB; *Penicombe* c1120-c50 EHC; *Pencoumbia* 1166 REB; *Penc(o)umbe* 1243 Fees, 1300 Ipm, 1341 NonInq, 1342 KPC.

The identification with the 11th century form *Pencofan* is not certain. All other evidence indicates *cumb* 'short, broad valley' as second element. The first element may be OE *pen* 'enclosure'. *Cumb* is a rare element in Herefordshire.

Grendon Warren (at Grendon Court 600548)

Gre(i)ndon' 1204 Cur (p), 1205 Pleas (p), 1317 Ipm.
Greuden 1210 SalopFF; *Grendene* 1224 Cur (p), 1276-82 Cant (p), 1300 Swin; *Grendaine* n.d. AcornC (p).
Grendene Waryn 1291 Tax; *Grandnewaryn* 1341 NonInq.
Grendon(e) Waryn 1316 FA, - *Waren* 1397 VR.

Probably 'green valley', with interchange between *denu* and *dūn* in the second element. A Warin 'of Grendon' was living in 1204, as was another in 1276-82.

Barnstone Farm (581533)

> *Bernes(ton)* 1303-1452, 1447 *Slocombe.*
> *Berneslond* 1359 *Slocombe.*

'Settlement or estate with a barn'.

Durstone Farm (597541)

> *Hurdiston* 1278-9 Early Deeds; *Thourdeston* 1403; *Thorston* 1438 *Slocombe.*

'Thored's estate'.

Fishpool (593530)

> *La Fyshpole* 1316 (p); *Fispol* 1336 (p); *La Fysspole* 1377 PT; *Fyshepole*
>   1437 *Slocombe; Fyschepole* 1486 *Wms.*

There was presumably an artificially-constructed fish-pond.

Gasbage (590522)

> *Garsbache* 1303 *Slocombe.*

OE *bæce* 'stream-valley' (presumably referring to the feature which runs south-east from the farm), qualified by *gærs* 'grass'.

Hennerwood Farm (561537)

> *Hualdeswood* 1236 *StGC; Honalwode* 1385 *Slocombe.*

More forms are needed for safe etymology.

Holly Grove (formerly **Bitterley Hide** 578517)

> *Butterley, Bytherleye* c1340 *Slocombe.*
> *Bitterleyhide* 1447 *Slocombe.*

Perhaps a manorial name, from a family deriving from Butterley in Wacton, a short distance north-east of here. 'Hide' refers to the taxation assessment of the estate.

Maidenhyde Farm (568548)

> *Maidenhide* 1303, *Maydenhythe* 1438 *Slocombe.*

Probably a one-hide estate with a lady owner.

Marsh Court (584520)

> *Merscourt* 1418, *Mersshcourt* 1429 *Slocombe*.

Self-explanatory. A post-Conquest name, as *court* is a French word.

Marston Stannett (571552)

> *Mer(e)stune* 1086 DB; *Merston* 1312 Ipm, 1318 Ipm, 1333 *Slocombe*;
>   *Mariston* 1304 *Slocombe*; *Mershton* 1326 Ipm.
> *Marston Stanward* 1546 HT.

'Marsh settlement'. 'Stannett' is presumably manorial in origin.

Nash Farm (formerly Hyde Ash 577541)

> *Assche* 1318 Orl.
> *Ash Hyde* 1304; *Hyde Ashe* 1305; *Asshehyde* 1361 *Slocombe*.
> *La Nasshe* 1377 PT; *Nassch* 1447 *Slocombe*.

'Ash tree'.

Sidnall (595516)

> *Suden(e)hale* 1100-35 GlouC; *Suthenhale* 1228-43 Patterson; *Suthale*
>   1263 -84 GloucC; *Sothenhale* 1303 Slocombe (p); *Sydenhale* 1312 Swin
>   (p), 1340 Capes (p).
> *Suthendale* 1278-91 Early Deeds.

Sidnall usually derives from *(æt thæm) sidan hale* 'at the wide nook', but in this instance the spellings indicate 'place south of the nook', OE *(bi) suthan hale*.

Sparrington Farm (568538)

> *Spar(e)weton(e)* 1265-72 Duncumb, 1437 *Slocombe*.

'Sparrow settlement'.

Stone (583528)

> *La Stone* 1339 *Slocombe*.
> *Stonhide* 1242 *Slocombe*.

'Stone', perhaps a rocky outcrop.

PENCOYD

Pencoyd (517266)

> *Pencon* 722 AnnCamb; *Pencoyt* 1291 Tax, 1334 SR; *Penncoet* 1397 VR;
> *Pencoid* 1535 VE.

'Wood's end'. This Welsh name has become Penge in Greater London and
Penketh in Lancashire. Another name which may be associated with this land-
unit is:

> *Cil Hal* c555 (c1130) LL.

The bounds of *Cil Hal* c555 (c1130) LL: '*Apalude magno usque adargan-
hell*.' 'From the great marsh as far as the (spring of) Ariannell.' LL equates *Cil Hal*
with Pencoyd, although its reasons for doing so are not clear, and Davies is not
convinced. However, the very brief bounds (brevity denoting an early date) do fit
the topography of the present parish. In the north, at 516274, is a group of houses
called The Marsh lying close to a dried-up meander of the river Gamber. If this
was at one time marshy (as the place-name suggests) then this may be the 'great
marsh' of the bounds. With 'great marsh' in the north, then presumably the feature
called Ariannell lay in the south. This name appears in the bounds (thought to
date from c860) of another estate in LL. This is St Maughan's in Monmouthshire
and it occurs there as *Licat Arganhell* 'spring (or source) of Ariannell', and with
this in mind it seems reasonable to suppose that in these bounds the word *licat*
has been omitted before *Arganhell*. This, therefore, would seem to be the name
of a spring and watercourse on the southern side of the estate, and at 516263 on
the southern boundary of Pencoyd parish there is indeed a spring that gives rise
to a small brook that runs west by south into the Gamber. This brook forms the
southern boundary of Pencoyd, as it probably did for *Cil Hal*.

Lenaston Farm (508272)

> *Hen Lenhic*; *(ecclesiam) Hennlennic super ripam amhyr* c758 (c1130) LL;
> *Hennaston* 1540 HT.
> *Lenniston* 1831 OS.

LL suggests that as Lenaston lies on the banks of the *Amhyr* or Gamber
it could well be *Henn Lennic*, where the first element is Welsh *hen* 'old' and the
second possibly a diminutive of *llan* 'church'. In c758 a certain Catuuth ap Coffro
gave to the Church an estate of three *modii*, that is, *ecclesiam Henn Lennic super
ripam Amyr* 'the church of *Henn Lennic* on the bank of the river Gamber'. A
century later the same three *modii*, *super ripam Amhyr fluminis*, were given by

178

two other men within these bounds: '... *uadam pallan ad fossam, fossa ducente ad cumulum glas, et acumulo Eregione usque ad amyr flumen cum parte illius agri desilua mamilet.*' (From the) ford of *Pallan* to the ditch, and following the ditch to the green mound and from this away as far as the river Gamber, with part of the woodland of *Mamilet*.

If these bounds included Lenaston, then they may have started at a ford across the small brook between Pencoyd and Lenaston that is affluent with the Gamber at Audit's Bridge (505258). The ford may have been at the point where the minor road between Pencoyd and Llanwarne crosses it at 515269. This road may in fact represent the line of the ditch the boundary then follows, passing a burial mound ('green mound'), which perhaps stood at the crossroads at 513272, before descending to the Gamber at 515275. The Gamber was then followed, passed Lenaston, as far as Audit's Bridge, from where the boundary went back up the small brook to the ford. On the other side of the lower reaches of this brook, possibly, stood the estate at Treberon (509259) given to the Church c890: see Treberon in Tretire with Michaelchurch.

In the earlier grant the church of *Hennlennic* is equated with the church of Llanwarne. This, however, seems to be a record of a much later, 11th century, amalgamation of two churches on the Llanwarne site, one dedicated to St Teilo and the other to St Dyfrig, resulting in a church at Llanwarne dedicated to both saints (LL). See Llanwarne. A chapel at Lenaston nevertheless survived into the Middle Ages (Duncumb).

❧ PETERCHURCH ❧

Peterchurch (345385)

Almundestune 1086 DB.

Sancti Petri 1160-70 HDB; *Sancto Petro* 13th AD.
Beati Petri (in Straddele) 1271 Swin.
Pat'church 1291 Tax; *Peterescherche* 1302 Pat; *Petreschirch* (in Straddel) 1341 NonInq; *Petruschirche* 1428 AD.

Almundestune is 'Ealhmund's estate'. The DB estate is annotated *Sancti Petri* in HDB, showing that Peterchurch is its later equivalent. This annotation does not show (cf. Tait in HDB) that the DB estate then belonged to St Peter's Abbey at Gloucester. The church and lands here were given to Great Malvern Priory early in the 12th century and it retained them until the Dissolution. See District Name Straddle. An earlier name for this estate may be:

Mafurn c605, c860 (c1130); *Podum Mafurn* c625, c745 (c1130) LL.

The bounds of *Mafurn* (incomplete) c605 (c1130) LL: '*Mafurn di guar alt rudlan ... dour.*' '(From) Maffrwn to the top of the wooded-slope at the red bank ... Dore'. As with *Garthbenni* or Goodrich, these bounds, even if not complete, are of the brief, early, variety. In the text there is a gap between *rudlan* and *Dour* that suggests one or two words are missing. So the whole may originally have read '(From) Maffrwn to the top of the wooded-slope at the red bank (as far as the) Dore'. *Rhuddlan* ('red bank') may have referred to the summit of the hills east of Peterchurch that separate the Golden Valley from the Wye plain, while the river Dore runs immediately west of the church.

Upper Godway Farm (351405)

> *Beltrou* 1086 DB; *Benitrou* 1160-70 HDB; *Bamptr'* 1213 P; *Bautre* 1232
>   Dugdale.

> *God(e)weye* 1232 Dugdale, c1250, c1265 AD; *Goodway* 1537 Dugdale.

The earlier-recorded name is French *bel trouvé* 'well found', a sort of name which is known to have been occasionally bestowed on monastic properties. *Goodway* is probably a similar name. Lands at *Bautre* were given to Dore Abbey in the 12th century and their grange there was known as Godway Grange. The two places must therefore have lain close to each other – even if they are not alternative names for the same place. See also 'Walterstone' in Vowchurch.

Hinton (341387)

> *Heneton (in Straddele)* 1302 Pat.
> *Hin(e)ton(e)* 1316 FA, - *(in Stradylvale)* 1318-61 Court, 14th AcornC;
>   *Hyniton* 1325 Orl (p), - *(in Stradhull)* 1370 AD (p).
> *Over(e) Hin(i)ton* early 14th AD, 14th AcornC.

'Monastic estate', OE *hīna-tūn*. 'in Straddle Valley (*Stradylvale*)' to distinguish it from other Hintons, of which there are at least four in Herefordshire. See also District Name Straddle.

Lyonshall (355391)

> *Lenhal'* 1160-70 HDB; *Linhale* 1232 Dugdale; *Lynhales* 1316 FA, 1368 AD (p);
>   *Lignhales* 1476 BM; *Lynnallys* 1540 HT.

Probably 'flax nook'. The modern forms suggest there has been association with Lyonshall parish.

(lost, but within the 'fees' of Godway and Wellbrook)

Maudon c1265, 13th AD.

See Mowbach, below.

Mowbach Farm (346394)

Maubache 1232 Dugdale, 13th AD (p), 1334 SR; *Mowbache* 1523 HT.

The *dūn* of *Maudon* and the *bæce* of Mowbach were probably a hill and a stream-valley named with the same qualifying element. The only word suggested by ME *Mau-* is *maga-*, 'stomach'. This is a possible term for the flood-plain of the river Dore.

Snodhill (320403)

Terra de Strada 1127 Regesta; *castellum de Stradel* 1136-48 Brockworth.

Snauthill 1196 P; *Snod(e)hull(e)* c1230 BM, 1250 Ipm, 1275 RH, 1291 Tax, 1305 Ipm, 1341 NonInq, 1431 FA; *Snothulle* 1280 Cant; *Snowdehulle*, *Snowdell* 1397 VR.

Penparke Snothill 1540 Dugdale.

For Snodhill DEPN suggests *snāwede* 'snowy', as first element. The castle is situated on a hill that may well have retained snow longer than in the valley below it.

Henry I gave lands in Peterchurch to Great Malvern Priory and these were called *terra de Strada* when the priory exchanged them for the manor of Hatfield with Roger de Chandos. The Chandoses built a castle on these lands and this was known at first as the 'castle of Straddle' as well as 'castle of Snodhill'.

'Tratlershope' (345377 site only)

Thurlokes(h)op(e) 1217 Bracton, 1243 Fees; *Thorlokeshop'* 1334 SR; *Throllokeshope* 1440 Ipm; *Trilloshope* 1523 HT; *Troloyshop(e)* 1542 HT; *Tratlershope* 1832 OS.

'Thorlac's remote valley'; perhaps originally a simplex name *Hope*, with the personal name (which is of Old Norse origin) prefixed in the late OE or early Norman period.

Urishay Castle (322376)

Alcamestune 1086 DB; *Alch Hemestona* 1160-70 HDB.

Haia 1166 RBE (p), c1212-17 RBE (p); *Haya* 1198 Fees (p).
Haya (H)urri c1200 *LeomC* (p), 1243 Fees; *La Haye Vrry* 1281 Select Cases;
   La Hay Urri 1296 Ipm (p); *Hay Urry* 1325 AD; *Hayuiry* 1334 SR; *Urysay*
   1397 VR; *Urryshay or Hay-Urry* 1399 Ipm (p); *La Hay Urry or Urreyshay*
   1425 Cl.

Alcamestune may be 'Alhhelm's estate. Hay is OE *(ge)hæg* 'enclosure', a term
particularly characteristic of forest areas.

The DB estate is almost certainly the one known later as Urishay. Hugh
Donkey had five manors in the Golden Valley in 1086 – *Beltrou, Wluetone,
Wilmestune, Almundestune* and *Alcamestune. Wilmestone* (Wilmastone) is
the only one to retain its name into the modern era. Of the others, *Beltrou*
can be shown to have been Godway, *Wluetone* Turnastone and *Almundestune*
Peterchurch, leaving only *Alcamestune* unidentified. But in fact it can be readily
identified as the fief at Urishay held by a family taking their name from that
place. At first known simply as 'Hay', it acquired the prefix 'Urry' from the *Urrio*
or *Ulric* 'of the Hay' living in 1136-48 (Brockworth; First Century). See also
'Walterstone' in Vowchurch.

Wellbrook Farm (351384)

Wurkebroc 1214 Cur; *Wirkebroc* 1243 Fees, 13th AD; *Wirkibroc* 13th AD;
   Wyrkebrok(e) 1275 RH, 1334 SR, 1490 Ipm; *Wirkebroke* 1440 Ipm.
Willbrooke 1663 MA.

The first element looks like *geweorc* 'work', sometimes used in place-names
to denote ancient fortifications. A rectilinear earthwork with a mound in the
centre was recorded at the back of the farm in 1922. The mound was demolished
in 1924, when a small flake of prehistoric flint was found beneath it (TWNFC
(1922) & (1924)).

Wilmastone Farm (340401)

Wilmestune 1986 DB; *Wulmestun'* 1243 Fees; *Wylmeston* c1265 AD (p), 1326
   BM, 1334 SR; *Wilmeston* 1278 Ipm, 13th AD; *Wilmarston* 13th AD.

'Wīghelm's estate'.

Peterstow (563249)

> *Lannpetyr* 1045-1104 (c1130) LL.

> *Peterestow'* 1207 Cur (p); *Peterustoye* 1307 Ipm; *Petrestowe* 1341 NonInq.

> 'Church of St Peter' (Welsh) and 'holy place of St Peter' (English).

Everstone (552250)

> *Yevaneston'* 1334 SR; *Evaston* 1443 Ipm; *Evorston* 1488 Ipm.

> Mr Morgan suggests 'settlement of Ieuan', although there may be some influence from the personal name Ifor.

Hendre (551235)

> *Hendre* 1334 SR, 1540 HT.

> A medieval Welsh name which can be translated as 'home farm'.

Wilson (558234)

> *Wilsston* 1505 Duncumb.

> More forms are needed for safe etymology.

𝔰 PIPE AND LYDE 𝔰

Arundel Farm ('Lyde Arundel', 'Lyde Godfrey' 496434)

> *Leode* 1086 DB; *Ludes* 1334 SR.
> *Lud Godfridi* c1225-50 Whitehead; *Luda Godefrai* 1232 AD; *Ludegodefrey*
>   1256 Ex; *Lude Godfrere* 1304 Swin; - *Godefray* 1316 FA; *Luyd Godfrey*
>   1381 QD.

Lyde is a well-evidenced OE stream-name *Hlyde* 'the loud one'. Even today, if one stands on the old bridge carrying the road from Hereford to Leominster over the stream north of Pipe Church, one can hear it chuckling loudly over the rocks and stones below. See also District Name Lyde, page 19.

In 1210-12 this part of Lyde was held by Godfrey of Moreton (RBE): his name may have become attached to it to distinguish it from the other Lydes. A DMV at 498440 and associated motte-and-bailey castle (499441) may mark the original manorial centre of 'Lyde Arundel' (Whitehead; TWNFC).

Lower Lyde Court ('Lyde Saucey' 519439)

Lude 1086 DB; *Liude* 1200 Pleas.
Luda Salcei 1160-70 HDB; *Lude Saucey(e)* 1243 Fees, c1310 *StGC*; - *Sause* 1303 FA.

The manor belonged to Ralph de Saucey in 1086. His family were from La Saussay, near Villers-Bocage, dépt. Calvados (Loyd).

Lower Lyde Farm ('Lyde Mucegros', 'Lyde Beauveys' 515443)

Lude 1086 DB, 1243 Fees; *Luda* 1173 Capes.
Luda Muchegros c1250 Capes; *Lude Muchegros* 1303, 1346 FA; *Luyde Muchegrosse* 1484 QD.
Lude Beaumyes 1316 FA; *Lude Bevis* 1426 Cl.
Netherluyd 1477 AD.

Ralph of Munsley held this part of Lyde in 1173 (Capes) and his daughter married Walter I de Mucegros. The family were from Mussegros, north of Les Andelys, dépt. Eure (Loyd). An heiress of Walter II de Mucegros (died 1237) married into the Beauveys family. They were from Beauvais, dépt. Oise.

Upper Lyde ('Lyde Prior' 497445)

Lude(s) 1086 DB, 1148-55 Foliot, 1163-7 *StGC*, 1291 Tax.
Lude Monach' Heref' 1160-70 HDB; - *Monachorum* c1250 Capes.
Ludeloged c1179-86 Barrow.
Lude Prioris 1268 *StGC*; - *Prior* 1316 FA; *Ludepriour* 1327 Banco.

Aubrée de Loges and Gerwy her son gave this to St Guthlac's Priory in 1148-55. –*loged* is probably a corrupt form of their surname, for which see Edvin Loach.

Pipe (502441)

(La) Pipe 1086 DB, c1179-86 Barrow, 1272, 1309 Capes, 1535 VE; *Pipa* 1218-36 AD; *(La) Pypa* c1225 Capes, 1247-72 LostC (p), 1291 Tax.

OE *pipe* 'pipe', perhaps referring to a canalised section of the brook, or some waterworks connected with it.

PIPE ASTON

See page 34.

PIXLEY

Pixley (661388)

> *Picheslai* 1086 DB; *Pykesleye* 1278 Cant, 1291 Tax, 1341 NonInq.
> *Picte(le)* 1162 P (p), 1206 Cur.
> *Pikesl(e) Clinton'* 1243 Fees.

DEPN suggests *Peoht* 'Pict' as first element. This was probably a personal name. Simon de Clinton had the manor in 1243 (Fees).

Court-y-Park (647396)

> *Parco* 1243 Fees; *Park* 1316 FA, 1334 SR, 1360 Ipm; *La Parke* 1357 Trill;
> *Part* 1291 Tax.

Welsh *cwrt-y-parc* 'court of the park'.

Mainstone Court (658398)

> *Maineston* 1206 Cur; *Maynestun'* 1243 Fees; *Mayn(e)ston(e)* 1305 Swin,
> 1312 AD, 1360 Ipm, 1377 QD, 1386 AD, 1507 Ipm, 1547 AD; *Mayanston*
> 1545 HT (p).

Probably OE *mægen-stān*, which has given rise to place-names with the same modern form in Devon, Derbyshire, Shropshire and Surrey, and which also occurs in Anglo-Saxon charter boundaries in Devon, Wiltshire and Berkshire. It may be significant that Mainstone Court is on the boundary between Pixley and Munsley.

mægen-stān has generally been translated 'great stone', but there is another possible explanation for Mainstone in Shropshire, where a small boulder, preserved in the church, was used by young men for trials of strength. 'Strength stone' is a possible translation, with OE *mægen* having the sense which it retains in the modern phrase 'might and main'.

Preston on Wye (383424)

> *Prest(r)etune* 1086 DB, c1175 Capes; *Presteton'* 1176 P; *Pruston* 1196 Cur;
> *Preston(a)*, *-(e)* 1252 Capes, 1291 Tax, 1375 Capes.
> *Prestone super Weye* 1221 Capes; *- super Waiam* 1437 Ipm.
> *Prestone Superior.*

'Estate of the priests'. '- Superior' to distinguish it from the smaller estate at Preston Wynne (Preston 'Inferior') that also belonged to Hereford Cathedral. Another place-name associated with this estate is:

> *Tir Conloc*; *agri Conloc* c575 (c1130) LL.

The location of *Tir Conloc* is given in LL as '*super ripam Gui infra insulam ebrdil usque Cumbarruc ynis stratdour*' or 'on the banks of the Wye within Efrdyll's Island as far as *Cum Barruc* in the vale of the Dore'. *Tir Conloc* was therefore on the Wye and not too far distant for an estate of reasonable size to have stretched as far as the hills separating the Golden Valley from the Wye plain. The places that would fit this sort of location most easily are Bredwardine, Moccas and Byecross, but as these appear elsewhere in LL it is unlikely to be them. Probably, therefore, LL is right in identifying it (tentatively) with Preston on Wye, the next place on the Wye closest to those hills. Egerton Phillimore agrees with this location (Owen's Pembrokeshire). Davies, however, locates it at Madley, but this is not *super ripam Gui*'. For 'Efrddyl's Island', see Madley and District Name Mawfield.

Bellamore (394406)

> *Bellimore* 1316 FA; *Bel(l)ymare* 1334 SR, 1388 Ipm, 1437 Ipm.

The *-a-* of *-mare* in all four spellings (1316, 1334, 1388 and 1437) indicates that the second element is likely to be *mere* 'pond', nor *mōr* 'marsh'. Norman-French clerks fairly frequently wrote *-mare* for *-mere*. The first element is probably *belg* 'bag', used occasionally in place-names of distinctively-shaped valleys or hollows.

Byecross(?)(375424)

> *Bolcros* c610, c620 (c1130); *Bolgros* c625, c745 (c1130) LL.

Bolcros lay near Moccas – the preamble of king Gwrfodw's grant of *Bolgros* says that it lay *super ripam guy eminus mochros*, 'on the banks of the Wye not far from Moccas' – and Byecross, even if it is not a form of *Bolcros*, seems a likely location. *Bolcros* is probably Welsh *bol* 'swelling, bulge, lump' and *rhos* 'promontory', and possibly refers to the twisting course of the Wye round two promontories between Moccas and Preston-on-Wye. It was the site of a monastery, an abbot occurring c620 and c625.

Huntley (384414)

> *Huntelaw* 1291 Skidmore (p); *Huntelowe* 1379 QD (p); *Henntlowe* 1379 PT;
> *Hontelowe* 1422-61 AD;
> *Hunt Low* 1663 MA.

'Huntsman's tumulus'; *Hunta* may be a personal name.

Ploughfield (385416)

> *(burgus de) Ploufeld* 1273 Capes, 1415 QD; *Plowfeld* 1345 Trill, 1545 HT.

Probably 'open land where sports are held', first element OE *plaga* 'play'. For the development to *Plow-*, cf. Vowchurch, from *fāg*. The bishops of Hereford had a small borough here. (There is no Ploughfield in Peterchurch as PNHe says.)

PRESTON WYNNE

Preston Wynne (559466)

> *Prestetune* 1086 DB; *Preston(e)* 1210-12 RBE, 1282 Swin, 1316 Ipm, 1334 SR;
> *- Inferior* 1316 FA.

'Estate of the priests'. Preston Wynne was Preston 'Inferior' to Preston on Wye's 'Superior'. Dionisia Wynne had this manor in 1303 (FA).

PUDLESTONE

Pudlestone (565598)

> *Pillesdun(e)* 1086 DB; *Pullesdone* 1211-12 RBE.
> *Putlesdun(a)* 1123 LeomC, 1158-61 Foliot; *Putelesdon'* 1209 P; *Putlesdon(e)*
> 1211-12 RBE (p), 1291 Tax; *Pitlesdon* 1220 Cur (p); *Pudlesden* 1221
> Cur (p); *Pud(e)lesdon(e)* 1222 Cur, 1291 Tax, 1334 SR; *Pudleston* 1287
> Ipm; *Puddelisdone* 1307 Ipm.

'Mouse-hawk's hill', OE **Pyttelesdun.*

187

Brockmanton (at Manor Farm 549594)

> *Brochemt'* 1086 DB; *Brocmanetun* 1123 *LeomC*; *Brokmenton'* 1137-9 HDB; *Brocmant(ona)* before 1160/70 *LeomC*, 1243 Fees; *Brockmonton* 13th KPC(p); *Brockmanton(e)* 1303 FA, 1334 SR.

'Settlement of the men by the brook'.

Ford Abbey (563585)

> *Ford* 1123 *LeomC*; *(La) Forda* 1158-61 Foliot, early 13th *LeomC*; *Le Foorde* 1577 KPC.

'Ford'; the Humber Brook was perhaps more of an obstacle than it appears on modern maps. 'Abbey' because it belonged to Reading Abbey, mother-house of Leominster Priory.

Whyle (558608)

> *Huilech* 1086 DB; *Whiale* 1123 *LeomC*; *Whilai* c1150 Capes; *Wielai* 1160-70 HDB; *Wihale* 1158-61 Foliot; *(Le) W(h)ile* 1211-12 RBE, late 13th BM, 1341 NonInq, 1354 Ipm, 1431 FA; *Wyle(y)* 1220 Cur, 1243 Fees, 1287 Ipm, 1303 FA, 1307 Ipm; *Whyle* 1334 SR.

The spellings indicate that this is a compound name with *lēah* 'wood, clearing' as final element. The first element is unexplained. The forms suggest **Hwi* or **Hwig*, but no such term is known.

❧ PUTLEY ☙

Putley (646376)

> *Poteslepe* 1086 DB.
> *Putteleghe* 1158-65 LostC; *Putelega* 1174-88 WalkerSC; *Puttesl'* 1205 P; *Putelehe* 1219 Capes; *Potteleye* 1291 Tax; *Putteley(e)* 1327 Banco, 1334 SR, 1362 St Katherine.

Probably 'hawk clearing'; Putta may be a personal name.

❧ CANON PYON and KING'S PYON ☙

Pyon (unassigned)

> *Pionia(m)* before 1066, c1200, 1219 Capes, 1240 Dugdale, 1294 Orig; *Peune, Pione* 1086 DB; *Pyonia* 1256 BM, 1273 Capes, 1291 Tax; *Pyon(i)e* 1230-4 Capes, 1292 QW, 1320 Capes.

Canon Pyon (450492)

> *Piona Can'* 1160-70 HDB, *Pyone Canonicorum* 1221 Capes; *Pyonia Canonicorum* 1316 FA, 1400 KPC.
> *Pionia Majori* 1246 Capes; *Pyonyia Majori* 1291 Tax.
> *Pionia Parva* 1256 Capes; *- Stephani* 1294 Swin.

King's Pyon (438506)

> *Pion(i)a Regis* 1160-70 HDB, 1291 Tax; *Pyonia* Regis 1397 VR.
> *Pyonia Eschetot* c1250 Roderick.
>
> *Kyngisfenne* c1280 Croft; *Kyngespanne* 1312 Orig; *Kyngespewne* 1535 VE.

DEPN suggests 'island of the gnats', OE *pēona ēg*, and no alternative etymology is to hand. The frequent *–ia* of the spellings may be a Latinisation, due to ecclesiastical influence. OE *ēg*, most characteristically used of slightly raised areas in marshland, is also used of high sites surrounded by marsh or by streams; Kersey in Suffolk is a clear instance. Pyon Hill could have been seen as an 'island'.

Canon Pyon belonged to the canons of Hereford Cathedral. The location of 'Parva Pyon' and 'Pyon Stephen' within Canon Pyon is not known. King's Pyon belonged to the king before 1066. Richard de Esketot held King's Pyon under the Lacys in 1160-70. His family was from Ectot, near Villers-Bocage, dépt. Calvados (Loyd).

Brook House (438508)

> *Brocpyon* c1270 Rawlinson.

Butthouse (441488)

> *Burthulse* 1350 Dugdale; *Buttas* 1638 MB, 1832 OS.

> *Villa Wallensica* c1250-71 Roderick.

> *Welkeslece* 1275 RH.

More spellings are needed for Butthouse, although it may be Welsh *betws* 'chapel' in view of the presence of a colony of Welshmen here in the 13th century. More forms would be needed, however, to confirm this. *Villa Wallensica* or 'settlement of the Welshmen' stood on *Walschebrok* (c1200 Dugdale), which is the brook running south of Butthouse to Canon Pyon and beyond, and below *Akhull* (c1200 Dugdale), which is Butthouse Knapp (440491). This is almost certainly the part of King's Pyon in the hands of Gruffudd ap Maredudd, pretender to the throne of Deheubarth, in 1086. Like *Curdeslege* in Brilley it may well have belonged to his family for a hundred years or more before DB.

(lost, but in Canon Pyon)

> *Gorewell(e)* 1230-4 Capes, 1291 Tax; *Gorwalle* 1535 VE.

> Possibly 'dirty spring'.

Lawton's Hope (472503)

> *Lautoneshope* 1355 Trill.
> *Parvam Hope* 1304 Swin.

Hope is the regular term for the settlement which nestles in the recesses round the edge of the Dinmore massif. Adam of Lawton had 'Little Hope' in 1304 and John of Lawton 'Lawton's Hope' in 1355.

(Westhope 464511)

> *Smetheleye* 1247 Ipm; *Smithlee* 1655 (TWNFC, 1939).

'Smooth clearing'. According to Silas Taylor, writing c1655, Westhope was the site of *Smithlee* 'locally pronounced Smirley' (TWNFC (1900)).

RICHARD'S CASTLE

Richard's Castle (484702)

See DEPN for forms. Named from Richard Scrope, who was a landholder in Herefordshire in the time of Edward the Confessor and who may have built the castle. Most of the parish of Richard's Castle is now in Shropshire.

Bilbury (494682)

Billebury 1373 QD.

Probably 'Billa's manor house'.

RODD, NASH AND LITTLE BRAMPTON

Little Brampton (304614)

Bruntune 1086 DB; *Brontona* 1160-70 HDB.
Brom(p)ton 1287 Ipm, 1292 Subs, 1307, 1376 Ipm.

'Broom settlement'. 'Little' to distinguish it from Brampton Bryan.

Nash (309624)

Essis 1244 Inspeximus; *La Ayse, (La) Asshe* 1287, 1307 Ipm.
Nasche 1239 Ch; *Nash* 1355 Ipm.

'Ash-tree', with *N*- from ME *atten* 'at the –'.

Rodd (322627)

(La) Rode 1220 Cur, 1244 Inspeximus, 1304 Ipm, 1355 Ipm (p).

'Clearing', OE *rodu*.

Bradleys Cottage (321617)

Bradelege 1086 DB; *Bradel(egh)* 1251 InqMisc, 1265 Cl (p).

'Broad clearing'.

ROSS ON WYE

Ross on Wye (598241)

DEPN suggests Welsh *rhôs* here means 'hill', but 'promontory' would suit the site better.

Alton Court (605234)

Aleton(e) c1215 Capes, 1228 Hart; *Aletunes (Broc)* 1282 Grundy.

Possible 'Ælla's estate.

Cleeve Farm (590235)

Clive 1086 DB; *Cliue* 1199 Cur; *Cliua* 1163-86 Dugdale; *Cleve* 1307 Ipm;
  (Le) Clyve 1334 SR, 1413 Ipm.

'Cliff', here used of a low bank overlooking the flood-plain of the Wye.

Over-ross (607235)

Uverores 1210 Cur; *Over Rosse* 1663 MA.

Penyard (618225)

Penthard 1216-72 BM; *Penerd* 1230 P; *Penyard* 1280 Hart, 1300 Swin;
  Peniord 1292 QW; *Penni'd* 1663 MA.
Penyerd Regis 1227 Ch.
Laxpeniard 1228 Hart.

A Welsh name meaning 'high hill'.

Rudhall House (625254)

Rudhale 1364 AD (p), 1396 Ipm (p).

Second element *halh* 'nook'. The first is probably a plant-name, OE *rūde* 'rue' or ME *rud* 'marigold'.

ROWLESTONE

Rowlestone (374271)

> *Rolueston* 1300 Ipm (p); *Rouleston* 1317, 1383 Ipm; *Rol(l)eston* 1338 Larking, 1540 Dugdale; *Rawlston* 1542 HT.

'Rolf's estate'; probably a late manorial name.

ST DEVEREUX

St Devereux (441312)

> *(Ecclesie) Sancti Dubricii* 1279 Cant, 1291 Tax, 1320 Capes, 1428 FA; *Sancto Dubricio* 1353 Trill.

'Church of St Dyfrig'. The modern form is doubtless due to influence from the name of the Devereux family, who were widespread in Herefordshire from soon after the Conquest.

Didley (452322)

> *Dodelige* 1086 DB; *Duddele(ia)* 1166 RBE (p), 1228 Cur (p); *Dod(d)eleye* 1210-12 RBE, 1316 Swin; *Dudele(ye)* 1210-12 RBE (p), 1231-4 Capes; *Duddelegh* 1228 Pat (p); *Dud(d)eley(a)* 1303 FA, 1334 SR, 1431 FA.

'Dudda's clearing'. See also Kenderchurch.

Trelough (432312)

> *Treyloghe* 1335 Charl; *Traillough* 1388 QD.

'Settlement by a pool (or marsh)', from Welsh *tref* and *llwch*.

ST MARGARET'S

St Margaret's (353338)

> *Llanvarged* 1543 HT.

'Church of St Margaret'.

Whitewall Farm (325364)

> *Wythewell* 1232 Dugdale; *Whitewell* 1248 AD; *Wytewell* c1264-c91 AD;
> *Hytewall* 1537 Dugdale; *Whitewall* 1540 Dugdale.

'White spring'.

❧ ST WEONARD'S ☙

St Weonard's (496244)

> *Lann Santguainerth* 1045-1104 (c1130) LL.
> *Sancti Wenarch* 1143-55 BreconC; *Sancti Waynard* 1291 Tax; *Sancto*
> *Waynardo* 1320 Orl; *Sancti Warnardi* 133- Capes; *- Waynardi* 1356 Capes;
> *Seint Waynard* 1341 NonInq; *S'c'i Waynardi* 1535 VE.

'Church of St Gweinardd'.

Llanfernach (510233 – **Llangunnock** on modern OS maps, but Llanfernach on
the 1831 OS Map.

> *Llanfirnach* 1815 OS (ex inf. Mr Morgan).

Thomas Wakeman (CBSS notes) thought this might be named from the
Mainerch ap Milfrit who gave the local bishop an estate situated on the Gamber
c855 (LL). However, Mr Morgan thinks it is more likely to be 'church of Bernach',
a name thought to be a variant of Brynach.

Penrose Farm (482218)

> *(capella de) Penros* 1397 VR; *Penrose* 1525 HT.

A Welsh name, perhaps to be construed as 'top of the promontory'.

Rhydicar (482248)

> *Rydekyr* 1313 Duncumb.

Mr Morgan suggests 'ford of the carts or sledges', from Welsh *rhyd* with the
definite article and *ceir*, plural of *car*.

Treago (490239)

> *Treyago* 1578 Charles, 1599 BM.

> Welsh *tref* plus the personal name Iago.

Treferanon Farm (471245)

> *(capella de) Treferanon* 1397 VR; *Trevraneth* 1524 HT.

> *Tref* plus an unidentified personal name.

Velindra (494225)

> *Velyndre* 1488 Ipm; *Phelyndrey* 1579 AD.

> Welsh *melin-dref* 'mill village'.

❧ SALTMARSHE ☙

Saltmarshe Castle (671572)

> *Sautemareys* 1316 Cl; *Sautmersh* 1415 Ipm; *Santmarshe* 1433 Ipm. *(Norton) Saltmarshe* 1501 Ipm.

'Salt marsh'. It lies close to the township of Norton-by-Bromyard. DEPN's references under this place-name are to the family of Saltmarsh, of Saltmarsh in Henbury, Gloucestershire.

❧ UPPER SAPEY ☙

Upper Sapey (682636)

> *Sapina* 1180 P; *Sapy* 1210-12 RBE, 1221 Cur, 1282 Swin (p), 1291 Tax, 1341 NonInq, 1397 VR; *Sapi* 1256 Salop Eyre.

DEPN suggests a stream-name, from OE *sæpig* 'full of sap'. Lower Sapey is in Worcestershire.

Sarnesfield (374509)

> *Sarne(s)feld(e)* 1086 DB, 1199 Pleas (p), 1291 Tax, 1324 ReadingC (p),
> 1331 AD; *Serne(s)feld* 1123 *LeomC*, 1158-63 LostC (p); *Cernef(f)eld*
> 1166 RBE (p), 1265 Cl (p); *Senesfelda* 1198 Cur (p); *Sarnusfeuld* 1220
> CMAD (p); *Saresfeld* c1252 IrishC; *Serenfeld* c1260 RATD (p).
> *Sarnesfeud Philippi* 1243 Fees.
> *Sarnesfeld Water* 1493 Ipm.

'Open land by a road', a hybrid Welsh/English name. The road concerned was a Roman one (now the A4112) which passed right by the church. The 1243 form may be from Philip of Sarnesfield, who then had the manor, or an earlier Philip living in 1148-63 (Foliot). 'Wa(l)ter' is presumably another member of the family. Another part of Sarnesfield, 'Sarnesfield Roger', lies at Little Sarnesfield in Weobley (which see). There were also 'Middle Sarnesfield' in Weobley (now The Dairy House: 382514) and Hyatt Sarnesfield in Norton Canon (380500). Richard Hyatt of Sarnesfield was sheriff of Herefordshire in 1601 (Robinson). Sarnesfield was evidently an estate of considerable extent.

Hallaston (362407)

> *Halewarston* c1306 AD; *Holaston* 1545 HT.

The first element may be a personal name, but more spellings are needed.

Woodmanton (369505)

> *Wodemanton* c1306 AD; *Wodemanten'* 1359-60 *KinRR*; *Wodemonton'* 1379
> PT (p).

'Woodmen's settlement', a variant of the recurrent name Woodmancote. There is another Woodmanton in Yarkhill.

Sellack (566277)

> *Lann Suluc* c866, 1045-1104 (c1130) LL.
> *Sellak* 1344 Charl, 1397 VR; *Sellek* 1535 VE; *Sellick* 1654 BM.

The church is today dedicated to St Tysilio, the chief saint of Powys. Mr Morgan doubts whether the parish name is derived from a postulated hypocoristic version of his name (*Ty-suluc or *Ty-sulio), as DEPN suggests.

Baysham (573276)

> *Baissan* 1086 DB, 1251 Capes; *Bay(e)sh(a)m* 1134-9 Barrow, 1148-55 Foliot, 1306 Swin (p), 1325 Ipm, 1441 Pat; *Bais(s)am* 1273 Capes; *Beisham* 1176 P, 1208 Cur (p); *Beissam* 1179 P; *Be(y)sham* 1207 Cur(p), 1230 P, 1246 Capes; *Beyssam* 1216-72 BM; *Bays(s)am* 1252 Capes, 1285 Ipm, 1294 Capes; *Baisham* 1252, 1273 Capes, 1322 Orl, 1510 Ipm.

'Land in a river-bend belonging to Bæg'. On topographical grounds the generic is likely to be *hamm*, though none of the spellings points specifically to this.

Caradoc Court (559276)

> *Cayrcradok* 1293 Ipm; *Kari Craddok* 1308 Ipm; *Caer Caradock* 1334 QD; *Cartodok* 1334 Charl; *Kaercradok'* 1334 SR; *Kaire-Cradock* 1488 Ipm; *Crocradocke* 1540 HT.

Duncumb says that in the vicinity of Caradoc Court is 'an ancient encampment which gives its name to the locality. It is supposed to have been constructed by the Silures under Caratacus when resisting the Roman invasion. Another tradition calls it the castle of 'Caradog Vreichvras, Knight of the Round Table.' There is no trace today of any fortification of the site, and the reference may be to the hillfort at Gaer Cop in Hentland, within whose territory Caradoc Court may have come (Stanford). Caradog Vreichvras ('Strong Arm') appears in many Arthurian romances under various guises. In the 12th century 'Lives' of St Tatheus and of St Padarn, however, he is a king in Gwent (VSBG). He seems to have been a real 5th-century character that may once have ruled over Archenfield and Gwent (Chadwick). Craddocke or 'Sir Cradoc', who is the hero of the early English ballad called 'The Boy and the Mantle' and whom Robinson connects with this place, is the same person. In his mythical aspect he is probably a version of Nodens or Nuadu Argetlam ('Silver Arm'), the Irish god worshipped at the Lydney Roman temple. He had a silver arm made to replace one lost in battle, the principal characteristic of this new arm being that it was stronger than the one it replaced.

The Grove (557260)

> *La Grave* 1279 Cant, 1291 Ch; *Grava* 1334 Charl.

'Grove'.

Pengethley (543257)

> *Penkelle* 1334 Charl; *Penkelly* 1540 HT.

A Welsh name meaning 'place at the head of the grove', probably referring to the same area of woodland as The Grove.

Strangford (584282)

> *Strangef'* 1160-70 HDB; *Strang(e)ford(e)* 1229 Pat (p), 1443 Cl; *Strongeford(e)* 1242 GloucC, 1278 Ipm; *Strengeford* 1272 StGC.
> *Stranguard Ford* 1763 FFW.
>
> *Capulfford* 1410 Ipm.

'Ford through a strong current'. There was another 'Strangford' (now Strangworth) in Pembridge. The late Mrs Elizabeth Taylor of King's Caple said that this ford was also known as 'Caple Ford'.

❧ SHOBDON ☙

Shobdon (401629)

> *Scepedune* 1086 DB; *Skopindona* 1143-8 WalkerCh (p); *Sopedun'* 1200 Pleas (p).
> *Sob(b)edona* 1160-70 HDB, 1291 Tax; *Sobbedune* 1243 Fees;
>   *Schob(b)edon(e)* 1291 Tax, 1346 KPC (p), 14th Chronicle; *Shob(be)don(e)* 1328 Banco (p), 1334 SR, 1535 VE; *Schebbedon* 1369 BM.

'Sceobba's hill'. Shobdon Court stands on the type of hill which is often called *dūn* in place-names.

Easthampton (406630)

> *Esthamptone* 1278 Cant.

'East settlement' (in relation to Shobdon).

Ledicot (414620)

> *L(e)idecote* 1086 DB; *Ledicote* 1210 Cur; *Ledkote* 1243 Fees; *Lydecote* 1317 Ipm; *Ledecote* 14th Chronicle.

The first element is obscure, the second element OE *-cot*, 'cottage'.

SOLLERS HOPE

Sollers Hope (612331)

> *hop* 'Valley', see DEPN. For the Sollers family, see Bridge Sollers.

STANFORD BISHOP

Stanford Bishop (682516)

> *Stanforde* 1174-86 Capes (p).
> *Stanford Superius* 1243 Fees.
> *Stanford(e) Episcopi* 1316 FA, 1334 SR, 1397 VR.

'Stone ford'. The ford from which this place, 'Stanford Faucon' (below) and 'Stanford Regis' (King's Stanford) in Bishop's Frome were named is across the Frome at 671502, now replaced by a bridge. 'Superior' to distinguish it from 'Little Stanford' or 'Stanford Faucon'.

Court Farm ('Stanford Faucon', 'Little Stanford' 690517)

> *Stanford* 1086 DB.
> *Stanford Malgerii* 1160-70 HDB; *Stanford' Walteri* 1249 Fees;
>   *Stannfordesfaucon* 1317 Ipm.
> *Parva Stanford* c1267 Swin.

A John Falcon (*ffaukun*) was a citizen of Barton in Hereford c1285 (Red Book). Mauger and Walter may have been members of his family.

Hyde Farm (667521)

> *(La) Hyde* 1274 St Katherine, 1307 Swin (p).

'Estate assessed for taxation as one hide'.

Wofferwood Common (693578)

> *Wafferedwode* c1285 Red Book.

More spellings are needed. The first element might be the ME present participle of the verb *waver*, though this should have given *Waf(f)erend-* not *Waffered*. An element *wæfer* is associated with trees and woods in the place-names Wavertree, Lancashire, and Waverley, Surrey.

⅀⅀ STAPLETON ⅀⅀

Stapleton (325655)

> *Stapleton'* 1207 PatR; *Stepelton(e)* 1259, 1287, 1355 Ipm, 1402 BM;
> *Stepulton* 1399 BM, 1473 BM.

'Settlement on a steep slope', OE **stepel-tūn*. This is also the origin of Stapleton in Shropshire. Other Stapletons are 'post settlement' from OE *stapol*.

⅀⅀ STAUNTON ON ARROW ⅀⅀

Staunton on Arrow (370601)

> *Stantun(e)* 958 BCS, 1086 DB, 1243 Fees; *Stantona* 1175 P (p); *Staundon*
> 1303 FA.
> *Stauntone juxta Pennbrugge* 1397 VR.
> *Nether Staunton* 1305, 1368, 1371 Ipm.

'Settlement on stony ground', a common place-name. 'on Arrow' and '- juxta Pembridge' to distinguish it from Staunton on Wye, though that has a different derivation. 'Nether' because it is on lower ground than 'Over Staunton', now Staunton Park (below).

The bounds of this estate given in a deed of 958 in BCS have been explored in detail by Lord Rennell of Rodd (TWNFC (1959)) and also in ECWM. Nothing new can de added here.

Mowley (335604)

> *Maldelega* 1160-70 HDB; *Malleye* 1277 Cant (p); *Moldeleya* 1287 Ipm;
> *Mallelegh* 1305 Ipm; *Mouldley* 1535 VE.

'Wood or clearing near a domed hill'. This is an interesting addition to the small corpus of place-names containing OE *molda* 'crown of the head', used in a topographical sense.

Staunton Park (361611)

> *Stantune* 1086 DB.
> *Overstanton* 1305 Ipm; *Overstaunton* 1368 Ipm.
> *Staunton Logerous* 1371 Ipm.
> *Stanton Waples* 1558 Old Rectories.

The 1371 suffix is unexplained; the 1558 one presumably refers to Wapley (below). Both 'Over' Staunton and Wapley were in the hands of the lords of Richard's Castle, who made them part of their marcher lordship of Stapleton. The boundary of this lordship divided 'Over' Staunton from 'Nether' Staunton or Staunton on Wye.

Stocklow Manor (371616)

Stocklowe 1305 Ipm; *Stokkelowe* 1334 SR.

'Tree-stump tumulus'. Stockley Cross to the south and Stockley House to the north probably contained Stocklow.

Wapley Hill (346625)

Wapletone 1086 DB; (?)*Walpretone* c1285 Red Book.
Wapelit(h) 1293 Rodd, 1304 Ipm; *Wappelyth* 1305 Ipm; *Wapelethe* 1399
    Ipm.
Wapleys Eaves 1635 *Faraday*.

-lith, later *–ley*, is OE *hlith*, used in Shropshire and Herefordshire for a distinctive type of concave hill-slope. The place-name element *wapol* is variously interpreted as 'marsh' and 'spring'. There was presumably a settlement, since hill-names do not appear in records such as the above references, and the DB form probably represents an alternative name with *tūn* as generic. This settlement may have been at Stansbatch (349612). Stansbatch is the name of the nearby brook (*Tanes bæc* 958 BCS). As a place-name it does not appear to have any antiquity and may have been transferred to the DB settlement in comparatively recent times.

STAUNTON ON WYE

Staunton on Wye (375448)

Standune, Stantune 1086 DB; *Staundun* c1150 StGC; *Standon* 1243 Fees;
    Staundon(e) 1273 Capes, 1315 Ipm; *Staundene* 1355 Capes.
Standon Leurici; *Stand' Mah'* 1160-70 HDB.

'Stone hill', second element *dūn*. '- on Wye' to distinguish it from Staunton on Arrow, though they have different derivations. '- Leofric' refers to the DB holder of the manor and '- Mahel' to Mahel or Matthew du Mans, whose family long held the manor. Neither affix survived into the 13th century.

Letton Court Farm (343461)

> *Over Letton* 1291 Ch.

> See parish name Letton.

✣ STOKE EDITH ✣

Stoke Edith (604406)

> *Stoches* 1086 DB.
> *Edithe Stok(a)* 1160-70 HDB, 1292 QW; *Edithestoc'* 1174-86 Fr; *Edidestoc*
>   c1180-6 Barrow; *Edythestoke* 1314 BM.
> *Stok Edith* 1281 Tax, 1341 NonInq.

OE *stoc* 'dependent settlement'. 'Edith' is the wife of Edward the Confessor, who had this estate before 1066. The affix effectively distinguished it from the other two 'Stokes' in the county, Stoke Prior and Stoke Lacy.

Perton (597404)

> *Pyriton'* 1334 SR; *Pyrton, Piriton* 1372 QD (p).

> 'Pear orchard'.

✣ STOKE LACY ✣

Stoke Lacy (621494)

> *Stoches* 1086 DB, c1174 Capes; *Stoca* 1102-2 Regesta; *Stoka* 1143-8
>   Barrow; *Stokes* c1225 Capes.
> *Hodestoca, Oddestoca* 1216-28 StGC.
> *Stok(e)lacy* 1234-9 GloucC, 1341 NonInq; *Stoke Lacy* 1243 Fees, 1246 Ipm,
>   1291 Tax.

'Dependent settlement'. The Lacy family acquired the manor soon after the Conquest. *Odde-* is probably Odo, their subtenant in 1160-70 (HDB).

Lower Hopton (631493)

> *Hopton Hagurner* 1358 PNHe; - *Habernel* 1373 Ipm; - *Havarnel* 1522 Jones.

'Settlement in a secluded valley'. Hopton Sollers in Avenbury (636496), which is in the same valley (Hopton Dingle), being on much higher ground, was 'Upper' Hopton. The Hagurner or Hagurnel family held this manor under the lords of Brecon (BreconC). Richard Hagurner was living in 1166 (RBE) and Gerald of Wales tells an extraordinary story about Gilbert, Richard's relative, who lived in the lordship of Brecon. See also Munderfield Farm in Avenbury, page 36. For the Sollers family, see Bridge Sollers, page 53.

Mintridge Farm (635525) and **Rough Mintridge** (640541)

> *Munt(e)rich(e)* c1138-c58 *StGC* (p), 1243 Fees, 1262-71 LostC, 1349 AD;
>   *Muntric* 1159-60 *StGC* (p).
> *Muterich* 1283-6 Kirby's Quest (p).
> *Myntrythe* 1377 PT (p).
> *Myntrygge* 1543 HT (p); *Myntredge* 1575-80 Bromyard.

This name is unexplained. The second element looks like OE **ric*, used in place-names of a raised linear feature, sometimes natural (e.g. a glacial morain), sometimes artificial (e.g. the spoilbank of a drainage channel). There is no suitable feature apparent on the map of the area. The first element is unlikely to be Welsh *mynydd*, as that gives ME *Munde-*, not *Munte-*. The spellings suggest OE *myn(e)t*. There is a word *mynet*, which means 'coin', but it is very doubtful whether this would be used in a place-name formation.

❧ STOKE PRIOR ☙

Stoke Prior (520565)

'Dependent settlement'; once in the hands of Leominster Priory.

(at c508572)

> *Folk(eia)* 1186-99, 1216-28 *LeomC*; *Volkeye* 1216-28 *LeomC*.
> *Volca Meadow* 1832 OS.

Perhaps originally a simplex name from OE *ēg*, 'island, raised ground in marsh', with the Old French personal name *Fulco* prefixed.

Wickton Court (523546)

> *Wigget(one)* 1200-13, 1213-26, 1272 *LeomC*; *Wyg(g)eton(e)* 1268-75 *Red Book MS* (p); *Wikton* 1485 Ipm; *Wyckton* 1564 KPC.

'Wicga's estate'. A pool at 527542, south-west of Wickton, is possibly *Wigemere* in 1213-26 (*LeomC*) and not far away is Wig Wood, which is *Wygewod* in 1270 (Ch). Meanwhile, across the Lugg in this vicinity was *Wigheford* (1226 Cur), all of which may be abbreviations for 'Wickton Mere', 'Wickton Wood' and 'Wickton Ford'.

Witsets Farm (533555)

> *Wytese* early 13th *LeomC*; *Witsey* 1261-91 ReadingC.

More spellings are needed for safe etymology.

❦ STRETFORD ❧

Stretford Court (444557)

'Ford by which a Roman road crosses a river' (DEPN), in this case the Stretford Brook.

❦ STRETTON GRANDISON ❧

Stretton Grandison (633441)

'*tūn* on a Roman road', see DEPN. The manor was once in the hands of the Grandison family.

❦ STRETTON SUGWAS ❧

Stretton Sugwas (466429)

> *Stratone, -a* 1086 DB, 1142 Holzmann; *Strattun'* 1198 CartAntiq; *Strat(t)on(e)* 1285 Capes, 1292 QW; *Strettone* 1340 Capes; - *by Sugwas* 1347 AD.

'Settlement on a Roman road'. The bishop of Hereford had two estates within the parish of Stretton – Stretton and Sugwas (now Sugwas Court) – the latter being in his manor of Eaton Bishop in 1086. Sugwas remained in the parish of Eaton Bishop until the late 19th century, long after it had become detached from the manor.

Sugwas Court (454408)

> *Sucwessen* 1086 DB; *Sugwas* 1160-70 HDB, 1292 QW, 1356 Capes;
> *Suggewas* 1506 BM.

Final element OE *wæsse*, used in a group of west midland place-names for land by a meandering river which floods and drains with spectacular speed. Rotherwas, a few miles lower down the Wye in Dinedor, is another Herefordshire example. The first element of Sugwas is probably OE *sucge* 'sparrow'.

ꙮ SUTTON ꙮ

Sutton St Michael (526458) and Sutton St Nicholas (534454)

'South settlement', perhaps so called because it was in the southern part of the district called Maund (see District Name Maund). See also Freen's Court (below), which was 'Sutton Freen'.

Freen's Court ('Sutton Freen' 520459)

> *Mage* 1086 DB; *Magen(a)* 1137-9 HDB, 1185-6 *StGC*.
> *Sutton et Magene* 1243 Fees.
> *Sutton Frene* 1316 FA, 1334 SR, 1376, 1516 Ipm; *Sutton' ffrer'* 1377 PT;
>   *Sutton alias Sutton Frene* 1470-4 Court.
> *Netherfrenescourt* 1419 BM; *Sutton Overcourt* 1452 BM.

Another portion of Sutton. Nigel the Doctor's DB manor of *Mage* was held in 1243 by Hugh de Fresne (or Fraxino) as the manor of *Sutton et Magene* (Fees). The 'Maund' part was then dropped and the family surname added to become 'Sutton Freen'. Eventually the 'Sutton' part was also dropped and the estate divided into 'Over' and 'Nether' portions of 'Freen's Court'.

Sutton Lakes (544469)

See under Marden, page 160.

Tarrington (618407)

> *Tatintune* 1086 DB; *Tadintona* c1135-44 Barrow; *Tatin(g)ton* 1200 Pleas,
> 1246, 1279 Ipm; *Tattindon* 1291 Tax; *Tatynton* 1447-8 Court.
> *Magna Tatynton(e)* 1272-c90 BM, 1303 FA, 1334 SR; - *Tadynton* 1306 Orig.

Probably 'estate associated with *Tāta*', the spellings suggest an *–ingtūn*
formation. The change to Tarrington is analogous to that seen in Dorrington
in Condover, Shropshire, from ME *Dodinton*. In that name the *–r(r)-* spellings
appear in the late 16th century.

Little Tarrington (625413)

> *Parva Tatintune* 1243 Fees.

'Radlow' (c610416)

> *Radelau, Radenelau* 1086 DB; *Radelowe* 1355 Capes.

'Red tumulus', which could be either an ancient burial mound or a mound
constructed to mark a meeting-place. It was the site of one of the DB hundred-
moots. Its approximate position is given in Thorn.

Tedstone Delamere (695586)

> *Chetestor* 1086 DB; *Ketestorna* 1160-70 HDB; *Kedestone, Kedestorhne* 1199
> Cur; *Chesdesthorn* c1200 CRCG (p).
> *Tedestorna, -e* 1160-70 HDB, 1200 Cur; *Teteshorn* 1200 Cur; *Tedestorhna*
> 1216-c40 BM; *Tedesterne* 1271 Swin.
> *Thoddesthorne la Mare* 1243 Fees; *Thedestone la Mare* 1275 RH; *Teddesthorne*
> *Delamare* 1283 Ipm; *Thedest'ne de la Mare* 1291 Tax; *Tedesterne la Mare*
> 1292 QW; *Tedethorne de la Mare* 1296 Ipm; *Tudesternelamare* 1341
> NonInq; *Tedston Delamare* 1373 Ipm.

'Tēod's thorn-tree'. This was a name that French speakers found difficult,
and the earliest forms show a good deal of corruption. It is unlikely that *Tetistorp*
(Testone Wafre, below) is a different name with OE *thorp* 'hamlet' as generic. The
Ch-, K- forms are probably due to a desire to dissimilate the initial consonant from

the following *d* and *t*. The descent of the DB manor of *Chetestor* into the hands of the Delamare family leaves no room for doubt that it is Tedstone Delamere. Robert and Jordan de la Mare were disputing possession of it in 1199 (Cur).

⚜ TEDSTONE WAFRE ⚜

Tedstone Wafre (677591)

> *Tetistorp* 1086 DB; *Thoddesthorne* 1243 Fees; *Tetestern'* 1292 QW.
> *Tedestorna R. Wafr'* 1160-70 HDB; *Teddesthorne Wafre* 1249 Fees; *le Waffre in Tedestherne* 1271 Swin; *Tedesterne Waffre* 1334 SR; *Tedston Wafre* 1373 Ipm; *Tedstern Waffour* 1416 Ipm.

R. Wafr' here in the 1160s is Robert Wafer (*le Wafre*), who also had Hampton Wafre at the same time. See Hampton Wafre.

⚜ THORNBURY ⚜

Thornbury (622597)

> *Torneberie* 1086 DB; *Tornebire* 1181 P; *Thornebir'* 1216 ClR; *T(h)ornebur(i)* c1225 Capes, 1251 Cl; *Tharbury* 1291 Tax; *Thorn(e)bury* 1292 QW, 1382 Ipm.

'Thorn-tree fort'. The estate was probably named from the Iron Age hillfort now called Wall Hills. This is surrounded by a ring of thorn-trees.

Kyrebatch (621612)

> *Cur(e)bache* c1250 KPC (p), 1439 KPC; *Kiere Batch* 1635 KPC.

'Stream-valley of the Kyre'. One of the headwaters of the Kyre Brook rises near here.

Netherwood (633608)

> *Nethewod(e)* 1301 Pat, 1418 KPC; *Nethwode* 1382, 1425 Ipm; *Netherwood* 1586 KPC.

Perhaps '(Place) beneath the wood', later interpreted as 'nether wood'.

Thruxton (437347)

> *Torchestone* 1086 DB; *Turkelestona* 1160-70 HDB; *Thur(c)lestun'* 1243, 1249
> Fees; *Thurkeleston* 1265 AD; *Thurcleston(e)* 1291 Tax, 307 Swin (p), 1341
> NonInq, 1346 FA, 1375 Capes (p); *Throleston* 1373 Ipm; *Thonglestone*
> 1378 Ipm; *Thorcleston* 1381 QD, 1395 Capes, 1428 FA; *Throkeston* 1485
> Ipm.
> *Turneston'* 1243 Fees; *Thornston* 1316 FA.

'Thorkell's estate'. This is likely to be a name of relatively late origin, coined
when Scandinavian personal names were common in the land-owning class.

Titley (331602)

> *Titel(l)ege* 1086 DB; *Titellega* 1123 LeomC; *Titileia* 1147 Fr; *Titele(a)* 1194 P,
> 1292 Subs; *Tyteleye* 1304 Ipm.

Second element *lēah* 'wood, clearing'. The first might be a diminutive, **titel*,
of OE *tit(t)* 'teat, breast', which occur occasionally in place-names. Some of the
hills which surround Titley may have shapes which would prompt an anatomical
allusion.

Titley seems to have been the site of a Welsh religious community in the
pre-Conquest era. According to a Winchester College document there was once a
church dedicated to *Tylliar* or *Tyliard* (clearly a Welsh name, with hypocoristic ti-)
adjacent to what became (after 1120-1) the priory church of Titley (Land of Lene).
And one of the boundaries of Staunton on Arrow in the document of 958 (BCS)
faced a certain *lionhina gamæra* or *leonhina gæmeres*, 'religious community of
Leen boundary', which may refer to Titley.

Eywood (318596)

> *Eiwde* 1130-5 LeomC; *E(i)wda* 1148-63 ReadingC.

'Island wood'. This a noteworthy instance of the occasional use of *eg* for
places in high situations.

Flintsham Farm (320588)

Flintesham(e) 1279 Cant, c1280 *StGC.*

'Flint's enclosure'. Second element *hamm*, here probably used in one of its later senses, 'cultivated plot in marginal land'.

Oatcroft (314597)

Atcroft 1292 Subs (p), 1304 Ipm; *Otecrofte* 1399 Ipm; *Otekrofte (in Lughurnes)* 1481 Howse.

'Oat enclosure'. See also District Name Lugharness.

TRETIRE WITH MICHAELCHURCH

Tretire (520239)

Rythir 1210-12 RBE; *Ryttyr* 1265 Ipm; *Retir* 1276 Cant, 1314 Swin; *Ret(t)yr* 1277 Pat, 1292 Staffs Pleas, 1308 Ipm; *Reyteyr* 1281/2 Abbr; *Ri(c)tir(e)* 1291 Ipm, 1334 SR; *Rit(t)yr* 1291 Tax, 1341 NonInq; *Retbyr* 1292 QW *Ryctir* 1293 Ipm; *Rythyr* 1349 Trill.
Ryguarda 1211-12 RBE (p).

A Welsh name *rhyd-hir*, 'long ford', the ford being where the B4521 crosses the Gamber. The order of elements, with the generic (*rhyd*) first suggests that this is a name coined after the Roman period. *T-* must be a relatively modern addition, probably due to association with *tre* 'homestead'.

Michaelchurch (522255)

Lann Mihacgel cil luch 1045-1104 (c1130) LL.

Mycheleschyrch 1334 SR; *Michelchirche* 1488 Ipm.
S'ti Michaelis 1341 NonInq.

Self-explanatory. *Cil luch* refers to Gillow Manor in Hentland, only a short distance away.

Kilbreece (527235)

Kylbrest' 1334 SR, 1540 HT.

Mr Morgan suggests that Welsh *cil* 'nook' is here qualified by *brisg* 'track, trail'.

Treberon (509259)

Trebereth 1302-3 LWE; *Treberyn* 1334 SR; *Treberen* 1540 HT.

Mr Morgan suggests *tref* + personal name *Peren* or *Beren*. This may be the site of:

Villa Cair Birran c890 (c1130) LL.

The bounds (incomplete) of *Villa Cair Birran* c890 (c1130) LL: '*Oguorlurch iudgual usque adfrut elhaith, hac obrenan picet in ...*'. 'From Guorlwrch Idwal to the stream of *Elhaith*, and from *Brenan Picet ...*'. Arthfael, a king in Gwent, gave four *modii* of land within these bounds to the local bishop. If they were located at Treberon, they will have bordered an estate at Lenaston (*Hennlennic*) in Pencoyd along a short stretch of the small brook ('*Elhaith* Stream'?) that descends from the direction of Pencoyd to reach the Gamber at Audit's Bridge (505258): see Lenaston in Pencoyd. 'Birran's Fort' may have been on the hill now occupied by Trevase Farm.

Trevase Farm (512256)

Trevays 1334 SR, 1540 HT.

Mr Morgan points out that this is *tref* + *maes* 'field'.

❧ TREVILLE ☙

Treville (425324)

Triueline 1086 DB; *Trivel(a)* 1141 Regesta, 1158-9 RBE, 1224 AD, 1227 Ch; *Triuel* 1159 P; *Triveleye* 1211-12 RBE; *Trivell'* 1216 Cl; *Tryvel* 1298, 1364 Ipm.

The name is unexplained. DEPN suggests Welsh *tref* + *melin* 'mill settlement', but this does not suit the forms. It may however be the source of the personal name 'Traveley' that occurs in medieval records for Breconshire and Herefordshire, and which has become the name of a township, Travley or Trafle, in Llowes, Radnorshire (now Powys).

❧ TURNASTONE ☙

Turnastone (358365)

Wluetone 1086 DB.

Tornerieton' 1210 P (p); *Thorneston(e)* 1242 Cur, 1299 Swin; *Thurneistun'*
   1243 Fees; *T(h)urneston(e)* 1243, 1251-2 Fees, 1291 Tax, 1315 Ipm, 1316
   FA, 1334 SR, 1341 NonInq, 1356 Ipm; *Turneyston* 1250 Ipm; *Tornaston(e)*
   1311 Swin (p), 1428 FA; *Turnaston* 1348 Ipm; *Thornastone* 1397 VR.

A manorial name derived from Tournay (*Turuei, Tornai*), the name of the
family who held the DB estate of *Wluetone* ('Wulfa's estate') from at least the 12th
century. The family were from Tournay-sur-Dive, near Argentan, dépt. Orne
(Loyd). Robert de Tournay had *Wluetone* in the 1160s (HDB), but this earlier
estate was probably centred near a chapel of St Leonard at Lower Slough (EpActs;
Swin), rather than at Turnastone. The chapel (now lost) stood at 343357.

❧ TYBERTON ☙

Tyberton (380399)

Tibrintintune 1086 DB; *Tibritona* 1160-70 HDB; *Tybyrtone* c1218 Capes;
   Tyberton(e) 1279 Cant, 1324 Capes, 1327 Banco, 1428 FA; *Tebrychton*
   1281 Select Cases; *Tybreton* 1291 Tax; *Tib(b)erton(e)* 1300 Swin (p),
   1325 QD.

Most of the spellings indicate 'Tīdbeorht's estate', a name which has become
Tibberton in Gloucestershire and Shropshire. The absence of genitival –*s*- is
characteristic in compounds of *tūn* with personal names ending in –*beorht*. The
DB form, however, may indicate an original *Tīdbeorhtingtūn*, which is the OE
form of Tibberton in Worcestershire.

❧ ULLINGSWICK ☙

Ullingswick (597500)

Ullingwic 1086 DB; *Olingewiche'* c1127 AC; *Ullingwika* 1167 GlouC;
   Ollingewike 1188-1205 GloucC; *Ullingwike* 1210-12 RBE; *Elli'gwyk'* 1261
   Patterson; *Ullyngwick* 1292 QW; *Ullynchwyke* 1397 VR.

'Dairy farm associated with Ulla', OE *Ullingwīc. DEPN gives two forms (*Willyngwiche* 1167 and *Wylynwyche* c1200) from GloucC, but these are 14th century forms of the 1167 form given above and of a similar one dating from 1192.

Broxash (603507)

Brockeshes 1186 GloucC; *Brockes esse* 1243 Fees; *Brockeshashe* 1316 FA.

'Brocc's ash-tree'. This was the site of one of the late medieval hundred-courts.

ৡ৵ UPPER SAPEY ৵ৡ

See page 195.

ৡ৵ UPTON BISHOP ৵ৡ

Upton Bishop (650273)

Uptune 1086 DB; *Uptona, -e* c1200, 1226-30, 1246 Capes; *Huptona* 1200-19 Capes, *Huptun'* 1243 Fees; *Upton(e)* 1334 SR.

'Higher settlement'. The relationship is probably to Ross on Wye. These places, together with Walford, were part of the land at Ross that king Edmund Ironside gave to the bishop of Hereford in 1016 (ECWM).

Coldborough Park Farm (636288)

Calcheberge 1086 DB; *Calkeberga* 1160-70 HDB; *Cakeberge* c1215 Capes; *Kaukeberge* c1250 Capes (p); *Caleberg* 1302 Swin.
Calberue 1226-30 Capes (p); *Calkebarwe* 1292 QW; *Calbar(e)we* 1303, 1346 FA; *Caldebarewe* 1428 FA.
Kalkeb(rigge) 1200-19 Capes (p), c1234-9 StGC (p); *Calkebrigg* 1239 Capes (p).

'Chalk hill', from OE (Anglian) *calc* and *beorg*.

Gayton (631266)

Gayton(e) 1220-4 StGC (p), 1230-4 Capes (p), 1348 Trill; *Gaitun'* 1233 Barrow; *Kayton* 1547 HT.

This name is an addition to the corpus discussed in DEPN under Gayton. Gayton le Wold in Lincolnshire is a Scandinavianised form of OR *gāt-tūn* 'goat settlement', but there are several other Gaytons which cannot be explained in this way, and these and the few names with other generics indicate a place-name element *Gǣge, Gǣga*. A stream-name *Gǣging* is the source of Ginge, Berkshire. *Gǣge* may have been a name for a winding stream, derived from the verb *gǣgan* 'to turn aside'. This would suit the stream that rises near Gayton Hall. But there is a well-documented meadow-name, The Gay in Shrewsbury, and Jay on the Shropshire/Herefordshire border is earlier *Gay*, so there may be an as-yet-unidentified noun which could be used as a simplex place-name as well as being a qualifying element.

Tedgewood (663272)

> *Ted(d)eswode* 1155 (1291) Swin, 1316 Pat.

'Tēod's wood'. The development of *Tedes-* to Tedge- can be paralleled in several names. Mudgley in Somerset, for example, was *Mudesle* in the 12th century.

❧ VOWCHURCH ☙

Vowchurch (362365)

> *Fow(e)chirch(e)* 1291 Tax, 1294 Swin, 1316 FA; *Fowechurch* 13th AcornC, 1358 Court; *Fowechyrch* 1334 SR; *Fou(e)chirch(e)* 1341 NonInq, 1428 FA; *Vowechurche* 1397 VR, 1508 Ipm; *Fowerchurch (and the Moore)* 1573 DM.

'Multi-coloured church'. 'The Moore' is a former name for White House in St Margaret's (349357).

Chanstone Court Farm (364356)

> *Elnodestune* 1086 DB; *Elnodestona* 1160-70 HDB; *Alnatheston* 1201 Abbr; *Elnotheston* 1206 Cur (p); *Auleneston'* 1207 Cur; *Eylnathestona* 1224 Bracton.

> *Chenestun'* 1243 Fees; *Cheyn(e)ston(e)* 1303 FA, 1334 SR, 1346 FA, 1356 Ipm, 1508 Ipm; *Cheynest(re)* 1317, 1336 Ipm; *Cheineston* 1428 FA.

Elnodestune ('Ægelnōth's estate') is an earlier name for the estate that became Chanstone. Chanstone is probably a late manorial name with the French surname Cheney. A Laurence *Canuti* or *Chanu*, who appears in 1207 in association with *Auleneston'*, may be a member of this family.

(lost, but possibly at or near The Yewtree 395361)

Fookesyate 1300 Ipm; *Fokefyn* ... 1302 Cl; *Foukesyate* 1391 Ipm.

Second element OE *geat* 'pass through hills', the pass in question being the place where the B4348 road goes through the hills dividing the Wye plain from the Golden Valley at The Yewtree and Blackhole. The first element is from a man called Fulk whose son Richard appears in 1196 and 1224 (Cur) in association with Monnington Straddle (below). His descendants used his Christian name as a surname. In 1243 Richard Foukes's portion of the manor of Monnington Straddle is called *Asse* ('ash-tree') but in 1303 *Fookesyate*. A Hugh *atte Yate* occurs in 1350 (Trill).

Monnington Straddle (Monnington Court 383368)

Manetune 1086 DB; *Monitone* 1220 Cur (p); *Monitun'* 1249 Fees; *Monyton* 1334 SR.
Monintona 1160-70 HDB; *Monintun* 1243 Fees.
Molitone 1224 Cur.

Monynton in Straddel 1300 Ipm; *Monyton Straddel* 1316 FA; *- in Stradhull* 1376 Ipm.

'Communal estate'; see also Monnington on Wye and the lost 'Monnington' in Ewyas Harold. For *Straddel* see District Name Straddle.

Poston Court Farm (352372)

Poscetenetune 1086 DB; *Pos(s)inton* c1132 EpActs, 1137-9 HDB; *Puscetone* 1224 Cur; *Puscytone* 1232 Dugdale; *Pustune* 1249 Fees; *Puscetun* 1264-9 AD (p); *Po(u)ston'* 1316 FA, 1379 PT; *Puston'* 1334 SR, 1373 InqMisc.
Pocintona W. Huard 1160-70 HDB.
Puston in Straddel 1300 Ipm.
Putston 1377 PT.

The DB spelling suggests a formation with *–sǣte* 'inhabitants'. There is a series of *–sǣte* names along Offa's Dyke in Shropshire and Herefordshire, and Poston could be a *tūn* in the territory of one of these units. But the first element is unexplained. OE *pusa* 'bag' would suit formally, but there is no striking landscape feature here to which it might refer. For *W. Huard* see 'Walterstone' (below). For *Straddel* see District Name Straddle.

'**Walterstone**' (lost, but possibly the DMV at 364362)

Edwardestune 1086 DB.

Villa Huardi 1160-70 HDB.

Waltereston' 1224 Cur, 1316 FA, 1327 Banco, 1334 SR, 1399 Ipm, 1425 Cl.
Walterestun' *cum Byford* 1249 Fees.

Edwardestune is annotated *Villa Huardi* ('Howard's estate') in HDB. Howard
is probably W(alter?) Howard (*Huard*), who also had Poston at this time. If so,
this connection between *Edwardestune*/'Howard's estate' and Poston was maintained into the 13th and later centuries. By this time, however, the former had
become 'Walterstone'. Walter was the name of the holder of *Edwardestune* in DB
and it may have taken its later name from him. There has been considerable confusion in the records between this 'Walterstone' and Walterstone in Ewyas. 'Byford'
may be the location of the motte-and-bailey castle at 366259, which seems to have
been built to control a nearby crossing of the river Dore.

Edwardestune was among several DB estates in the Golden Valley whose
names did not survive the Norman conquest and settlement of Herefordshire.
There were nineteen settlements with English names there before 1066 and of
these only ten have retained this name into modern times; of the other nine,
two (*Burcstantestune* in Dorstone and *Wadetune* in Bacton) are lost altogether
(together with their settlement-sites) and the other seven renamed. These seven
are, besides *Edwardestune*, *Ruuenore* (now Mynydd Brydd), *Alcamestune* (now
Urishay), *Beltrou* (now Godway), and *Almundestune* (now Peterchurch), all in
Peterchurch; and *Wluetone* (now Turnastone) and *Elnodestune* (now Chanstone)
in Vowchurch. The reason for this is probably that the Golden Valley was ravaged
by the Welsh at the same time as they attacked Archenfield in the time of Edward
the Confessor, leading to the situation revealed in DB whereby there were only
twenty-three working ploughs in a valley, that could support 112 ploughs. It may
be, therefore, that when the Normans took control many settlements were simply
too ruined to be economically viable, leading to the clearance and resettlement
of some, either on the old or possibly (as at Turnastone) on a new one, and the
abandonment of others. As part of this process several of the DB estates acquired
new names.

❧ WACTON ঌ

Wacton (616574)

> *Waketon(e)* 1189 P, 1268-75 *Red Book MS* (p), 1316 FA, 1334 SR, 1431 FA; *Wacto(u)ne* 1397 VR, 1585 BM.
> *Wakintun'* 1243 Fees; *Wakyntone* 1283 Swin; *Wakyngton* 1547 HT.

'Estate associated with Wac(c)a', probably an *–ingtūn* formation.

Butterley Court (613580)

> *Butrelie* 1086 DB; *But(t)erlega* 1123 *LeomC*, 1158-61 Foliot; *Buterley(a)* c1177-91 IrishC, 1428 FA; *Buterl(ie)* c1190 CMAD (p), 1243 Fees; *Buterle(ye)* 1303 FA, 1317 Ipm, 1346 FA; *Botterley* 1318 Orl; *Boturleye* 1327 Banco.

'Butter pasture', there are several instances of this name in other counties. *lēah* is used in its late OE sense in this compound.

❧ WALFORD ঌ

Walford (587204)

> *Walecford* 1086 DB; *Valford* 1148-55 Fr (p); *Wal(e)ford(e)* 1166 RBE (p), 1200 Cur (p), 1226-30 Capes, 1300 Swin, 1341 NonInq; *Wau(l)ford(e)* 1219 InqMisc, 1258 Capes (p); *Welleford* 1280 Hart.
> *Wanford* 1188 P.

'Welshman's ford', First element OE *Walh*. The ford is across the Wye at 576202. See Goodrich, page 104.

Callow Farm (573212)

> *Calewe* 1302 Swin; *La Calowe* 1473 AD.

'Bare hill', OE *calu*.

Cobrey Park (607214)

> *Cokebury, Coughbury* n.d. Robinson.

Probably 'manor house by *Cocc*'. See Coughton, below.

216

Coughton (600212)

> *Cocton(e)* 1216-72 BM, 1286 Swin; *Co(c)kton* 1280 Hart, 1365 QD.
> *Koctere* 1282 Grundy.
> *Cotton* 1328 Ch.

First element *cocc* 'hillock', perhaps a reference to the pyramidal shape of the hill occupied by Chase Wood. The same name occurs in Warwickshire.

Howle Hill (601205)

> *Hule* 1280 Hart, 1300 Swin, 1334 SR.
> *Hule Cnoll* 1286 Swin.
> *Cnolmule* 1291 Tax.

This name and Howle in Shropshire are considered to derive from OE **hugol* 'small hill'. *cnoll*, also meaning 'small hill', appears to have been added to the 1286 form. This is not DB *Hulla* as has been thought (cf. Thorn), which is probably Huntsham Hill in Goodrich.

(lost)

> *Wytehaya* 1148-55 Capes; *Wydyhay* 1280 Hart; *Wydehay* 1300 Swin.

Second element ME *hay* 'forest enclosure'. The first could be 'wide' or 'white'. It was in the Forest of Dean.

❧ WALTERSTONE ☙

Walterstone (341249)

'Walter's estate', possibly named from Walter de Lacy (died 1085); see DEPN. See also 'Walterstone' in Vowchurch.

❧ WELLINGTON ☙

Wellington (497482)

> *Weolintun* 1016-35 ASCh; *Walintone* 1086 DB, 1230-4 Capes; *Walintona(m)* 1123-7 Capes, c1155-c58 Foliot, c1227 Capes (p); *Welint(one)* 1148-63 HDB, c1163 Foliot, 1275 RH; *Walentunia* c1189 Capes; *Welintun'* 1243 Fees; *Welynton(e)* 1247 Ipm, 1291 Tax, 1308 Capes (p), 1314 Orig, 1334 SR. *Waligtona* 1123 Regesta.

There are four Wellingtons in England, the others being Wellington Heath (below), Wellington in Shropshire and Wellington in Somerset. The etymology is uncertain. 'Estate associated with Weola' would suit, but there is no other trace of the personal name, and it is unlikely that it would be found only in four *–ingtūn* formations.

Adzor Bank (480476)

> *Eaddesour'* 1185 *StGC*; *Eddeshoura* 1216-72 AD; *Addesore* 1319 AD, 1429 Cl, 1516 Ipm.

'Æddi's flat-topped ridge', second element OE *ofer*, which suits Adzor Bank perfectly.

Auldberrow (493474)

> *Orlebarwe* 1216-72 AD; *Aldborewos(wey)* 1349 AD; *Auborough* 1832 OS.

The forms are too inconsistent for etymology.

Burghope (501504)

> *Bur(e)hop(e)* 1101-2 Regesta, 1143-8 *StGC*, 1166 RBE, 1217 ChR (p), 1243 Fees.
> *Burghopa* 1216-28 *StGC*; *Bo(u)rghope* 1316 FA, 1319 AD, 1428 FA; *Burghope* 1334 SR.
> *Burchope Henry* 1243 Fees.

'Secluded valley with a fortification'; an Iron Age hillfort has been discovered recently on Dinmore Hill, one mile to the north. 'Henry' is from either Henry of Burghope, who was living in 1216 (ChR), or another of the same name living in 1243 (Fees).

Wootton (488486)

> *Wudetona* 1229 Bracton; *Wudetun'* 1243 Fees; *(La) Wodeton* 13th AD; *Wotton* 1303 FA.

'Settlement near a wood'.

❧ WELLINGTON HEATH ☙

Wellington Heath (714202)

> *Walynton(e)* 1200-15 Dugdale (p), c1285 Red Book, 1303 FA, 1305 Swin (p);
> *Wel(l)in(g)tone* 1210-12 RBE, 1295 Swin (p); *Waliton(e)* 1230-4 Capes;
> *Welynton* 1328 Banco.
> *Walynton in Ledebur' sub Maliverna* 1219-27 Barrow; *Over Walinton* 1432
> St Katheribe; *Walyngton by Ledbury* 1507 Ipm.
> *Wallyngton Holywater* 1547 HT.

See Wellington (above). 'Holywater' tithes were payable to the minster within whose *parochia* the place lies, in this case Ledbury church.

(lost)

> *Houlande* 1300 Swin (p).

'Cultivated land on a hill-spur', OE *hōh-land*.

❧ WELSH BICKNOR ☙

See page 41.

❧ WELSH NEWTON ☙

See page 168.

❧ WEOBLEY ☙

Weobley (401519)

> *Wibelai(e)* 1086 DB, 1162/3-85 HDB, 1187 P; *Webbele(ya)* 1101-2 Regesta,
> 1271 Ipm; *Webbelegge* 1138 JW; *Wibeleia* 1169-76, 1205-16 StGC,
> *Webbeleia* 1186-98 StGC; *Webbeleye* 1327 Barrow.
> *Wilbeleye* 1107-15 StGC; *Wilbel'* c1225-7 Barrow.

'Wibba's clearing'. The *-lb-* spellings might be scribal error for *-bb-*.

Burton (394498)

> *(la) Buryton(e)* 1319 Orl, 1355 Ipm, 1424 AD; *Buryngton* 1426 Cl.

'Settlement at a fort', OE *byrigtūn*. There is a cluster of names with this significance in north Herefordshire and south Shropshire.

Fenhampton (390503)

> *Fenhampton* 1355 AD, 1357 Ipm, 1424 AD; *Fannanton* 1426 Cl.

'Fen settlement'.

Fernhill (390497)

> *Fernehalle* 1086 DB; *Frenhal'* 1252 StGC; *Fernhalle* 1315 InqMisc; *Fernehale* 1429 AD.

Probably 'fern nook', in spite of the *–ll-* of two of the forms. OE *hall* 'hall' is rare in pre-Conquest names, and does not seem likely.

Garnestone Castle (404502)

> *Garn(e)ston* 1355 Ipm, 1372 AD; *Gernerston* 1385 AD (p); *Germaston* 1426 Cl.

A late *tūn* name with the Old French personal name *Gerner*. In 1252 John Garner gave land in Weobley to St Guthlac's Priory (*StGC*).

The Ley (392512)

> *(La) Lega* 1166 RBE (p), 1171 P; *Leghe* 1231 Cur (p); *(La) Ley* 1341 NonInq, 1424 AD.

Perhaps a late name using *lēah* in the sense 'meadow' or 'pasture'. It is near Fenhampton.

Nunsland (379539)

> See Broxwood Court in Pembridge.

Little Sarnesfield (386521)

> *Sarnesfeud Rogeri* 1243 Fees; *Sarnesfield Cosyn* 1424 AD; *- Coffyn* 1532 Robinson. *Little Sarnsill* 1594 AD.

See Sarnesfield. Roger of Sarnesfield had the manor in 1243.

WESTHIDE

Westhide (586442)

> (La) Hide 1086 DB, 1157-62 First Century, 1174-86 Fr, 1196 P; Hyde 1291 Tax.
> Hida Walteri, Hid(a) W(illelmi) 1160-70 HDB.
> Westhyde 1243 Fees, 1292 QW; Westhide 1359 Ipm.

'Estate assessed for taxation at one hide'. Hugh Donkey had two further manors in this vicinity in 1086, one unnamed and the other called *Lincumbe* ('flax coomb'), which may have lain near Shucknall Hill. In 1160-70 the unnamed manor was called *Hida Willelmi* while *Lincumbe* was described as being *in Hida Walteri*. Walter and William were two sons of Arnold of Powys, the subtenant of Westhide. West- to distinguish it from Monkhide and Little Hide (in Yarkhill), both of which are east of it.

In 1086 Roger de Lacy had a manor of one hide at *Hide* (DB). In 1160-70 Richard son of Robert held it. In 1243 the manor is called *villa Ricardi*. Richard of Hide held a moiety of this *de Kaerdin* and Richard of Hurstley the other moiety, which was at Whitwick (in Yarkhill). *Kaerdin*, which may be a Welsh name involving *caer-* 'fort', may relate to the Roman building (fort?) at 578443, which is on a hill called 'Chester Hill' in the 19th century tithe award (TWNFC, **48** (1996)).

WESTON BEGGARD

Weston Beggard (584413)

'West settlement', in relation to Yarkhill, which seems to have had some local importance, with a family name (whose origins are unknown: Robinson) attached.

WESTON UNDER PENYARD

Weston under Penyard (631233)

> Westune 1086 DB; Weston 1280 Hart.
> Westun' Bret 1243 Fees.
> Weston subtus Penyord 1376 Orig.

'West settlement', the counterpart of Aston Ingham's 'east settlement'. They lie either side of the estate containing Linton and the Roman town of Ariconium. The Bret or Brito family were lords of the manor from early in the 12th century.

Bollitree Castle (637240)

>*Bolletre* 1282 Grundy.

>Probably 'Bolla's tree'.

Kingstone (631246)

>*Chingestune* 1086 DB; *Kyngestona* 1154-89 Swin; *Kingestone* 1226-30 Capes; *Cigestona* 1240 Dugdale.

>'Royal estate'. Before 1066 Kingstone was an outlier of the Gloucestershire manor of Westbury on Severn. Earl William fitzOsbern joined it to Herefordshire in 1070.

Pontshill (637218)

>*Panc(e)hille* 1086 DB, 1208 P; *Paunteshull* 1219-34 LostC; *Penshulle* 1300 Swin.

>Probably 'Pant's hill'.

Ryeford (641226)

>*Ryford* 1300 Swin; *Ruford* 1306 Ipm; *Riford* 1663 MA.

>'Rye ford', perhaps of a similar significance to those instances of Barford which mean 'barley ford'.

Old Walton Farm (635211)

>*Walton* 1306 Ipm.

>Perhaps 'spring settlement', but more spellings are needed.

Lower Weston Farm (623239)

>*Nethere Westune* 1282 Grundy.

Whitbourne (725570)

> *Witeberne* 1163 Foliot; *Wyteburn(e)* 1219 InqMisc, 1272, 1356 Capes;
> *Whyteburne* 1241 Capes, 1291 Tax; *Wyteborne* 1412 Capes.

'White stream', OE *burna* is a rare term in the west midlands.

Badley Wood (695578)

> *Baddeleye, Baddelithe* 1268-75 *Red Book MS* (p).

'Badda's concave hill-slope', second element OE *hlithe*.

Bringsty Common (705551)

> *Brinkesty(e)* 1219-34, 1277 Cant; *Bryngsty* 1268-75 *Red Book MS*; *Brenkesty*
> 1307 Swin; *Brynkstre* 1540 *Wms*; *Bringstie* 1575-80 Bromyard; *Brinxtie*
> 1575 *Wms*.

'Brink path', the road here follows the curving edge of a hill-spur.

Crumplebury Farm (700569)

> *Grymalbury* 1495 Ipm; *Cromolbury* 1663 MA; *Crumblebury* 1675
> Whitbourne.

byrig is probably 'manor house' here. The first element is OE *crymel* 'small piece', the precise meaning of which in place-names has not been ascertained.

Elmores End (**Upper** 713545, **Lower** 710546)

> *Ellemer* c1285 Whitbourne; *Elinor* 1492 Whitbourne.
> *Elmers Bellowes* 1577 Whitbourne.

'Ella's pool', second element OE *mere*. Bellowes is probably a personal name.

Old Gaines (718554)

> *Gynes* 1234-7 BreconC (p), 1291 Capes (p), 1292 Swin, 1328 KPC, 1355 QD.

A manorial name derived from Guines, near Calais (Whitbourne).

Huntlands (718558)

> *Huntiland(a)* 1140-8 Capes (p), 1170 P (p); *Huntelande* 1166 RBE (p); *Huntin(ge)land* 1200 Cur (p), 1210 P; *Huntilande* 1200 Cur (p), 1228 Pat (p); *Huntelond* 1304 Swin.

'Hunting land'.

Linceter Farm (691573)

> *Lynsete* 1240-68 Whitbourne (p); *Lincestre* c1285 Red Book; *Lyncestre* 1577 Whitbourne.

More spellings are needed. OE *ceaster* 'walled Roman site' does not seem likely, even in the less precise usage found in western counties. Names in *–sete* are usually ascribed to *geset* 'dwelling, camp, place for animals', and those in Lin- to OE *līn* 'flax'.

Longlands Farm (704564)

> *Longelond* late 13th AD.

'Long land'.

Moorhall (714560)

> *Mearhalles* 1577 Whitbourne.

More spellings are needed before an etymology can be attempted.

Lower Poswick (709571)

> *Possewike* c1285 Whitbourne; *Possewyc* late 13th AD (p).

'Possa's dairy farm', the same name has become Postwick in Norfolk.

Tedney (731589)

> *Tedenee* c1285 Red Book.

'Tēoda's island', final element probably *eg*. This is a promontory jutting into the flood-plain of the river Teme.

❧ WHITCHURCH ☙

Whitchurch (556175)

> *Lann Tiuinauc* 1045-1104 (c1130) LL; *Fendenerac* 1277 Cant; *Landeuenok*
> 1334 SR; *Landonenok* 1436 CRCG.
> *Albi Monasterii* 1148-63 MonC; *Albo Monasterio* 1281 Tax; *Album
> Monasterium* 1313 Duncumb.
> (church of) *St Tiburcius* 1325 Ipm.
> *Wytechirche* 1320 Orl; *Whitchirch* 1325 Ipm; *Wytechurche* 1346 Trill, 1397
> VR; *Whit Church* 1535 VE.

The name of this place has come from a description of the appearance
of its church – 'white church'. However, the name of the saint to which it was
dedicated produced a different set of place-names. This saint may have been St
Gwynnog (Tywynnog, with hypocoristic *ty-*), who also has a church dedication at
Llanwonog in Clodock (Harris). By 1325, however, the dedicatee had become St
Dyfrig, to whom it is still dedicated.

Lewstone (534173)

> *Leweston* 1282 Duncumb; *Cleuston* 1397 VR; *L(l)ewston* 1609-13 Lancaster,
> 1655 Duncumb; *Luston* 17th Duncumb.

Perhaps 'Lēofwig's estate', with some Welsh influence in the spelling.

❧ WHITNEY ☙

Whitney (268474, but original site by Old Whitney Court (274466); moved to
present site after 18th century flooding)

> *Witenie* 1086 DB; *Witteney(e)* c1130 GloucC, 1233 Cl; *Wytteneia* 1219
> InqMisc; *Wytteneye* 1230 Cur (p), 1291 Tax; *Hwytene* 1217-1307 BM;
> *Wytheneye* 1300 Ipm (p); *Whiteney* 1316 FA; *Whytney* 1412 Capes.

'Hwīta's island' or 'white island'. Old Whitney Court has a typical *eg* site.

Millhalf (278482)

> *Halvehyd* 1424 Winforton.

Probably takes its name from the half-hide manor the king had in Whitney
in 1086.

Stowe (282471)

> *Stowa* 1193 P; *Stennia'*, *Steuwa* 1219-34 Dugdale; *Stowe* 1237-64 Winforton.

stōw in place-names means 'venue for an activity', the activity frequently being religious. Aerial photography has shown that a sub-circular enclosure or ring-ditch, possibly defensive in origin, lies just to the north of the A438 here. This may be the location called *Aldbury* or *Oldbury* close to which Winforton hermitage had lands (Duncumb).

❦ WIGMORE ❧

Wigmore (413691)

> *Wig(e)more* 1086 DB, c1194-1214 BM, 1535 VE; *Wygimor* c1250-72 BM; *Wyg(g)emore* 1262 BM, 1319 Orig, 1387 BM, 1535 VE; *Wyggmora* 1406 BM.

This name refers to the peculiar nature of the marsh (OE *mōr*) in the basin overlooked by Wigmore Castle. It is an unstable marsh in which wet patches erupt in different places. The first element is OE *wicga* 'beetle, something which wriggles'.

Brinshope (421677)

> *Brunshope* 14th Chronicle.

Apparently the same name as Brinsop parish.

Deerfold (c380686 and c380670)

> *Dereford* 1301 Pat; *Dorfaud* 1304 Ipm; *Darveld* 1535 VE; *Dorwalde* 1542 Dugdale.

'Deer fold'. This compound has become Darfoulds in Worksop, Nottinghamshire, and Derfald, a Shrewsbury street-name. It probably meant 'park'. Deerfold was the name of an extensive chase on the west side of Wigmore Castle.

Paysure Wood (421675)

> *Peysure* 1292 QW.

Perhaps a manorial name from the surname Poyser, Peiser.

(**lost**, but c394684?)

Tumbelawe 1086 DB.

Second element *hlāw* 'tumulus'. The first element is OE *thūma* 'thumb', which could be a person's nickname, or could refer to some visual characteristic of the burial mound. The chapel of St Leonard, which formerly stood at Chapel Farm at the grid reference above, may mark the site of the DB estate.

❧ WILLERSLEY ☙

Willersley (312473)

> *Willaueslege* 1086 DB; *Willelmesle* 1142 Holtzmann; *Willameslea* 1188 P;
>   *Wilageslege* 1219 InqMisc; *Wylardesl(eye)* 1291 Tax, 1316 FA, 1327 Banco;
> *Weere Lesey* 1663 MA.
> *Little Wylardesleye* 1328 Banco.

Second element *lēah* 'clearing'. The spellings are inconsistent as regards the first element. It was probably a personal name, but *Willaues-*, *Willelmes-*, *Wylardes-* suggest different ones. 'Little Willersley' may have stood at the crossroads near Old Crow Farm (316475), now in Eardisley.

The Wydenhams (306464)

> *Wybbenham* 1365 Winforton, 1377 Ipm.

'Wibba's land in a river-bend', second element *hamm*.

❧ WILLEY ☙

Willey Hall (324671)

> *Wileleghe* 1292 Subs; *Wylyleye* 1304 Ipm; *Wylleley* 1490 Ipm; *Wylley* 1546 HT.
> *Wylileg' Welshry* 1259 Ipm.

'Willow wood or clearing'. Willey formed part of the Welshry of the marcher lordship of Stapleton. DEPN's references under this name refer to Willey in Barrow, Shropshire.

❧ WINFORTON ☙

Winforton (298470)

> *Widferdetune* 1086 DB; *Wilfreton(e)* 1219 InqMisc, 1237 Pat; *Wynfreton(e)* 1219-34 Dugdale, 1265 Ipm; *Wlfretone* 1278 Abbr; *Wynferton* 1316 FA; *Wynforton* 1535 VE.

Perhaps 'Winfrith's estate', with some Norman-French confusion of *–l-* and *–n-* and a corrupt DB spelling.

'Winforton Hermitage' (hermitage site at Court Barn 302464, chapel site at 293456)

> *(Chapel of) St Keneder in Wilfreton* c1250-83 BM.
> *(Stephanus capellanus de) insula de Wilfreton* c1250-83 BM.

Walter de Mucegros patronised hermits of St Cynidr living on 'Winforton Island' in 1219-34 and one of his successors gave it to Wormsley Priory in 1264 (Dawson). At DB the island was included in the estate of Middlewood. This place-name is now only to be found south of the Wye in Clifford (which see) but when the main course of the Wye ran more towards Winforton it included this location.

❧ WINSLOW ☙

Winslow (**Upper** 617533, **Lower** 615532)

> *Wivesell'* 1224 Cur (p).
> *Win(n)eslawe* 1224 Cur (p), 1268-75 *Red Book MS* (p); *Wyn(n)eslowe* 1268-75 *Red Book MS* (p), 1303-1452 *Slocombe* (p).
> *Willyslowe* 1303-1452 *Slocombe* (p).
> *Wynesleslade* 1305 *Slocombe*.
> *Wynslowe Halywat'* 1545 HT.

'Wine's burial mound', the same name occurs in Buckinghamshire. 'Holywater' tithes were payable to the minster within whose *parochia* the place lies, in this case Bromyard church.

Hardwick Manor (643556)

> *Her(e)d(e)wyk(e)* c1250 *StGC*, 1268-75 *Red Book MS* (p), 1334 SR, 1359
> Trill; *Hardewyke* 1307 Swin (p).

'Dairy farm'.

Keephill (637543)

> *Chipelai* 1086 DB.
> *(Le) Cuple* 1143-55 WalkerCh, 1268-75 *Red Book MS* (p), late 13th *StGC*,
> 1356 Bromyard, 1420 Lacy; *Cuplelai* 1160-70 HDB.
> *Kepyll* 1545 *Wms*; *Keepul* 1768 Bromyard; *Keephill alias Keepel* 1845
> Bromyard.
> (?)*Cipeltone* 1307 Swin (p).

The first element is probably OE *cȳpe* 'osier basket'. A **cȳpe-lēah* could be a
wood from which materials were obtained to make these.

'Plegelgate' (651552)

> *Plegeliet, Plegelgete* 1086 DB; *Pleggeny(e)ate* c1286, 1589 *Wms*.

The final element appears to be OE *geat* 'gap', though the topographical
reference is not obvious. Plegel- may represent OE **plega-lēah* 'sport clearing',
which has become Plealey in Shropshire and Playley in Worcestershire.

Rowden Abbey (630564)

> *Ruedene* 1086 DB; *Rugedona* 1137-9 HDB; *Rugedun'* 1243 Fees; *Rugheden',*
> *Rughedun'* 1225 Cur; *Raden* 1226 Cur; *Rouden* 1268-75 *Red Book MS* (p),
> 1373 Ipm; *Roudon(e)* 1303 FA, 1334 SR; *Royden* 1316 Ipm; *Rowdon* 1418
> KPC (p).
> *Little Rowden* 1619 KPC.

'Rough valley'. Hackley Brook has the sort of valley which is called *denu* in
place-names. The 'Abbey' affix is said to come from the d'Abbetot family, though
no connection between them and the manor is known. The same family are also
said to have given their name to 'Debitots Barn' (which see) in Avenbury (TWNFC
(1893-4)). 'Little Rowden' may have been at Tack Farm (639571).

Steward's Hyde (613528)

> *Stewardshide* 1268-75 *Red Book MS.*

Possibly the site of the hide of land the reeve of Bromyard had in 1086 (DB).

Wallcroft (644558)

> *Wellecroft* c1240 St Katherine; *Wallecroft(e)* 1268-75 *Red Book MS* (p), c1330 KPC.

'Croft with a spring'.

The Wells (623540)

> *Welles* 1204 Cur (p), 1243 Fees (p), 1283 Ipm (p); *(la) Walle* 1268-75 *Red Book MS.*

'Springs'.

❧ WITHINGTON ☙

Withington (566435)

> *Widingtune* 1086 DB; *Wit(h)inton(e)* 1228 Pat (p), 1252, 1355 Capes; *Wythinton(e)* 1320 Capes, 1341 NonInq; *Whyttynton* 1377 QD. *Chircwithinton* 1266 InqMisc; *Churiswythynton* 1334 SR.

Eau Withington (**Court** 545343, and **Builth Farm** 545429)

> *Eywytington* 1291 Tax; *Ewythynton'* 1334 SR; *Ewethynton* 1516 Ipm. *Wythyngton aquosa* 1294 Swin.

Withington Marsh (553445)

> *Parva Wythyntone* 1294 Swin.

'Settlement by a willow copse', OE *wīthegn-tūn*. Three settlements within Withington seems to have become known as Church (or Great) Withington, Parva Withington and Eau Withington. The last named is the one nearest the Lugg, and the affix is probably *ea* 'river', influenced by the French word *eau*.

Nunnington Court (552431)

> *Nunniton* 1272 Ipm (p); *Nonynton(e)* 1284 Swin, 1328 Banco; *Neuynton'*
> 1334 SR.

'Settlement of the nuns', OE **nunnena-tun*. This is probably named from
the *moniales de Hereford* ('nuns of Hereford') who had lands in the bishop of
Hereford's manor of Withington in 1086 (DB). Duncumb notes that there was
formerly a nunnery in Hereford whose chapel had a painting of St Catherine
of Alexandria and her wheel on the front. This lady's cult arrived in England in
the 12th century, with returning Crusaders, however, so this is unlikely to be
the nunnery of DB. Nevertheless, it could have been a refounding of an older
house, perhaps originally founded by the nuns of Wenlock Abbey to supervise
the thirty hides of land they had at Lyde by Hereford (and just across the Lugg
from here) given to them by king Merewalh (see District Name Lyde). It has been
noted under Kenderchurch that the bishop seems to have been the inheritor of
Wenlock's lands in Herefordshire, and it may be significant that the nuns of 1086
held their land at Nunnington under him. In addition to the thirty hides in Lyde,
Merewalh also gave Wenlock five hides in the district of *Magana* or Maund, and it
is possible that these were at Nunnington. Nunnington eventually became the site
of a prebendary of Hereford cathedral, probably when bishop Reinhelm (1107-
15) first established a regular chapter of clergy. This may mean that the Hereford
nunnery then no longer existed and that the way had therefore been cleared for a
refounding of it under the patronage of St Catherine.

Thinghill (**Court** ('**Great Thinghill**') 567448 and **Grange** ('**Little Thinghill**')
552453)

> *Tingehall, Tingehele* 1086 DB; *Tinghulla* 1160-70 HDB; *Tinchull* 1232 Pat;
> *Thinghall* 1251 StGC; *Yngel* 1291 Tax; *Thynghull* 1303 FA.
> *Parva Yynghull'* c1179-86 Barrow; - *Thunghull* 1334 SR.

'Assembly hill'. It may be significant that Thinghill Court is close to the
parish boundary, where meetings between peoples are likely to have taken
place.

Veldo (557435)

> *La Felde* 1328 Banco.

The early spelling means 'open land'. The settlement is at the tip of a spur,
and the modern name probably has *hōh* as second element. Intermediate spellings are required.

Wolferlow (669617)

> *Wilferlau, Ulferlau* 1086 DB; *Wulferlaw'* 1160-70 HDB; *Wolfrelawe* 1291 Tax; *Wlverlowe* 1292 Ipm; *Wollefolowe* 1529-30 Court.
> *Wulfarslowe* 1342 Ipm; *Wolfreslowe* 1357 Ipm.
> *Wulferlay Phylippi* 1169 P.
> *Wlfrelowe et Frome* 1249 Fees; *Wolfrelowe et Frome* 1303 FA; *Wolfrelowe et Frene* 1346 FA.

'Wulfhere's burial mound'. 'Philip' (1169 P) must have been a current or former tenant under the Lacys. In 1086 Roger de Lacy had six hides at Wolferlow and another at *Frome*. Thorn says this is in Bishop's Frome, but Little Froome in Avenbury is perhaps more likely.

Poswick Farm (669631)

> *Pownswyk* 1434 KPC; *Ponsewick* 1493 KPC.

Probably 'Pūn's dairy farm'.

Underley (657614) and **Upper Underley** (657622)

> *Underlide* 1160-70 HDB; *Wuderlithe* 1226 Cur (p); *Underlithe* 1230 Cur (p); *Underlich* 1303 FA (p); *Underlythe* 1334 SR; *Underlight* 1362 Ipm; *Underleth* 1429-30 Court, 1434 KPC.
> *Underley* 1582 KPC; *Underleigh* 1586 KPC.
> *Underlide Adam* 1160-70 HDB.
> *Hunderlithe Walter* 1243 Fees.

'(Place) under the concave hill-slope', second element OE *hlith*.

Woolhope (612358)

Hopam pre-1066(?) Capes; *Hope, -a* 1086 DB; c1153-5, c1200, 1273 Capes; *Oppam* 1219 Capes.

Wolvythehope 1219-27 Barrow; *Wulveve Hope* 1243 Fees; *Wlwyneope* 1246 Capes; *Wolvinehope* 1252 Capes; *Wolnythehop* 1327 Banco, *Wolvythope* 1341 QD; *Wulvenehope* 14th AD; *Wulhope* 1526 AD.
Hope Wolnith 1221 Capes, 1341 NonInq; - *Wulume* 1291 Tax; *Hard Wolnyth* 1375 QD; *Hopewolnyth* 1407 BM; *Hopewolvyche* 1429 Cl.

OE *hop* 'secluded valley', with the feminine personal name *Wulfgifu* affixed. According to Fees, 'Hope' was given to Hereford Cathedral before 1066 by *Wulveve* (Wulfgifu) and *Godheve* (Godgifu).

Lower Buckenhill (365336)

Bo(c)kenhull(e) mid-13th *StGC* (p), 14th AD (p), 1407 BM; *Buckenyll* 1526 AD.

Probably 'hill of the he-goat', but Bucca may be used as a personal name. There is another Buckenhill in Norton-by-Bromyard.
A 'chapel of St Dyfrig' (*capella Sc'i Dubricii*) stood at Lower Buckenhill in 1535 (AD). This is referred to as *the priour* in 1526 (AD); it was not the site of a religious community after the coming of the English. See also Capler Camp (below).

Capler Camp (592329)

Caplefore 1086 DB; *Capelore* late 13th Patterson (p); *Capullore* 1298 Kirby (p); *Capeloure* 1310 CRCG (p).
Capellar or Wobury 1732 Jack.
Woldbury n.d. Jack.

Capler is the name *Caple* ('look-out place') with the addition of *ofer* 'flat-topped ridge'. According to Jack, two fields on the southern slopes of Capler Hill are today called Upper and Lower Walboro, and Walboro would seem to be an alternative name for the Iron Age hillfort. *Woldbury* is 'ancient fortification'.
Capelfore contained five 'English' hides and three 'Welsh' hides in 1086. HDB says that the 'English' hides lay at Brockhampton (Brockhampton-by-Ross), but does not give a location for the Welsh ones. These, however, probably lay at the 'Welsh' centre at Lower Buckenhill, where, as noted above, until the 16th century there was a chapel of St Dyfrig. *Caplefore*, with King's Caple, How Caple and Lower Buckenhill, may represent a pre-Conquest land-unit called 'Caple' dependant on Capler Camp.

❧ WORMBRIDGE ❧

Wormbridge (428306)

> *Winebruge* 1199 Dugdale; *Wermebrige* 1207 Cur; *Womebrigge* 1217 Capes; *Worm(e)brigg(e)* 1292 QW, 1334 SR, 1338 Larking; *Wirmebrug* n.d. Owen.

'Bridge over Worm Brook'. See also Kenderchurch.

(lost)

> *Spechele* 1207 Cur (p); *Spekele* 1208 P (p).

There is a place-name element *spēc*, from which Speke in Lancashire derives, which is thought to be a term for some kind of brushwood. This would be a likely qualifier for *lēah*.

❧ WORMSLEY ❧

Wormsley (428478)

> *Wermeslai, Wrmesleu* 1086 DB; *Wormest* 1291 Tax; *Wurmesley* late 13th BM; *Wormesley(e)* 1312 Orig, 1316 FA, 1332 Capes, 1397 VR; *Wormeslaye* 1341 Non Inq.
> *Wemelee* 1206 Cur (p); *Wirmeles, Wurmeleys* 1243 Fees; *Wrmelegh* 1256 Salop Eyre (p); *Wormele(ye)* 1272 Capes, 1287 Swin, 1291 Tax.

Either 'snake clearing' or 'Wyrm's clearing'.

❧ YARKHILL ❧

Yarkhill (608426)

> *Geardcylle* 805-11 ECWM.
> *Archel* 1086 DB; *Hiarchull* 1101-2 GloucC; *Yarchull(e)* c1158 Foliot, 1291 Tax, 1350 Ipm; *Serchelle* c1158-63 Foliot; *Archil(l)(a)* 1158-85 HDB, 1194 P, c1203 Patterson; *Iarchul(le)* 1177-86 *StGC*, 1179-c80 Barrow; *Arkil* 1187 P; *Yar(e)hull(e)* 1219-31 Barrow, late 13th Patterson; *Hyerkell* 1232 Capes; *Yarculle* c1250 Early Deeds; *Gerchull* c1260 Early Deeds; *Yark(e)hull* 1316, 1399 FA; *Yarkle* KPC.
> *Varcullne* c1230 Patterson.
> *Iarculn'* 1243 Fees.

'Kiln with an enclosure'. OE *cyll* (a reduced form of *cyln*) has been confused with *hyll* 'hill'. It is doubtful whether this name would have been interpreted correctly without the survival of the OE spelling, though *Iarculn'* (1243 Fees) suggests some memory of the true nature of the second element persisted.

DB records only two hides in Lacy hands in the parish of Yarkhill, but later evidence shows that there were five, four at Yarkhill itself and one at Monkhide that William Devereux gave to Gloucester Abbey.

'Little Hide' (somewhere between Monkhide and Whitwick)

> *Villa Ricardi* 1243 Fees.
> *Parva Hyda* 13th Patterson, 1316 FA; *Parva Hida* 1334 SR.
> *Little Hyde* 1329 St Katherine; *Lyttlehyde* 1339 Kirby; *Lutel Hyde* 1365 Kirby;
> *Lyttel Hyde* 1563 KPC.

This was the hide of land in Radlow Hundred that one Tezelin held from Roger de Lacy in 1086. In 1243 this hide of land, now called *villa Ricardi*, was held in two moieties, one by Richard of Hide *de Kaerdin* and the other, located at Whitwick, by Richard of Hurstley (Fees). *Villa Ricardi* ('Richard's estate') is possibly named after Richard son of Robert, who held Tezelin's hide of land in 1160-70 (HDB). 'Little' to distinguish it from Monkhide (below) and Westhide. For *Kaerdin*, see Westhide.

Monkhide (614440)

> *(La) Hyda, -e* 1114-30 (13th) Patterson, 1273 Capes.
> *Hida Monachorum* 1243 Fees; *Hyde, -a Monachorum* 1319 Kirby, 1329
>   St Katherine, 1480 Kirby.
> *Monkshide* 1321, 1413 Kirby.

William Devereux gave a hide of land in Yarkhill to Gloucester Abbey in 1114-30. Monkesbury ('manor-house of the monks')(619439) was on the manor of Monkhide.

Showle Court (611437)

> *Solla,-e* early 13th, 1254 Patterson; *Solles* 1254-7 Dugdale; *Shelle* 1256 Salop
>   Eyre (p); *Sholle(e)* 1256 Salop Eyre (p), 1283-84 Early Deeds, 1334 SR,
>   1347 KPC; *Scholle* 1365 Kirby, 1397 VR, 1413 Kirby; *Schulle* 1377-99 BM.

A manorial name from William *de Stolle* or *Scholle* (the former is probably a transcriptional error for *Scolle*, a rare occurrence for Round) the tithes of whose lands in Yarkhill Ralph de Tosny gave to St Peter de Castellion before 1102 (Fr). William left descendants who called themselves *Solla, Solles* or *Scholle*, their surname eventually becoming attached to their Yarkhill lands. He and they may have hailed from Soulles, south-west of St-Lô, dépt. Manche (Adigard de Gautries).

Whitwick Manor (610457)

> *Witewiche* 1086 DB; *Witewike* c1210 Kirby; *W(h)ytewyk(e)* 1243 Fees, 1334 SR, 1362 Ipm; *Wytewike* 1321 St Katherine (p).

> Probably 'Hwīta's dairy-farm', but the adjective 'white' is possible.

Woodmanton (601437)

> *Wudemont'* c1200 (p), *Wodemonnetun'* c1250 Patterson (p).

> 'Woodmen's settlement'. There is another Woodmanton in Sarnesfield.

❧ YARPOLE ❦

Yarpole (470648)

> *Larpole* 1086 DB; *Garepolla* 1135-54 OxfordFacs; *Iarpol(e)* 1160-70 HDB; *Yarpol(le)* 1173-86 Kemp, c1200-c50 *LeomC*, 1287 Ipm, 1316 FA, 1328 Banco; *Jarpol(e)* 1249 Fees; *Jarypol* mid-13th RATD (p), *Yerpole* 16th BM.

> 'Pool with a fish trap', OE **gear-pol*.

Bircher (476657)

> *Birchour'* 1173-86 Kemp; *Birchou'* 1200-50 *LeomC*; *Byrchore* 1388 QD.

> 'Birch-tree ridge'.

❧ YATTON ❦

Yatton (627304)

> *Getune* 1086 DB; *Giet(t)ona* 1137-9, 1160-70 HDB; *Yatton* 1307 InqMisc, 1399 Ipm.

> 'Settlement at a pass through hills', first element OE *geat*. The hills in question were those of the Woolhope massif.

❧ YAZOR ❧

Yazor (406467)

> *Lavesofre* 1086 DB; *Iagashor* 1142 EpActs; *Iagesoure* 1160-70 HDB, 1243
> Fees; *Iagosoure* 1179-82 Patterson; *Iawesore* 1198 CartAntiq; *Eausore*
> 1243 Fees; *Yaveso(u)re* 1277 Cant, 1303 FA; *Yanesore* 1291 Tax; *Yausore*
> 1313 Ipm; *Suavesour* 1317 Ipm; *Yasoure* 1334 SR; *Yavesovere* 1336 Ipm;
> *Yazore* 1397 VR; *Yasor* 1428 FA, 1540 Dugdale.

'Iago's ridge'; the personal name is Welsh.

(lost)

> *Berchull* 1198 CartAntiq; *Brechull* 1199 Dugdale.

Probably 'birch-tree wood'.

Foxley (412467)

> *Foxleg(am)* 1152 Holtzmann, 1233 Cur; *Foxle(ia)* 1198 CartAntiq, 1199
> Dugdale.

'Fox wood or clearing'.

Yarsop (409475)

> *Ardeshope* 1086 DB, 1198 CartAntiq; *Edreshope* 1086 DB; *Erdeshop(e)*
> 1086 DB, 1143-55 WalkerCh, 1243 Fees, 1291 Tax, 1337 QD, 1397 VR;
> *Erdes(s)op(e)* 1086 DB, 1233 Cur; *Ardep'* c1155-c58 Foliot (p).

Probably 'Ēadrēd's remote valley'.

Index of Place-names

241

Huntington 114, 121
   (in Hereford) 19, 114, 121
Huntlands 224
Huntless 62
Huntley (Huntleys; in Much Marcle) 158
   (in Preston on Wye) 187
Huntsham 105, 106
   Hill 104, 217
Hurstley 140
Hyatt Sarnesfield, see Sarnesfield, Hyatt
Hyde (in Leominster) 138
   (in Stanford Bishop) 199

Ingestone 99
Insulam Ebrdil, see 'Ynys Efrddyl'
Ivington 138

Jetelynde (in Goodrich) 106

Kaerdin (in Westhide) 221, 235
Keephill 229
Kenardesl' (in How Caple) 63, 130
Kenchester 121
Kenderchurch (*Stane*) 17, 121, 193, 231, 234
Kentchurch (*Lann Cein*) 123, 124
Kilbreece 210
Kilbury 133
Kilforge 74
Kilpeck 124
Kilreague 146
Kimbolton 18, 124
King's Caple, see Caple, King's
Kingsland 17, 126
King's Pyon, see Pyon, King's
'King's Stanford', see 'Stanford Regis'
Kingstone 23, 127
   (in Weston under Penyard) 127, 222
Kingswood 129
Kington 39, 55, 128
Kinley 140
Kinnersley 55, 63, 130
Kinsham 18, 131
Kinton 135
Kiperlegh (in Kingstone) 127, 128
Kivernoll 77
Knill 132
Knoakes 139, 174
Kynaston (in Hentland) 112, 158
   (in Much Marcle) 158
Kyrebatch 207

Lagademar, see Garway
Langarewi, see Garway
Langstone 147
Lann Budgualan, see Carey

Lann Cein, see Kentchurch
Lann Celinni, see Ganarew or St Wolstan's
Lann Cinfall, see Llangunville
Lanncusthennin Garthbenni, see Hentland (in Goodrich)
Lann Deui, see Much Dewchurch
Lanndougarth, see Ganarew
Lann Ebrdil, see Madley
Lann Guern, see Llanwarne
Lann Guorboe/Lannguoruoe, see Eaton Bishop
Lann Hunapui, see Llandinabo
Lann Idoudecsent, see Welsh Bicknor
Lann Iunabui, see Bredwardine
Lann Loudeu, see Llancloudy
Lann Martin, see Marstow
Lann Mihacgel supra Mingui (in Garway) 104
Lannpetyr, see Peterstow
Lann Ridol, see Llanrothal
Lann Santfreit, see Bridstow
Lann Suluc, See Sellack
Lann Timoi, see Foy
Lann Tisauuc, see Ganarew or St Wolstan's
Lann Tiuinauc, see Whitchurch
Larport ('Frome Henry'; 'Little Frome') 165
Lawton 126
Lawton's Hope 190
Lea 132
   (in Kimbolton) 125
Leadon 101
Lecche, see Dulas
Ledbury 13, 58, 101, 132, 133, 134
Ledicot 198
Leen district 17-18
   (in Pembridge) 17, 173
Leighton 71, 140
Leinthall Earls 135
   Starkes 135
Leintwardine 135
Lenaston (*Hen Lenhic*; *ecclesiam Hennlennic*) 151, 178-9, 210
Leominster (Llanllieni) 17-18, 96, 108, 125, 137, 183
Letton ('Nether Letton') 139, 202
   (in Letton, Walford and Newton) 31, 140
   Court ('Over Letton') 140, 202
   Lake 57
Levithe Rugga (in Eastnor) 91
Lewstone 225
Ley (in Weobley) 220
Leysters 18, 118, 141
Licat Amr ('Llygad Amr'), see Garway
Lilwall 129
Limebrook 142
Linceter 224
Lincumbe (in Westhide?) 221

Index of Persons, peoples and organizations

Hamonis (Halmond) (fl. 1160-70) 100
Hampton, Richard of (fl. 1242) 119
Harold Godwineson, earl (died 1066) 102
    John (fl. 1383) 37
    son of earl Ralph of Hereford (fl. 1086) 15, 94
Hay, Urry de la (fl. 1136-48) 182
Helion, family of 158
Henry I, king of England (1100-35) 26, 100, 181
    II, king of England (1154-89) 62, 168
    III, king of England (1216-72) 28
Hereford, bishop of 13, 19, 31, 100, 107, 122, 187,
    205, 212, 231
    dean and chapter of 166, 169, 186, 189, 232
    family of (at Larport) 165
    Gilbert Foliot, bishop of (1148-63) 13
    Henry of (of Larport) 165
    nuns of 231
    Ralph, earl of (died 1057) 94
    Reinhelm, bishop of (1107-15) 231
    St Guthlac's priory in 84, 93, 97, 115, 165,
    172, 184, 220
    St Peter's church in 172
Herewald, bishop in Archenfield, 41
Hide, Richard of (fl. 1243) 221, 235
Hingan (fl. 1127) 35, 54
Hospitallers 122, 168
Howard (*Huard*), W(alter) 214, 215
Huard, see Howard
Huntington, lordship of 55
Hurstley, Richard of (fl. 1243) 221, 235
Hwicce 158
Hyatt, Richard (fl. 1601) 196
Hywal Dda, king of Deheubarth 55

Ingan, Richard (fl. 1212) 35
Ithel ab Arthrwys, king of Gwent (fl. c685) 155
    ap Morgan, king of Gwent (fl. c745) 27, 85,
    155

Kent, Richard of (fl. c1185) 118
Kingstone, Laurence of (fl. 11160-70) 128
Kington, lordship of 55
Kinnersley, Richard of (fl. late 12th century) 77

Lacy, family of 17, 117, 202
    Hugh I de (died c1115) 122, 151
    Roger de (fl. 1086) 221, 232, 235
    Walter I de (died 1085) 68, 172, 217
Lawton, Adam of (fl. 1304) 190
    John of (fl. 1355) 190
Layamon 29, 103
Ledbury, church of 101, 134, 219
'Leen, religious community of' (at Titley?) 208
Leofric (fl. 1086) 201
Leominster, nunnery of 18
    priory of 110, 118, 188

Limebrook Priory 38, 56, 88, 142, 173
Llanthony Prima, priory of 102, 115, 151
Loges, Aubrée de (fl. 1148-55) 184
    Gerwy de (fl. c1170) 93, 184
Longchamps, Henry de (died 1212) 64
Lyre, abbey of (Normandy) 171

Mainerch ap Milfrit (fl. c855) 194
Magonsaete 76, 158
Mamintone ('Monnington'), Godfrey of (fl. 1166) 95
Mans, Matthew (Mahel) du (fl. 1160-70) 201
Mansell, Henry (fl. c1160) 118
Mapnors, Adam of (fl. 1160-70) 119
Mapson, Godric (fl. 1086) 104
Mare, de la, family of 93
    Jordan (fl. 1199) 207
    Robert (fl. 1199) 207
'Marlborough', Alfred of (Alfred Maubanc)
    (fl. 1086) 94
Marshal, William, earl of Pembroke (died 1219) 49
Maubanc, Alfred, see 'Marlborough'
    Ruald (12th century) 124
Maund, Brian of 47
    Maurice of (fl. 1148-62) 47
    Nicholas of (fl. 1148-55) 47
Mercia, kingdom of 15
Merewalh, king of the Magonsaete 17-18, 19, 122,
    231
Monmouth, Baderon of (died 1170/76) 168
    family of (at Larport) 165
    Geoffrey of (author) 29, 103
    Henry of (fl. 1243) 165
    lords of 118
Morcar, earl (fl. 1072) 87
Moreton, Geoffrey of (fl. 1265) 166
    Godfrey of (fl. 1210-12) 183
Morien (fl. 9th century) 75
Mortimer, Edmund de, earl of March (died 1382) 90
    Robert de, of Richard's Castle (died 1219) 18
    Roger III de (died 1282) 90
Mortimers of Wigmore, family 56, 173
Mucegros, Walter de (fl. 1201) 184
    Walter de (died 1237) 184, 228
Munsley, Ralph of (fl. 1173) 184

Nigel the Doctor (fl. 1086) 205
Nodens, see Nuadu
Nothheard, ealdorman of the Magonsaete
    (fl. 823-5) 76
Nuadu (Nodens) Argetlam, Irish god 197

Odo (fl. 1160-70) 202
Offa, king of Mercia (757-796) 15
Owain ab Edwin ab Einion 55

251